THEY CALLED IT
NAKED FANNY

Helicopter Rescue Missions During the Early Years of the Vietnam War

SCOTT HARRINGTON
with JOE BALLINGER

HELLGATE PRESS   ASHLAND, OREGON

THEY CALLED IT NAKED FANNY
©2016 Scott Harrington

Published by Hellgate Press
(An imprint of L&R Publishing, LLC)

All rights reserved. No part of this publication may be reproduced or used in any form or by any means, graphic, electronic or mechanical, including photocopying, recording, taping, or information and retrieval systems without written permission of the publisher.

Hellgate Press
PO Box 3531
Ashland, OR 97520
email: sales@hellgatepress.com

Editor: Harley B. Patrick
Cover & Interior Design: L. Redding

Library of Congress Cataloging-in-Publication Data available from the publisher on request

ISBN: 978-1-55571-837-4

Printed and bound in the United States of America
First edition 10 9 8 7 6 5 4 3 2 1

This book is dedicated to the memory of Duane Whitney Martin. Born January 2, 1940, Duane was a 1st Lieutenant in the United States Air Force, assigned to Detachment 1 of the 38th Aerospace Rescue and Recovery Squadron at Nakhon Phanom Royal Thai Air Force Base, Thailand. On September 20, 1965, his rescue helicopter was shot down over North Vietnam. He made his way across the border into Laos where he was captured by the Pathet Lao. Following his escape from a Laotian prisoner of war camp, he was brutally attacked and died July 3, 1966. He was one of the nearly 60,000 Americans who lost their lives during the Vietnam War. His name is enshrined on Panel 2E, Line 91 of the Vietnam Wall in Washington, D.C. He was one of the men of Naked Fanny: He was one of us.

Duane was posthumously promoted to captain and, since his remains were not recovered, his name is inscribed on the Courts of the Missing at the Honolulu Memorial. There is also a memorial headstone at Fort Logan National Cemetery in Denver, Colorado.

Left to mourn his death were his young widow and two small daughters. Jack Fellows, a renowned member of the American Society of Aircraft Artists, thought enough of his cousin's late husband to establish the Captain Duane Whitney Martin, USAF Award, an annual $500 award honoring the best art commemorating aviation that reflects events during the war in Southeast Asia.

CONTENTS

FOREWORD... ix
PREFACE.. xiii
INTRODUCTION... xvii
ACKNOWLEDGMENTS... xxi

1. NAKED FANNY: A SPECIAL PLACE....................................1
2. A BASE IN THE MAKING..7
3. THE BIRD...13
4. THE HH-43 DEPLOYMENT TO WAR....................................17
5. TIME TO MOVE IN... 33
6. AS IT WAS IN THE BEGINNING...39
7. INVERT CONTROL...49
8. DOWNTOWN NKP—JIM BURNS'S STORY........................55
9. FRED, IZZY, JAY, JIM, NEIL AND WARREN......................73
10. 1ST NVN HH-43 RESCUES AND FIRST NIGHT
    MISSION AT NKP..77
11. A PICKUP THAT DIDN'T COUNT.. 89
12. 1ST RESCUE OF A HUN PILOT IN S.E.A............................93
13. 5TH TCG AND 605TH TCS ROADRUNNERS.....................105
14. MEET JOE BALLINGER, CAPT. USAF................................117
15. PREPARING FOR TDY: THE KIRTLAND STORY...............123
16. NKP ARRIVAL: THE WORK BEGINS..................................133
17. A REBUFF; THEN A BUFF...141
18. HECK OF A WAY TO SPEND A RAINY DAY.....................147
19. THUD DRIVER IN A TREE... 153
20. AIR AMERICA AND LIMA SITES...159
21. UDORN GETS A SAVE..169
22. CH-3s: FROM EGLIN AFB, FL TO NKP................................177
23. THE JOLLY GREENS ARRIVE...183
24. TWICE IN, TWICE OUT: LEFT HIGH AND DRY.................187
25. SAM HAS HIS SAY AND A BAD WEATHER PICKUP.........191
26. FIRST HH-43/CH-3C COMBAT RESCUE UNIT IN S.E.A.....195

v

27.	A PIECE OF CAKE	217
28.	JOLLY GREENS MAKE IT NUMBER TWO	223
29.	THE INEVITABLE HAPPENS	231
30.	JOLLYS MAKE THIRD RESCUE	253
31.	DEPARTURE AND CHILLY HOMECOMING	259
32.	CATS AND DOGS MISSIONS	263
33.	OFFICERS' LOUNGE—NKP AIR BASE	271
34.	THIS AND THAT MEMORIES	275
35.	BATTLEFIELD COMMISSIONS	281

AFTERWORD ... 305
APPENDICES ... 311
   (A) HELICOPTER PERSONNEL ASSIGNED TO NKP ... 313
   (B) INVERT PERSONNEL ASSIGNED TO NKP ... 317
   (C) NEW HONOR COURT STATUE ... 319
   (D) WHERE ARE THEY NOW? ... 321
   (E) AIRCRAFT TIMELINE ... 323
   (F) MISSION TIMELINE ... 325
GLOSSARY ... 331
ABOUT THE AUTHOR ... 335

THEY CALLED IT
NAKED FANNY

**Helicopter Rescue Missions During the
Early Years of the Vietnam War**

FOREWORD

When our F-105D Thunderchief squadron arrived in the theater in early 1965, we were originally based at Da Nang Air Base (Republic of Vietnam). We immediately became familiar with NKP, a VOR (Visual Omni Range) station in northeastern Thailand. It was the only VOR that was close enough to Laos to be used as a navigation aid when going to targets in Laos and later into North Vietnam. Within a month we were moved to Korat, Thailand. From that base we started flying missions into North Vietnam, an operation called "Rolling Thunder." We always refueled on a radial off the NKP VOR and took our original headings to the targets from that VOR.

We saw the small air base below but didn't originally realize that (many of) the SAR helicopters that would provide our hope for rescue were stationed there. It didn't take long for us to understand how important that base would become and how many lives would be saved because of the tremendous rescue efforts that would originate from that single location known as "Naked Fanny."

The stories between the covers of this book bring to life the valor and courage needed day in and day out and animate the cold facts hidden in mission statements for almost half a century.

Finally, the first-person accounts bear witness to the enormous dangers and raw emotions behind the military after-action reports written by these "men of steel." It became especially important to me on July 27, 1965, when I found myself on the ground in North Vietnam and in serious need

THEY CALLED IT NAKED FANNY

of the SAR professionals at NKP if I was ever to see my wife and two daughters again.

It's hard to put into words how I feel about these brave individuals doing their jobs to their utmost that ended up with a successful rescue under horribly dangerous conditions. All of the F-105 pilots knew that most of the rescue efforts started at NKP so we held that location in special esteem. Being on the ground that close to Hanoi; with North Vietnamese soldiers clamoring in the elephant grass looking for me; and firing volleys of gunfire to get me to bolt is horrifying beyond description.

I had been involved in rescue attempts, both successful and unsuccessful, during my tour and I knew my situation was grim. It was two Navy A-1 pilots, Ed Greathouse and Holt Livesay, who located me and brought George Martin's helicopter, based at NKP, to my position. I can never describe how I felt when I saw that chopper coming in over me in spite of the ground fire. As you will read later in this book, we had our problems that day with one of the chopper engines and with the sling motor, but they persevered and carried me to a dry rice paddy; set me down and landed next to me so I could get in.

All of this was done under fire—gunfire that would be attested to by a number of holes in the fuselage. What unbelievable courage that took. We were complete strangers but it didn't matter; they did their job, they saved my life! Coming out of Naked Fanny, George Martin, the chopper pilot; Orville Keese, the co-pilot; Curtis Pert, the crew chief and Gordon Thayer, the PJ, risked their lives that day to rescue someone they didn't know. I am extremely proud to have been associated with this crew and all those in the SAR community that continually did this enormously important work.

This would be repeated time after time, as witnessed to in the pages of this book, over the next number of years with the same exhibition of bravery, selflessness and valor. Sadly, sometimes their efforts would prove to be fatal. Where do we get such men?

—Frank J. Tullo

Scott Harrington

FRANK TULLO JOINED THE AIR FORCE in October 1959, serving for seven years as a fighter pilot flying F-100s and F-105s. This included a tour in Vietnam (Thailand) where he was shot down on the outskirts of Hanoi and rescued by helicopter.

Tullo joined Continental Airlines as a pilot in 1966 and spent thirty-three years with them until he retired in 1999. During his career with Continental, he flew the Boeing 707, 727, DC-10, DC-9, MD-80, Boeing 757/767, Sabreliner and Lear Jet. While at Continental, Tullo held the positions of: Flight Engineer Instructor, Flight Instructor, Boeing 727 Fleet Manager, Director of Human Factors (CRM), Chief Pilot of Los Angeles and Honolulu, and Vice President of Flight Operations.

He is currently a part-time faculty member at the University of Southern California. Mr. Tullo also has an aviation consultant business specializing in human factors, working for domestic and foreign airlines including United Space Alliance, the organization that currently maintains the Space Shuttle. He currently flies for the Civil Air Patrol flying light airplanes on Search and Rescue missions in Southern California.

His education includes a BA from University of Maryland Overseas and an MS from Pepperdine University.

Awards include a Distinguished Flying Cross with Oak Leaf Cluster, Air Medal with Oak Leaf Cluster, Purple Heart and the FAA Master Pilot Award.

THEY CALLED IT NAKED FANNY

PREFACE

U NLIKE WITH WORLD WAR II AND PEARL HARBOR, U. S. involvement in the Vietnam War was not the result of a single event, although some may link it to the Tonkin Gulf incident when the USS *Maddox* was supposedly attacked by North Vietnamese torpedo boats in the Gulf of Tonkin. While it was the basis for the Tonkin Gulf Resolution that committed major American forces to the war in Vietnam, our involvement was actually a gradual process that gained momentum as the communist Viet Minh, led by Ho Chi Minh, failed to abide by the 1954 Geneva accords that ended the French Indochina War. Less than two months after the treaty was signed the Viet Minh moved into Laos to support the communist Pathet Lao in gaining control of Laos. Two years later North Vietnam invaded northern Laos, occupying a portion of the country. Fearing a communist takeover of Southeast Asian countries (the Domino Theory), the U. S., through both overt and covert actions, continued to escalate its involvement in Laos and Vietnam.

Dubbed "Yankee Team," classified aerial reconnaissance missions were begun over northern Laos in May of 1964, to provide intelligence to Laotian Loyalists. Two U.S. aircraft were lost during the early days of Yankee Team—one during a reconnaissance mission and the second during a failed Air America combat search and rescue attempt (CSAR) to recover the downed pilot.

THEY CALLED IT NAKED FANNY

That brings us to U. S. Air Force Captain Earl H. Tilford, Jr.'s writing in the book *United States Air Force, Search and Rescue in Southeast Asia*, written while he was assigned to the Office of Air Force History, United States Air Force, Washington, D.C., 1980. The following material begins on page 51 of his book and is in the public domain:

Meanwhile, in accordance with the Joint Chiefs of Staff directive in May, directing the Air Force to send search and rescue units to Southeast Asia, two ARS HH-43Bs, their crews and mechanics, were sent from the 33rd Air Rescue Squadron at Naha Air Station, Okinawa, to Bien Hoa. Because of the Yankee Team rescue requirements, they were diverted and rerouted to Nakhon Phanom Royal Thai Air Force Base on the Thai-Laos border. Arrangements also were made to have two U.S. Marine H-34s placed on alert at Khe Sanh in northern South Vietnam whenever a Yankee Team mission flew over Laos. Simultaneously, the 33rd Air Rescue Squadron at Naha sent two HU-16Bs to Korat Royal Thai Air Force Base to perform as airborne rescue control ships during search and rescue missions. During this same period, the 31st Air Rescue Squadron, Clark Air Base Philippines, sent three HU-16Bs to Da Nang for rescue duties in the Gulf of Tonkin.

Since the 6,000-foot pierced-steel planking runway at Nakhon Phanom could not handle loaded C-97 cargo planes, the plan was to land the unit at Udorn, have the helicopters unloaded, assembled, and then fly them to their final destination. Major Saunders (Major Alan W. Saunders, Commander, Detachment 3, Pacific Air Rescue Center) flew up to Udorn to make final arrangements and to greet the men. Unfortunately, he failed to obtain the necessary support items such as JP-4 fuel, bedding and rations for the men at either Udorn or Nakhon Phanom. Consequently, when the rescue unit reached Udorn on June 17, and began unloading and assembling their choppers, Saunders discovered there were no facilities to accommodate the men for that night. Saunders had the men flown to Nakhon Phanom for the night where he assumed there were suitable facilities. Only a few rickety open-sided sheds awaited the tired crewmen when they reached the dusty, riverside base. The exhausted party made a campfire, barbecued their C-rations, and slept under the stars. At dawn most of the men returned to Udorn where they continued assembling their choppers. By the following morning the helicopters were ready to fly to Nakhon Phanom, but then the crews discovered that the fuel had not arrived. Another day was spent in securing fuel, but finally, late on the afternoon of June 20, the HH-43Bs reached Nakhon Phanom.

During the next few weeks, barely livable conditions continued at Nakhon Phanom. Officers and enlisted men endured a lack of suitable latrine facilities, electric power, and even potable water. On June 27, an Air Force electrician arrived from Bangkok and installed a generator and some wiring for light. Three days later, four Thai carpenters began refurbishing the sheds and building a kitchen. Meanwhile, the rescue personnel worked at putting in a latrine and constructing a shower. Such as it was, Nakhon Phanom was the only base in the world with an Air Rescue Service officer as its American commander. Substantial problems remained, but at last Air Rescue Service helicopters were entrenched in Southeast Asia. Pilots who flew over Laos had trained Air Rescue Service forces to support their mission. (In reality this training didn't happen until the fourth unit had been on scene at Nakhon Phanom for at least a month.) The effect on morale was favorable, though not entirely warranted.

The HH-43B was limited to a relatively small radius of action that varied between 125 to 140 miles. Due to this range limitation, the Nakhon Phanom-based Huskies were not able to provide search and rescue services for the Plain of Jars or areas southeast of Pakse in the Laotian panhandle. An aircraft damaged by enemy fire over the center of the Plain of Jars had to be flown at least fifty miles south to be within range of any Nakhon Phanom-based Air Force rescue choppers.

THEY CALLED IT NAKED FANNY

INTRODUCTION

THIS BOOK FOLLOWS FIVE TEMPORARY DUTY (TDY) Search and Rescue groups as they appeared at Nakhon Phanom Royal Thai Air Force Base. The initial group was comprised primarily of personnel from the 35th Air Rescue Squadron (some sources list the unit number as the 33rd or 36th ARS) from Naha Air Base, Okinawa, along with HH-43B helicopters, and was augmented by personnel from other bases. They were accompanied by personnel from the 507th Tactical Control Squadron at Shaw Air Force Base, South Carolina, which had already set up a radar Control and Reporting Post at Tan Son Nhut Air Base outside of Saigon. (Call sign for the new CRP at Nakhon Phanom would be "Invert.") Four months later a second helicopter rescue group, comprised of personnel from rescue units at other bases but previously based at Da Nang would arrive to fill the gap until the next group of TDY personnel from the U.S. would arrive. The third group brought together officers and men from assorted U.S. Air Force bases. It would be pilots and crew members from this group that would execute the first rescue from NKP of a pilot shot down as part of Operation Rolling Thunder. The fourth group would be a different combination of personnel. Half would come from a scattering of units with the other fifty percent being transferred as a unit from Kirtland AFB, at Albuquerque, New Mexico. This group would be joined by a small detachment of CH-3C helicopters—two aircraft—from Eglin AFB, Florida. The bulk of the rescues during 1964-1965 would be made by these two groups.

THEY CALLED IT NAKED FANNY

Since the commanding officer of the fourth group (Captain Joe Ballinger who headed up the Kirtland group) kept copious notes of his TDY tour, and because my TDY tour as a Weapons Controller coincided with their stay at NKP, it will be their actions that will be most prominent in this book. Their story includes their transition from a peacetime Base Rescue unit to a Combat Search and Rescue unit at NKP.

In total, these TDY units were responsible for the rescue of eleven pilots who were shot down during Operation Rolling Thunder.

To give the reader an understanding of the process of constructing an air base in what was virtually a jungle environment the complete story of that endeavor is told by the Navy Seabee officer who was second in command of the operation.

And, because it is important for the reader to know, I have included, in Chapter 3, the history behind the decision to send a helicopter designed for air base rescue into a war zone to perform combat search and rescue missions over enemy territory, unarmed, without armor plating, with a range of just seventy-five miles and without self-sealing fuel tanks.

Other written materials include descriptions of rescue missions, detailed and presented in reportorial and feature story form in both print media and on Internet websites. Also included, as documentation of a story I had been told by my POW friend Tom Curtis—the heartwarming story of "battlefield commissions" awarded to the only three enlisted prisoners of war by their fellow POW officers.

Many of the missions are detailed via mission logs, official mission reports and from detailed notes about the specific missions in which the pilots were involved. I have compiled the various documents, media and oral histories to reflect this historic period in the annals of the Air Rescue Service. The efforts of these men and others like them should not be taken lightly as noted by the following (from *The Story of Air Rescue in Vietnam as Seen Through the Eyes of Pararescuemen*, by Robert L. LaPointe):

Scott Harrington

At the end of July, 1965, Air Rescue Service celebrated its first anniversary in Southeast Asia. Considering the limited resources they began the war with, Air Rescue achievements were remarkable. Between 1 August 1964 and 31 July 1965, 8780 sorties (missions) were flown in support of combat operations throughout Vietnam and Laos. The skill, aggressiveness and courage displayed by rescue crews resulted in 74 lives saved. (Eleven of those rescues were made by the HH-43 and CH-3 crews from Nakhon Phanom.) Equally impressive was the fact that over 250 decorations were awarded to ARS crewmembers including 16 Silver Stars and 10 Purple Hearts.

So there will be no misunderstanding, this book is an account of the early years of Nakhon Phanom Royal Thai Air Force Base, Thailand. The "early years" include the construction of the air base by the Seabees; the early occupancy of the base by the five temporary duty or TDY helicopter detachments; TDY radar operations and communications units and the initial cadre that made up the base support group. No one should misconstrue the descriptions of, or references to missions or events described here-in as in any way referring to, undermining or diminishing any event, mission or accomplishment that may have occurred or originated from any other location during this time period or at any other time during the remainder of the Vietnam War. The contents of this book pertain to and describe, or are made claim to only with the knowledge of those who were at Nakhon Phanom during the period from 1962-1965; the only exception being the missions described at the beginning of Chapter 10.

To assist the reader, as a history lesson the first-person description of the building process will leave you amazed at the effort it took to get the airfield constructed. The status of the Air Rescue Service and the subsequent assignment of an ill-equipped aircraft to perform Combat Rescue Missions will cause a heightened appreciation for what was accomplished by the little machines described as having "blades of wood," and the "men of steel" who flew them.

THEY CALLED IT NAKED FANNY

Life on the small base, and for some who lived "on the economy" in the nearby town of Nakhon Phanom, is shared by those who experienced it firsthand. For many of the men their tour of duty at Nakhon Phanom was life defining and formed the basis for many lifelong friendships.

Also shared are the experiences encountered in preparing a stateside detachment to "go to war" as it turns its focus from a peacetime mission to a combat mission. It is also the story of their commanding officer, his memories and his missions.

Accounts of missions, told by those who experienced them, often provide the reader with the perspectives of those being rescued as well as those doing the rescuing. And, since the military has its own lexicon, a glossary is available in the last few pages of the book to aid in the understanding of "Air Force speak."

This book is long on its insight into the men who put their lives on the line for their brothers in those early years at NKP.

—Scott Harrington

ACKNOWLEDGMENTS

I WANT TO THANK MY WIFE, JACI, FOR HER PATIENCE and support in my writing of this book.

Joe Ballinger was the commander of Detachment Provisional 2, PARC/Detachment 1, 38th ARS at Nakhon Phanom Air Base, Thailand, for six months, from April to October 1965. It is his recollection of the events of those several months, along with his belief that those who shared the temporary duty experience at NKP should be honored and recognized on a broader scale than within the Air Rescue community that prompted his desire to have this book written.

Without Joe's encyclopedic memory and the "first-person" contributions from others who served there and those whose rescues originated from there; the full story of Nakhon Phanom during the early years could not have been written.

Originally, Joe said, "My thoughts were to cover the time we were there, from April to October 1965, to ensure that the HH-43 (Pedro Community) got credit for their North Vietnam CSAR (Combat Search and Rescue)! And as sort of closure for us who left and scattered all over to never be a unit again. But as I got deeper into my research and contacts, I have realized that the 'Naked Fanny' story about three HH-43Bs and the men who flew and maintained them should cover at least the full TDY time—1964/1965. For sure, those who were there previous to our time prepared the basis for our success! They flew the first missions into Laos, configured the 43s, developed CSAR procedures and gave us enough knowledge to not be completely in the blind on our first mission. Also, I have found out that the Udorn detachment backed us up far more than I knew at the time. And for certain the two CH-3Cs and their men were a part of us, gaining permission to use the call sign 'Jolly Green' while with us, even though they officially became the 'Jolly Greens' when Baylor Haynes and his men took over as permanent party."

The CH-3C stories would have been sadly lacking were it not for George Martin's memories, with a "hat's off" to his wife Shirley (she manned the computer and took dictation from George so his story could be told), and for Phil Stambaugh's meticulous record keeping.

Also included, as a salute to those who set the bar for the HH-43 missions, is the story of the first rescue made by "Pedro" crews in North Vietnam.

My motivation for writing this book came from the respect that I have for and the esteem in which I hold these men who faced such danger and who looked death in the eye to rescue their Air Force and Navy brothers.

I am grateful for the recorded background information provided by CAPT George W. Fowler, CEC, USNR, Ret., which allows us a peek at the base during its construction stage and helps us to realize what a tremendous undertaking it was to move machinery from Bangkok to Nakhon Phanom and its subsequent return.

Also, my thanks to Lt. Col. Edward S. Marek, USAF, Ret., for his study and detailing of what led up to the deployment of the HH-43B helicopters to Southeast Asia.

The willingness of Frank Tullo to write the foreword for this book is but another example of this man's character, which he demonstrated on the third and fourth decade anniversaries of his rescue. It is also shown by his twenty-eight-year search to locate and make contact with the two A-1 pilots involved in his rescue.

Had it not been for my late friend Allen Childress's recommendation that I be a part of the Invert team, I would never have been blessed with having met these brave men or known of their achievements.

My deepest thanks and appreciation to the following for their contributions to this book:

CAPT George W. Fowler, CEC, USNR, Ret.
Col. Tom Curtis, USAF, Ret.
Col. Jay Strayer, USAF, Ret.

Col. Leo Thorsness, USAF, Ret., recipient Congressional Medal of Honor
Col. Walter Turk, USAF, Ret.
Col. Michael A. Wormley, USAF
Lt. Col. Robert Hanson, USAF, Ret.
Lt. Col. Byron Hukee, USAF, Ret.
Lt. Col. Edward S. Marek, USAF, Ret.
Major Joe Ballinger, USAF, Ret.
Major John Christianson, USAF, Ret.
Major William D. Hobbs, USAF, Ret.
Major George Martin, USAF, Ret.
Major Neil McCutchan, USAFR, Ret.
Major Phil Stambaugh, USAF, Ret.
SMSgt. James (Jim) Burns, USAF, Ret.
SMSgt. Wade Ketron, USAF, Ret.
SMSgt. Robert LaPointe, USAF, Ret.
Glenn Abernethy
David Cutillo
Israel "Izzy" Freedman
Bruce Hepp
Richard "Dick" Laine
Shirley Martin
Stephen Mock, Editor of Pedro News
Frank Tullo
George Warren

CHAPTER 1. References to Ban Ken Bridge come from "The First Bridge," published in the *Flight Journal*, December 2012, written by Lt. Col. Robert Hanson, USAF, Ret.

Permission for inclusion received from Lt. Col. Hanson and Budd Davisson, Editor-in-Chief, *Flight Journal*.

CHAPTER 2. The account of the construction of Nakhon Phanom Royal Thai Air Force Base was written by CAPT George Fowler, CEC, USNR, Ret. for Web Site Nakhon Phanom during the Secret War 1962-1975. Permission for inclusion received from CAPT Fowler.

THEY CALLED IT NAKED FANNY

CHAPTERS 3 and 4. Information on the deployment of and description of the HH-43B comes from http://www.talkingproud.us and was written by Lt. Col. Edward S. Marek, USAF, Ret., who also gave his permission to include it in this book. Additional first-person information about the Minot AFB HH-43 unit's deployment to Da Nang is courtesy of Maj. John Christianson, USAF, Ret. Major Christian also provided the accounts of the Da Nang unit's transfer to NKP and of the Ball 03 mission, which are reprinted from *S.E.A. Stories* with his permission.

CHAPTER 6. "As It Was in the Beginning" was written for www.pedronews.org. It is a series of recollections and comments by Leonard Fialko and Ken Franzel, who were two of the pilots in the initial deployment group that established Det. Provisional 2, PARC at NKP. Permission for inclusion received from Stephen Mock, Editor of Pedro News.

CHAPTER 8. Senior Master Sergeant Jim Burns, USAF, Ret. provided his story and several pictures from www.rotorheadsrus.us website.

CHAPTER 10. "First to go North" is reprinted courtesy of SMSgt. Robert LaPointe, USAF Ret. "The First Night Mission at NKP" is included with permission from its author, Israel Freedman.

CHAPTER 12. The "First Rescue of a Hun Pilot in SEA" was written by then-Captains Jay Strayer and Ron Bigoness, the principals involved, for www.rotorheadsrus.us and is included with the permission of SMSgt Jim Burns, Editor. Thanks also to Lt. Col. Byron Hukee, USAF, Ret., for information regarding the rescue of LTJG S. B. Wilkes.

CHAPTER 14. Information about Joe Ballinger was provided by Mary Kay Woodyard, from *The Norton (KS) Telegram*.

CHAPTER 21. Bill Wirstrom's story about the Udorn detachment appeared on Stephen Mock's www.pedronews.org website, and again appears with Editor Mock's permission.

CHAPTER 26. Frank Tullo's rescue story, "Tullo and the Giant," first appeared in *Air & Space/Smithsonian Magazine* and is reprinted with his permission and with that of the author, Lt. Col. Robert Hanson, USAF, Ret.

Scott Harrington

CHAPTER 27. The interview and article covering the rescue of Navy LT Grant Townsend by Peter Arnett is used with permission of The Associated Press, Copyright© 2013. All rights reserved.

CHAPTER 30. Senior Master Sergeant Robert L. LaPointe, USAF, Ret., from his book *PJs In Vietnam. The Story of Air Rescue in Vietnam As Seen Through the Eyes of Pararescuemen* provided information on the rescue of Capt. Frederick Greenwood and gave his permission to reprint it

CHAPTER 35. Major William Hobbs, USAF, Ret., gave his permission to reprint his story "Battlefield Commissions." "Commissioned in Hanoi," by Col. Leo Thorsness, USAF, Ret., himself a POW and Congressional Medal of Honor winner, is reprinted by permission from *Air Force Magazine*, published by the Air Force Association..

MISSION TIMELINE information is courtesy of www.rotorheadsrus.us and SMSgt. Jim Burns, USAF, Ret., who credits *PJs in Vietnam* by SMSgt. Robert LaPointe, USAF, Ret., "Vietnam Air Losses" by Chris Hobson, http://www.h43-huskie.info/framesetpedro.htm and http://en.wikipedia.org/wiki/38th_Rescue_Squadron.

My time at Nakhon Phanom was a defining four months of my life, and the writing of this book provides a window as to why I so treasure that experience.

—*Scott Harrington*

THEY CALLED IT NAKED FANNY

1

NAKED FANNY: A SPECIAL PLACE

A PLACE CALLED NAKED FANNY? ...That fosters memories? ...Must have been an after-hours hangout where GIs went at the end of their shift to help relieve the stresses of their work day.

In describing Naked Fanny I'm reminded of the "old saw" or adage about Indiana. It is said about the Hoosier State that "North Vernon is in the south; South Bend is in the north; and French Lick isn't what you think it is."

No, Naked Fanny wasn't a bar or, as they say in more polite circles, "a house of ill repute." In fact, its real name wasn't even Naked Fanny. But it's just as real as any of those other places and for thousands of Air Force veterans from the Vietnam War, it brings back tons of memories. You see, Naked Fanny was the nickname associated with a Royal Thai Air Force Base located near the northeastern town of Nakhon Phanom, Thailand. Leave it to a GI to slap a moniker lik[e that on a place] called Nakhon Phanom.

The following summation is based on factual [information] published in an article entitled "The First Bri[gade" by] Robert Hanson, USAF, Ret., which appeared in [an issue] of *Flight Journal*. Portions used appear with hi[s permission.]

THEY CALLED IT NAKED FANNY

For the record, in 1962, plans were well underway to build an American airbase on the site of what was called Nakhon Phanom Royal Thai Air Force Base. As a matter of fact, the Seabees had already begun actual work on building the base in August of that year. So, it was not a result of the information that follows that the base was constructed. But since the whys and wherefores of locating the air base at Nakhon Phanom are steeped in international diplomacy; for our purposes a brief summary will suffice.

Nakhon Phanom village welcome sign. Notice that the spelling on the sign is "NakornPanom," which is how the locals called it.

And while it was not the results of a specific U.S. Air Force mission that occurred on January 13th of 1965, that were responsible for its existence, the results of that mission do give credence to the need for the base's being and for the overall mission it supported.

The mission, ordered by General Curtis LeMay, Air Force Chief of Staff, involved the bombing of a wooden bridge on Route 7 in Laos. To accomplish the destruction of the Ban Ken Bridge, the General called on four F-100 and 16 F-105 fighter bombers from bases in Thailand; four F-100s based at Da Nang, South Vietnam; and a recce or RF-101 Voodoo reconnaissance aircraft for damage assessment.

Although the Ban Ken Bridge was destroyed, unanticipated anti-aircraft artillery (AAA) placements near the target area brought down an F-100 and an F-105. While both pilots ejected and survived, it was truthfully "only by the grace of God" that they were rescued by Air America H-34 helicopters.

Captain Al Vollmer, the F-105 driver, was rescued only because an Air America C-123 happened to hear his call on the universal emergency frequency known as the "guard channel" and was able to get in an H-34 that was nearby in Laos on a cargo and personnel run.

2

Captain Chuck Ferguson, pilot of the F-100, through the kindness of Laotian friendlies, was taken out of harm's way and picked up by another Air America H-34 the following day.

The fact that the two pilots were rescued almost entirely by chance, underscored the urgent need for locating U.S. Air Force Combat Search and Rescue (CSAR) men and aircraft nearer to what would become the field of air battle throughout the remainder of the war.

Nakhon Phanom Royal Thai Air Force Base (NKP- RTAFB), Thailand was located approximately 350 miles northeast of Bangkok and about 10 miles southwest of the town of Nakhon Phanom. More than 16,000 inhabitants lived in the northeastern Thailand town. The installation was operated continuously from the early 1960s, to approximately 1976, and the base population would swell to nearly 6,000. From this location, personnel supported several U.S. agencies in conducting what became known as "The Secret War." The dangerous missions carried out in Laos, Cambodia and Vietnam resulted in many aircraft and personnel being lost.

For every one of us who served at Naked Fanny, or NKP, as the VOR (Visual Omni Range) designator for the airstrip was called, the memories are imprinted in our minds as surely as a branding iron leaves its lasting mark on the hide of a steer. Many of the events that triggered those memories may have been similar to events that occurred at other bases in Southeast Asia during that time. But the memories of Naked Fanny were made special because there was a certain unique feeling about the place. From the earliest temporary duty (TDY) troops who bivouacked there with only tents for shelter as they set up communication links; waited for the call to respond to a search and rescue mission; or established an operational search radar site; to the Air Commandos who fought the "Secret War," there was a feeling of camaraderie. No matter what your duty or mission was, for every guy on that base—whether it was during the early days with fewer than 100 troops, or later on with thousands assigned there—there was a feeling of brotherhood. If you were fortunate to have been there and experienced that special feeling, you were blessed. It was something that the men with whom I served never experienced anywhere else.

THEY CALLED IT NAKED FANNY

To give the reader an idea of what it was like for those of us who were there during the early days, imagine you are an Air Force GI assigned to a radar operations crew. You are off duty, but are still very much aware of the sounds of the small base made up of a radar squadron, a helicopter rescue detachment, a small communications unit and base support personnel. You would often hear the sounds of F-4C and F-105D fighter/bombers passing overhead in flights of four heading toward, or returning from bombing runs over North Vietnam. All of a sudden you hear the "whoop, whoop, whoop" of the blades of the Kaman HH-43B helicopters coming to life along the flight line. You know what is happening. A call has come into the "chopper" unit that an aircraft is down somewhere between Naked Fanny and North Vietnam and its pilot is in harm's way. Now, eight of the guys—four officers and four enlisted troops—men you may or may not know or associate with, even on a casual basis, but who are your guys none-the-less because they live, eat and sleep around you, are being called on to risk their lives in an attempt to rescue a fellow American, on the ground in enemy territory. It becomes a personal thing—something very serious. And it causes you and others like you who are also off duty to draw into a shell. You go about your business; not making eye contact or talking with anyone else. The radar operations (Invert) crew members on duty draw into their own shells: totally focused on the mission at hand as they soon will be following those two helicopters as small "blips" on their radar scopes and "tracks" on the luminescent plotting board. They'll need to make sure they keep track of the locations of those fragile birds by keeping in close touch with the pilots on their radios. And they'll perform their jobs in the most professional way they know how, because eight or nine lives depend on them. And because the range of the radar may be less than where the choppers will go and those blips will disappear, their hearts will be in their throats while the rescue attempt is being made. For other members of the helicopter rescue team, all they can do is sit and wait and pray for their comrades' safety. The tension is so thick you can cut it with a knife. And it is present in every man on the base as every breath carries with it the hope that your guys can get out to the site where the pilot went down; pick him up and return safely to NKP. This day, everything goes as planned and in addition to the eight men who left Naked Fanny a few hours ago, there is a ninth man who may be the most thankful man on the face of the earth at that hour. You hear the choppers coming. There they are! They're home and it's "Katy bar the door!" It's time to celebrate.

But first, the base had to be built.

THEY CALLED IT NAKED FANNY

Construction sign left by the Seabees. (Photo by Jim Burns)

2

A BASE IN THE MAKING

THE FIRST U.S. MILITARY UNIT TO ARRIVE ON THE SITE that would become "Naked Fanny" was the U.S. Navy's Mobile Construction Battalion Three (MCB3) (Seabees). That was in August of 1962. Navy LTJG, now CAPT George Fowler, CEC, USNR, Ret., was the Assistant Commander of MCB 3 and told their story. It is reprinted here with his permission:

> **George E. Fowler:** *It was in August of 1962, U.S. Naval Mobile Construction Battalion Three (MCB 3) deployed to Camp Kinser in Okinawa to serve as the Alert Battalion in the Pacific. Orders were received to redeploy a major portion of the battalion to Nakhon Phanom (NKP), Thailand to construct a logistic support airfield. These orders were delayed several weeks by the Cuban Missile Crisis but, within a few weeks of arriving in Okinawa, Secretary of Defense McNamara personally approved the redeployment.*
>
> *The Battalion CO, CDR David P. Whyte; OPS Officer, LT Robert P. Phenix; and CDR Ben Saravia of the Commander, Naval Construction Battalion's Pacific (COMCBPAC) staff in Pearl Harbor visited the construction site in early August. Initially, the*

airfield was to be constructed adjacent to the west side of the town of Nakhon Phanom, but this site was subsequently moved ten miles farther west in order to place the airfield out of mortar range from Thakhek, Laos, just across the Mekong River. The airfield to be constructed was designed to be 100 feet wide; 5,000 feet long; would have 500 foot overruns on each end of the runway; a parking area; a marshaling area; and a taxiway/warm-up pad.

Upon receiving the redeployment orders, an advance party was formed and sent to NKP with the mission of building a camp area where everyone could live, while constructing the airfield. This camp was located on the west side of the town of Nakhon Phanom. Commander Whyte decided to deploy the main body of MCB 3 to NKP, which would consist of a portion of Headquarters Company, Alpha (heavy equipment) Company, and Delta (construction) Company. This amounted to approximately 325 personnel covering all necessary trades and skills. The remainder of the MCB 3 would remain in Okinawa at Camp Kinser.

The necessary equipment was loaded on the USNS Muskingum for transport from the port of Naha in Okinawa to Bangkok, Thailand. Several Seabees rode the ship with the equipment and upon arrival in Bangkok the equipment was off-loaded and everything that could travel by rail was sent by train to Udorn, Thailand, where it was off-loaded and then driven to NKP. Most of the Seabees being sent to NKP flew from the U.S. Air Force Kadena Air Base in Okinawa on November 4, 1962, in KC-135s and landed in Udorn, Thailand the same day. Upon arriving in Udorn we were greeted by several Buddhist Monks in saffron robes and several water buffalo next to the runway. At this time we split into three groups. One group flew to Bangkok to drive the large equipment to NKP; one group flew into the small dirt landing strip in NKP next to the base camp; and the other group stayed in Udorn to drive equipment that had arrived by train, over the road to NKP. It was 150 miles from Udorn to

NKP and the road was unpaved, rutted and buffalo wallered. Throughout the deployment, MCB 3 continued to haul equipment and supplies, such as Pierced Steel Planking (PSP), over this road.

Meanwhile, approximately 55 personnel went to Bangkok to drive the large equipment (too large to be carried on the train to Udorn) to NKP. LTJG Richard Y. Wisenbaker was the OIC of this convoy. The route from Bangkok to NKP was approximately 550 miles long and included 150 miles of paved road from Bangkok to Korat. Unfortunately, the remaining 400 miles were unpaved, rutted, buffalo wallered roads with bamboo bridges that could not support the weight of the heavy trucks and construction equipment. All rivers had to be forded and it took 16 days for the convoy to cover the 550 miles.

After 16 days on the road, the convoy of heavy equipment arrived in NKP and it was time to get to work on the airfield.

First the site had to be cleared, then all organic matter had to be grubbed out of the soil; then borrow pits had to be opened so we could get good fill dirt that could be properly compacted; then we started bringing the airfield up to grade. To do this we worked two 10-hour shifts (0600-1600 and 1600-0200) followed by a fuel and lube crew from 0200-0600, six days a week. (Military time is based on a 24-hour clock; hence 0600-1600 would be 6 a.m. to 4 p.m.)

Shortly after arriving at NKP and starting work, MCB 3 decided that it needed more prime movers and scrapers to move the laterite fill from borrow pits to the runway site. We also decided that the five ton sheepsfoot rollers that we had were not heavy enough to properly compact the laterite. Six additional prime movers, four more scrapers and two ten ton sheepsfoot rollers were ordered. This equipment was shipped from the Seabee Center in Port Hueneme, California to Bangkok. Once again the equipment had to be driven over the road 550 miles to NKP. LTJG George E. Fowler (author of this segment) was the

THEY CALLED IT NAKED FANNY

OIC of this convoy. During this convoy from Bangkok to NKP there was a major accident caused by the extremely poor roads. Unfortunately, a Seabee was killed when the steering apparatus on one of the prime movers failed; the tractor hit a tree and turned over on him.

Upon arriving back in NKP, the work went on at an accelerated pace. The goal was to have everything completed by June 1963.

As the airfield came up to grade, the drainage ditches across the center of the runway were put in and the conduits for future runway lighting were installed. Then, after final grade was achieved, it was time to "shoot" the airfield with emulsified asphalt and then cover it with PSP. Once the PSP was laid it was staked along the edges to keep it from rolling up in front of landing aircraft.

We were only approximately three weeks from finishing the entire job when the monsoon rains started. They were several weeks early that year. Because of the rain, we could not finish the airstrip at this time. A decision was made that everyone would return to homeport in Port Hueneme, California while the rains were coming down, except for a detachment of 35 Seabees who would remain in NKP. The detachment OIC was LTJG George E. Fowler and the mission was to maintain drainage at the airfield site, maintain the construction equipment and make sure that it would be ready to go back to work when the rains stopped, and to tear down a portion of the base camp that would not be required in November when everyone returned to finish the work.

Even though the warm-up pad, taxiway, parking area and marshaling area were not totally completed, an Opening Ceremony was held in mid-June 1963. An Air Force C-123 was the first plane to land on the airfield and it was followed by planes carrying members of the U.S. Embassy, the Commander of the U.S. Military Advisory Command, Thailand and the Thai Prime

Minister. The U.S. Ambassador to Thailand, Ambassador (Kenneth Todd) Young, was a speaker. The runway was officially opened.

The pilot of the C-123, the first aircraft to land on the new runway, said his instructions were to get Bangkok's international press corps to NKP before the official opening party arrived from Bangkok in a C-54. Flying it was Brig. Gen. Rollen Anthis, then-7th Air Division commander in Saigon. Seabees' officials in their Navy "whites" greeted the airplane. With no ramp or taxi strip, the C-123 pilot had to taxi his aircraft off into the mud and out of sight to make room for the C-54 in the formal picture.

After the ceremony was complete, several C-130s landed and all but 35 Seabees boarded the planes for the first leg of the trip back to the States. The Detachment that remained was known as Detachment Whiskey.

Finally, in November the rains stopped and Seabees returned to NKP to finish the airfield.

All work was completed and the equipment that could be sent to Bangkok via the rail system was driven to Udorn for loading onto the train. However, there were still approximately 25 pieces of equipment that were too large for the rail system and had to be driven 550 miles back to Bangkok. On the morning of December 24, 1963, at about 0600, the airfield to be known as NKP was turned over to 13 Thai Air Force Security personnel and the final convoy of equipment left NKP heading to Udorn, which was approximately 150 miles away. The convoy OIC was LTJG George E. Fowler with LT T.C. Schmitz, Medical Corps, and 38 Seabees who had volunteered to drive the equipment to Bangkok. The convoy arrived in Udorn at approximately 2330 that same day. On Christmas Day we worked on our equipment and got it ready for the next 400 miles to Bangkok and at 0600 on December 26, 1963, we left Udorn heading for Bangkok.

THEY CALLED IT NAKED FANNY

Overall, it took us six days to get to Bangkok. On December 30, we decided to keep driving as long as it took to get to Bangkok, day or night. We agreed to re-group outside of Don Muang Airport for the trip across town to the pier. The first piece of equipment got to the meeting point at 2300 and by 0200 on December 31, all equipment was there and we were escorted through Bangkok by the Thai Police. By 0400 the equipment was parked at the Klong Thoy pier, ready to be loaded aboard ship to return to Port Hueneme, California, and everyone went to a hotel and slept for most of the day. After about two days, we boarded a plane and headed back to Okinawa where we joined the main body of MCB 3 and started construction of facilities for the U.S. Marines at Camp Hansen.

For its efforts at Nakhon Phanom, MCB 3 received a "Well Done!" from CINCPAC (Commander in Chief Pacific).

3

THE BIRD

INFORMATION ABOUT THE HH-43B IS COURTESY OF *Talking Proud* website and Lt. Col. Edward S. Marek, USAF, Ret:

Lt. Col. Edward Marek: *Called the "Huskie," the HH-43 was the first U.S. Air Force Search and Rescue bird placed in service in the Vietnam and Laotian War. That was done in June of 1964, at Nakhon Phanom (NKP) Royal Thai Air Force Base (RTAFB).*

Initially designated as H-43, it was produced by the Kaman Corporation and was first flown in 1953. The emphasis was on ruggedness of construction and increased performance that would include medical evacuation capabilities at high altitudes. The Navy, Marines and USAF bought them. The Marines loved them, logging more than 10,700 flight hours in the western Pacific and western USA.

The Air Force saw the H-43 as a crash rescue and firefighting helicopter to be used near air bases, referred to as "Local Base Rescue" (LBR). This is because the Air Force had done a study that said the lion's share of its aircraft losses occurred within about 75 miles of an air base. As a result, the Air Force was satisfied with a 75 mile range for this helicopter. When there was

THEY CALLED IT NAKED FANNY

Kaman HH-43B Huskie.

a fire, or risk of fire, with a crash, the H-43 was seen as the first responder; aloft in a minute or so, and to the scene. The pilots would drop off the firefighters on the crew, and they in turn would use the FSK (Fire Suppression Kit) to suppress the fire as best they could until the fire trucks could get there. The rotor design was such that they created so strong a downwash that the smoke and fire would be blown away from the firefighters, allowing them to get in close to lay down the foam from the FSK. The H-43 would also bring along a medical technician.

In 1956, a Marine aircraft was tested with a new Lycoming T53 gas turbine shaft engine technology. The USAF liked that added power and in 1957 contracted with Kaman for the Huskie as a crash rescue helicopter, buying into the H-43A and the yet-to-be-flown H-43B. The Air Force took the first delivery of H-43As in November 1958, and assigned them to the Tactical Air Command (TAC), a fighter-oriented command. This reflected the requirement for the LBR mission for which the helicopter had been designed and was being procured. While the aircraft was not designed for combat SAR, you can see that it was designed as a "jack of several trades," which is why it was not a major conceptual leap to add a SAR mission to its list of trades.

Performance using the T53 turbine engine improved so much that the H-43B was developed and flown in 1958. Production began that year and the USAF took delivery of the first of 175 H-43Bs in June. In mid-1962, the USAF changed the H-43 designation to HH-43 to reflect its rescue role. The "Huskie" was retired in April 1973.

While this helicopter looked like a toy, it was a "heckuva"

flying machine. Two Air Force pilots, Major William J. Davis and Capt. Walter J. Hodgson, flew a production H-43B to an altitude of 29,846 feet in 1959, setting a new world altitude record for helicopters. By 1961, the H-43B set five new world records: two international altitude records and three new time-of-climb records that took the aircraft to 29,526 feet in 14 minutes 30.7 seconds. In 1962, the H-43B set two new records for distance: 655 miles closed course, 688 miles straight-line course.

In September of 1964, an upgraded version of the Huskie made its way to Southeast Asia. Curiously, the first two aircraft, which had been given a more powerful engine, armor plating and additional fuel capacity in self-sealing fuel cells as well as a hoist with 250 feet of cable, were sent to Bien Hoa, an airbase outside Saigon, rather than to NKP. It was only during the fourth group of TDY personnel that elements of the upgraded version were delivered piecemeal. As Joe Ballinger recalls, the spools with 250 feet of cable came first, followed later on by the self-sealing, expanded fuel cells that allowed them to do away with the barrel rigs (credited to Fred Glover in the third TDY group).

Realizing, of course, that since, according to their initial mission, the NKP birds weren't supposed to be flying into North Vietnam, they were way ahead of the war planning game.

THEY CALLED IT NAKED FANNY

4

THE HH-43: DEPLOYMENT TO WAR

THE HH-43 WAS THE FIRST USAF SAR (Search and Rescue) bird put into the Vietnam and Laos wars. That was done in June 1964, to Nakhon Phanom (NKP) Royal Thai Air Force Base (RTAFB). It was also the last USAF rescue helicopter to leave Vietnam, leaving Da Nang AB, Republic of Vietnam (RVN) after the peace treaty was signed in January 1973. We also believe it was the very last USAF SAR aircraft out of the region, leaving Utapao RTAFB in April 1975.

Stateside, the HH-43 was often referred to as Pedro, because of the radio call sign "Pedro" that was first used at Laredo AFB, Texas, prior to the war. In 1966, Pedro became the official USAF call sign used to designate the HH-43s and recognizing the radio call sign originally used at Laredo.

Thanks to Lt. Col. Edward S. Marek, USAF, Ret., from Talking Proud website, we were able to gain some insight about how the HH-43 SAR units were deployed and organized at the outset of the Vietnam-Laos wars:

> **Lt. Col. Edward Marek:** *While bureaucratic, it helps to better understand the environment in which the brave "Pedro" crews*

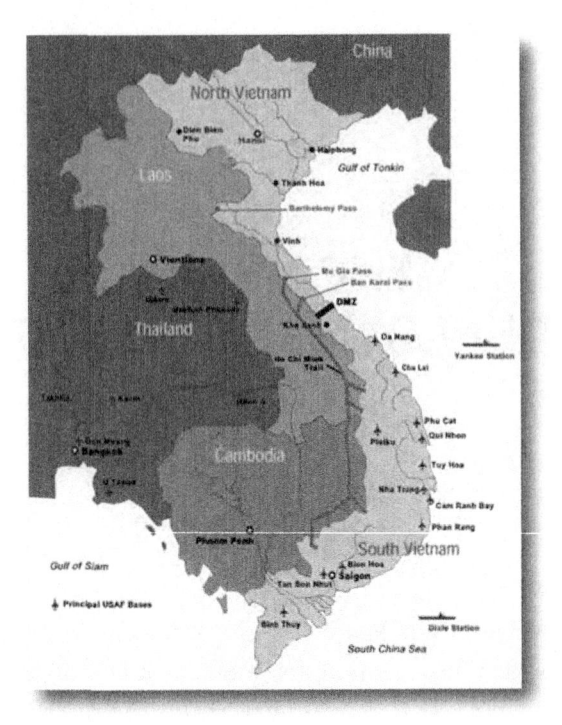

Map of SE Asia showing principal USAF bases.

operated. Here's a good example of why we say this. Lt. General George C. Kenney, Commander 5th Air Force and then-Commander, Allied Air Forces Southwest Pacific, arrived in the Pacific in July 1942, took a look around, and said this about the overall set-up: "It (5th Air Force) turned out to be another scrambled outfit...With so many lines of responsibility, control, and coordination that it resembled a can of worms as you looked at it..." General Kenney's initial assessment of command arrangements during WWII could also be applied to the command arrangements in Korea and Vietnam. In all three cases, we (the U.S. military) neglected to establish centralized command

and control of air power, which caused air resources to be spread out, and as a result we lost the advantage of having concentrated airpower. That's why this history is so important to understanding what the Pedros and others faced in Vietnam. It was a problem in WWII and Korea and was not solved when we entered Vietnam and Laos.

In fairness, employment of airpower started for the Americans in WWI, but really did not become a major factor until WWII. The USAF became a separate service in 1947, in part because of organizational and employment issues, and immediately had to face the Soviet nuclear threat, Sputnik, and the Korean War. Following Korea, the new service was immersed in the nuclear problem and simply was not ready for another Korea in Vietnam.

To help tell the Pedro story, we'll highlight three numbered Air Forces in the Pacific: the 5th, 7th and 13th.

Boiling down the histories of the three Air Forces, one might liken them to a kid on a trampoline—bouncing from hither to yon while turning summersaults and doing a juggling act at the same time. And all the while the Air Rescue Service, established in March of 1946, had to battle through all of the cobwebs in order to maintain its very existence.

Established under the Air Transport Command to provide rescue coverage for the continental United States, their mission was also expanded to include disaster relief.

Having shifted organizationally from one designation to another, i.e., Emergency Rescue Squadrons (ERS), to Air Rescue Service (ARS), to Air Rescue Groups (ARG), as well as consistently being reassigned from one Air Force or Command to another, when the Korean War broke out, they were ill-prepared to change from a SAR mission to a CSAR or combat SAR mission. And there is a massive difference between the two.

THEY CALLED IT NAKED FANNY

Lt. Col. Marek: *The Sikorsky H-19 flew the more tactical SAR missions. We'll underline yet again, however, that all these peacetime SAR outfits were not prepared to fight a war in Korea. Of course, they did it nevertheless and did so with enormous valor.*

In an essay published in the fall 1990, [in] Airpower Journal, Captain Edward B. Westermann, USAF, wrote this: "By using a combination of sheer guts, good luck, and a learn-as-you-go mentality, the ARS logged hundreds of combat saves and was responsible for the evacuation of 9,898 United Nations personnel by the end of the war."

At the end of that war (Korea), the USAF returned to its peacetime mentality for SAR operations. Westermann wrote: "By the end of 1960, the ARS was a skeleton command."

Remember, the strategic emphasis in the U.S. remained on the threat of a massive nuclear exchange, and the major investments were made in the strategic forces, bombers, submarines and ICBMs.

The net result was that once Korea was over, no one was thinking of another Korea in Vietnam, and certainly no one was thinking of a counterinsurgency style of war.

Well, Vietnam did happen and we're now ready to dig into the HH-43 deployment to that region. You will recall that the Commander-in-Chief Pacific (CINCPAC) approved that in May 1964. You'll also recall that the Gulf of Tonkin Resolution was passed in August 1964.

As we walk you through the HH-43 deployments, we want to emphasize that each air base to which the "Huskies" were deployed had many different missions and many different aircraft assigned to them. Furthermore, many aircraft, different from those stationed at these bases, came in and out, from all services, including Air America, for a wide variety of reasons. While we can only highlight a limited number of missions assigned to these bases, please keep in mind that no matter which base, the HH-43 crews had to be able to respond to the needs of each mission, each different kind of aircraft, from each service and Air America, and do long range or shorter range SAR missions to boot. That's a tall order for a limited number of HH-43 aircraft and crews. The crewmembers truly were walking aircraft data bases to be able to adjust their responses to each event that demanded their attention.

The USAF plan was to initially deploy the HH-43s to Da Nang AB, Republic of Vietnam (RVN), southeast of the border with North Vietnam, Bien Hoa AB on Saigon's northwest corner, and Soc Trang AB (not shown on map) to the south in the Mekong River delta region. The USAF SAR deployment began in June 1964.

Part of the deployment strategy was to send units into the theater on a temporary duty or TDY status in order to keep the official force level numbers down for permanent deployments. That's the way the 'Huskies' came in.

In response to orders from the Joint Chiefs of Staff (JCS), the USAF, in May 1964, instructed the 33rd ARS at Naha AB, Okinawa, Japan to send two HH-43Bs, their crews and mechanics to Bien Hoa AB and two HU-16 Albatrosses to Korat RTAFB, Thailand. We're not sure how this date crunches with the fact that CINCPAC did not approve the deployment until June, but will set that aside for other business. We'll also not worry about the "Albatross" in this report, but instead concentrate on the HH-43s. "Yankee Team" reconnaissance operations, which now were being escorted by USAF and Navy fighter aircraft over Laos, were incurring increasing losses, so, at the 11th hour, the two HH-43Bs were diverted from Bien Hoa to Nakhon Phanom RTAFB, nicknamed NKP (sometimes called "Naked Fanny," by those stationed there). A short time later, a third HH-43 came to NKP.

NKP was a better location, positioned in the northeast corner of Thailand, on the Mekong River, a stone's throw from Laos, and a short flight to respond to the "Yankee Team" area of operations.

THEY CALLED IT NAKED FANNY

The 33rd ARS helicopters were flown by transport into nearby Udorn RTAFB, just south of Vientiane, Laos, assembled, and then flown to NKP. These were the first USAF helicopter aircraft and crews in the Vietnam War specifically tasked with the combat SAR mission.

One of the fascinating, yet confounding occurrences in writing this book has come from the wonderful flow of information from, as it is currently phrased, "boots on the ground" or folks who actually experienced a described event. Such is the case with a section of Lt. Col. Edward Marek's information regarding what I call "the missing link." It involves the period from November through December of 1964, when the TDY unit from Okinawa returned home and prior to the arrival of a second four-month TDY unit in January of 1965. It was the TDY unit from Minot AFB, North Dakota, previously at Da Nang, that arrived to fill the two month span.

John Christianson, then a 1st lieutenant, was a part of that Minot unit and experienced the actual deployment of that group and its subsequent relocation to Nakhon Phanom. With apologies to Lt. Col. Marek, who, I believe would want all information to be correct, I have inserted, in brackets, Lt. Christianson's updated information.

Liutenant Colonel Edward Marek continues:

We haven't forgotten that the outfit at NKP consisted of men and machines TDY from [Okinawa] Japan. So, what did they call the outfit at NKP? It was called "Det Provisional 3 PARC." What's that, you ask?

There's an interesting bit of history here, so we need to pause before continuing with the other deployments.

The Air Rescue Service had divided the world into five rescue regions and had a rescue center located in each. Please remember, these were all peacetime organizations. In the continental U.S., there were the Eastern (EARC), Central (CARC), and Western (WARC) Rescue Centers. Overseas there were the Atlantic (AARC) and the

Pacific (PARC) Rescue Centers. Under normal circumstances, the Air Force organizes its basic units into squadrons, and, if required, detachments (Det—smaller elements) are subordinated to a squadron. In this case, however, each one of these rescue centers had detachments, an unusual organizational setup.

We believe that the 2nd ARG, which had earlier moved from the Philippines to Hawaii, became the PARC. Then, on April 1, 1962, Det 3 PARC was organized at Tan Son Nhut AB on Saigon's southeast corner, long before the USAF sent in any HH-43s. Det 3 PARC had no aircraft, but instead operated as a coordinating function only. It literally had to go out and find Army and Marine helicopters and persuade them to go on a SAR mission for aircrew recoveries. This could get hard if resources became short because of major ground operations that demanded these helicopters. There were instances where downed aircrews had to battle it out themselves.

Use of the nomenclature "provisional" was a holdover from the days of WWII when missions such as air-sea rescue were considered a minor part of the mission of any flying unit. In effect, with the nomenclature "Det Provisional 3 PARC," the HH-43 deployment connoted it was not primarily for SAR, but instead local base recovery (LBR) and local base firefighting. That supported the effort to keep it as quiet as possible that they were there to do SAR. But it also fit the reality that there was little forethought or planning attached to the SAR line of work. Using TDY crews not only covered the true number of forces in the theater, but also added to the temporary image the USAF was trying to create about all this.

Of course, the reality is the HH-43Bs did all three missions. This is what makes these Pedro outfits so special. They had to take care of all kinds of aircraft running into trouble on takeoff and those limping home and fighting to land in one piece; and also dart off on a more distant mission to save downed air crews or ground combat units trapped in tough fights.

THEY CALLED IT NAKED FANNY

A standard mission crew for the LBR-firefighting mission would consist of a pilot and co-pilot, flight engineer-crew chief, an aero-medical technician, and two airborne firefighters. Things got more complicated if they had to conduct a CSAR mission.

If they had formally trained pararescuemen, known in the USAF as "PJs," the crew composition would be pilot and co-pilot, one PJ and the flight mechanic. The PJ would be the one to go down on the hoist, retrieve the downed crewmember, and get him back in the aircraft. But if the unit did not have a PJ, then they might leave a couple crew members from the LBR-firefighting configuration behind and let the remaining crew, whether firefighter, flight engineer, or medic, handle the PJ's tasks. PJs did not start arriving until August 1964. They were assigned on temporary duty from Eglin AFB, Florida. They were few in number, and they served all over Southeast Asia, but mostly at NKP and Da Nang.

We've conducted a lot of business in discussing the deployment to NKP. It gave us a chance to explain a lot of things.

Let's go next to Da Nang AB, RVN, fondly known to many as "Rocket City." Two HH-43s came from Det 2 CARC, Minot AFB, North Dakota, arriving in early August 1964. [The two aircraft were actually from Det 3 CARC at Grand Forks, AFB, North Dakota, and were sent from Det 3 because the two HH-43s at Minot were too close to major component time change requirements. So it was, in fact Det 3's two aircraft that were shipped to Da Nang while the Minot HH-43s went to Grand Forks.] *They formed Det Provisional 2 PARC. A third aircraft arrived sometime in October 1964* [from Glasgow AFB, Montana].

This deployment was done with a tone of secrecy. On August 7, 1964, a call came into Captain Gene Graham, the Det 2 CARC commander, saying that a contingency plan [called OPS Plan 510] *for deploying LBR detachments was to be "exercised." Personnel were assembled, instructed that they were going on an extended temporary assignment to a classified destination, and were told what to bring. They were given no other mission-related information. In the meantime, they had to break down their HH-43s for shipment.* [The aircraft were not broken down for shipment as they were shipped on C-124s.]

Two C-124 transport aircraft arrived; two HH-43s were uploaded; the crews boarded the aircraft and then flew to Travis AFB, California. Following takeoff from Travis, Capt. Graham read the classified orders he had been given prior and read them to the crews: destination Da Nang AB, RVN, with a stop on the way for rest and fuel at Wake Island.

[Lt. Christianson: "All we had at that time was a classified message to deploy—no destination. Even when we left Travis after our night there, we still had no definite destination, although we all figured it was to Vietnam. We stopped at Hickam AB in Hawaii for a meeting with the Pacific Air Rescue Commander who ultimately gave us our destination. We did stop at Wake for a few hours while we refueled and had some food. Later, we stopped at Clark AB in the Philippines to pick up two Rescue Command personnel who would be stationed with us at Da Nang. As history would have it, these were the first three USAF Rescue helicopters in Vietnam."]

When the crews arrived at Da Nang, they learned that a handful of Grumman SA-16 "Albatrosses" formed the core of the USAF's SAR capability. Lending credence to the notion of being provisional at the SAR mission, the crews also found that their main job was LBR. The SA-16s were flying the deep penetration rescues and the HH-43s were used for the "local work," which included rescue missions in whatever was defined as the "local area." Do not minimize the importance or hazards associated with flying "local rescue" missions outside "Rocket City." As one HH-43 crewman put it, the region outside Da Nang was "Bad Indian Country." The HH-43B had no armor and was unarmed. Some folks at Da Nang might have called them LBR, but in anyone else's book, they were SAR missions (all part of the "provisional" mentality).

THEY CALLED IT NAKED FANNY

The Minot crews remained at Da Nang for about four months, until the end of the year, [actually until November 1964] when permanent crews started arriving. [This new unit came in with their new HH-43F models with armor plating and a bigger engine.]

Well, Det Provisional 2 PARC did not stay at Da Nang for very long. The air assault in Laos simply commanded more SAR resources be positioned at NKP. So the outfit moved to NKP in November 1964. Det Provisional 3 PARC was deactivated, and its forces joined with the Da Nang organization and all of a sudden Det Provisional 2 PARC was at NKP. NKP now had, for a few days we believe, six "Huskies." Then, the unit that originally set up shop at NKP, the group from the 33rd ARS from Okinawa, packed up and went home. So NKP went back to three aircraft.

[Before the Det 2 unit moved to NKP, two of its pilots were sent early to Don Muong Air Base at Bangkok. This was in order to try to obtain certain Aircraft Power Equipment (AGE) to provide electrical power to help start the aircraft engines, etc. This equipment was not currently at NKP. After receiving assurances that such equipment would be sent, the two pilots made their way to NKP and were immediately available for mission duty.]

[At the end of December], *while the Minot TDY crews left, their helicopters stayed behind and the crews returned to Minot with no aircraft.*

In April and May 1965, two more dets were set up at Ubon RTAFB and Udorn RTAFB, Thailand: Det Provisional 3 PARC and Det Provisional 5 PARC respectively.

In July 1965, the USAF got rid of most of this "provisional" and Det PARC stuff and formed the 38th Aerospace Rescue Squadron (ARS) at Tan Son Nhut, AB, RVN. Det 1 was at NKP with three aircraft; Det 2 at Takhli with two aircraft; Det 3 at Ubon with three aircraft; Det 4 at Korat with two aircraft; Det 5 at Udorn with two aircraft; Det 6 at Bien Hoa with three aircraft; and Det 7 at Da Nang with three aircraft.

Det 1, 38 ARRS was set up with two HH-43s at Phan Rang

AB, RVN on January 15, 1966, when Det 1 at NKP RTAFB moved there when the Jolly Greens took over at NKP.

In this section, we have tried to describe the deployments and highlight interesting features about each that would give you a broad brush look at the wide variety of missions the Pedros had, the wide variety of aircraft they had to worry about and know about, and the immense area of responsibility they had. While no one will ever shortchange the Jolly Greens, which, as mentioned above, ended up at NKP RTAFB and Da Nang, in South Vietnam, for the work they did and how they did it. We only wish to be sure everyone understands what these little "Huskies" were doing as well, spread around South Vietnam and Thailand at 14 bases, and doing so with aircraft not designed for many of the jobs undertaken and crews that had to discard their Air Force specialty codes and simply do what the moment called for.

Lieutenant Colonel Marek indicates there were six HH-43s at NKP at one time. Through conversations with men who were "on the ground" with the first and second TDY groups we have learned that the first group, from Okinawa, initially had only two "43s." A third aircraft arrived in August. Those three aircraft went back to Okinawa at the end of the TDY. When the Okinawa TDY group completed its tour of duty in mid-November, 1964, it was replaced by Det. Provisional 2 personnel and three helicopters from Da Nang. So, it is entirely possible that there was an overlapping short period of time during which there were six HH-43s at NKP.

Then-1st Lt. John Christianson wrote the following on the website S.E.A. Stories, and it is reprinted with his permission:

John Christianson: *Jim Sovell, a pilot classmate of mine at Stead AFB, NV, and who was deployed with us from Grand Forks AFB, ND, and myself, were sent to NKP several days before the rest of the unit moved over. We were to head to the AGE shop at Don Muang AB in Bangkok to try to get some AGE sent to NKP as they had no power units or other equipment* there. *After a couple of days in Bangkok, Jim and I descended upon NKP on 14 November 64. Being the good guys that we were, we offered our services to the unit there and would pull alert with them. "Pretty safe" we thought, as they had had no rescue missions of any consequence since their June arrival.*

On 18 November, however, that changed when Ball 03, one of two F-100s escorting a "Yankee Team" reconnaissance mission, was shot down while exchanging fire with an enemy antiaircraft gun position. Ball 03's wingman called "Dropkick" (a distress signal used in place of "Mayday" to confuse enemy troops) to the Air America Air Operations Center in Vientiane, reporting that Ball 03 had crashed just south of Ban Senphan in central Laos near the North Vietnamese border. The Air America Operations Officer in the Operations Center diverted a C-123 to reconnoiter the area and act as an Airborne Controller until relieved by a USAF HU-16 from Korat RTAFB. Once in position, Tacky 44, the HU-16, requested that U.S. Navy A-1 Skyraiders fly to Ban Senphan, to search for wreckage and the pilot, and suppress any enemy opposition if it were encountered.

Within minutes of their arrival on the scene, the Navy Skyraiders received ground fire from Pathet Lao emplacements near the location that Ball 03 was believed to have been shot down. The A-1s attacked the gun positions taking minor flak and small arms hits to their aircraft. During the action, one of the Skyraider pilots spotted what appeared to be a burning crash site in the jungle approximately five miles away from the coordinates originally furnished.

Two HH-43Bs were put on alert and launched with Det. 3 crew members, then proceeded the 10 miles to the Mekong River near Nakhon Phanom and Thakhek, Laos. At that time, the U.S. Ambassador's permission was required to cross the Mekong River into Laos and the crews did not receive this permission during their holding orbits on the Thai side of the river. Running short of fuel, both aircraft returned to NKP for refueling.

At the same time, a C-124 landed at NKP with its destination of Okinawa. Two of the original pilots, knowing that they were being replaced by Det 2 guys, asked Jim Sovell and myself if we would take their place. Jim and I said yes.

They got on the C-124 and went home and a few minutes later both aircraft (HH-43s) were launched, this time with clearance to cross the Mekong and with Jim and me on board as co-pilots. I believe Jim Crabb was Aircraft Commander; TSgt. Reed was the Flight Engineer and SSgt. Bennett the PJ.

Shortly after we crossed the Mekong, we picked up two U.S. Navy Skyraiders for cover. We were sent to investigate a fire in the jungle which approximated the shootdown coordinates. The call signs for our two HH-43s were Pansy 88 and 89. We flew blindly into Laos with no intel as to where the bad guys were. To our knowledge, we encountered no ground fire nor did we see any bad guys. The fire was just that—a jungle fire and not one caused by a crashed F-100. We made our way back to NKP without any complications.

Before darkness temporarily ended the rescue efforts, the HU-16 coordinated thirteen F-105s, eight F-100s, six Navy A-1s, two HH-43Bs, and a pair of Air America H-34s in a concerted effort to find and rescue the downed pilot. The coordination and control of these diverse elements provided a preview of SAR efforts that would be conducted over the next decade.

In an exchange of e-mails about the Ball 03 mission, Christianson wrote:

This mission crossing the Mekong into Laos made the history books (Tillford's "USAF SAR in SEA") as the first official rescue mission into Laos. As we crossed the river, we picked up

THEY CALLED IT NAKED FANNY

Rescue crew at NKP awaiting orders to cross the Mekong River into Laos, Nov. 1964. Shortly after the picture was taken the crew received clearance to fly into Laos. Shown in the photo are Lt. John Christianson (*far left*); co-pilot, 1st Lt. Crabb; Rescue Crew Commander (RCC), TSgt. Al Reed; crew chief and SSgt. Robert Bennett. (Photo courtesy John Christianson)

two Navy A-1s and also an Air Force Rescue HU-16, which became our Command and Control bird. We didn't find anything, but it is listed in the book as the first official mission. After we got back we talked to some Air America H-34 guys and they were surprised that we didn't get shot down as there were a lot of "bad guys" along our route. Not good, but we didn't notice anything.

From the RotorheadsRUs.us website, Jim Burns credits Chris Hobson's "Vietnam Air Losses," (http://www.h43-huskie.info/framesetpedro.htm) and *PJ's in Vietnam,* by Robert L. LaPointe, with the following:

1964—November 18-19*: The first large scale CSAR operations of the Vietnam War took place when two HH-43Bs (possibly*

#62-4564 and #62-4565), call signs "Pansy 88 and Pansy 89" from Nakhon Phanom RTAFB, Thailand attempted to rescue the pilot of an F-100D (call sign "Ball 3"), Capt. William Reynolds Martin, whose aircraft had been hit by AAA fire and shot down near Ban Senphan, Laos on 18 November 1964. The search for him was unsuccessful on the 18th, however his wreckage was located on the 19th and an Air America H-34 lowered their co-pilot and he discovered that Capt. Martin died during his ejection when he hit the rocky ground. The H-34 recovered his body.

Detachment Provisional 2 PARC Personnel—Da Nang AB, RVN and Nakhon Phanom RTAFB, Thailand.

Capt. Alva G. Graham	Det CO	Minot AFB, ND
Capt. Tom Kelly	RCC	Minot AFB, ND
Capt. Joe Leech	RCC	Minot AFB, ND
1st Lt. John Christianson	RCC	Minot AFB, ND
1st Lt. Jim Sovell	RCC	Grand Forks AFB, ND
1st Lt. Robert Osik	RCC	Selfridge AFB, MI
A1C George Fink	ADM	Minot AFB, ND
MSgt. Robert Bradfield	Maint Sup	Minot AFB, ND
MSgt. Eldrid Lusk	Maint NCOIC	Minot AFB, ND
SSgt. Charles Husby	FE	Minot AFB, ND
SSgt. Robert Julian	FE	Kincheloe AFB, MI
SSgt. James Tabor	FE	Glasgow AFB, MT
A1C Roman Jennissen	HM	Minot AFB, ND
A2C Larry Smith	HM	Minot AFB, ND
A2C John Zielinsky	HM	K. I. Sawyer AFB, MI
SSgt. Robert Bennett	PJ	
A2C Andre Raymond	PJ	
A2C Albert Dobson	PJ	
A2C Richard L. Graham	PJ	
SSgt. Arthur Saintheart	ABR	Minot AFB, ND
SSgt. William Dickerson	ABR	Minot AFB, ND
A1C Jerry Wolford	ABR	Minot AFB, ND
A1C Edward Bevens	ABR	Minot AFB, ND

THEY CALLED IT NAKED FANNY

NKP, November 1964. Unloading one of the three HH-43Bs flown in from Da Nang AB, RVN by a C-124. (Photo courtesy John Christianson)

Alert crew at NKP. *Left to right*: Lt. John Christianson; Lt. James Sovell, SSgt. Robert Bennett and A2C John Zielenski. (Photo courtesy John Christianson)

5

TIME TO MOVE IN

THERE ARE CONFLICTING CLAIMS AS TO WHETHER the 507th Tactical Control Squadron was the first U.S. Air Force unit to arrive at NKP, or Det Provisional 3 of the Pacific Air Rescue Center with its three HH-43B Huskie helicopters. And then again, it may have been the 1st MOB Group that established the initial communication base at NKP. According to the comments that follow, the "Huskie" drivers were the Gold Medal winners; 1st MOB took the Silver Medal and the Invert radar operations guys got the Bronze. But to keep peace in the brotherhood, let's just call it a photo finish with everyone getting a piece of the "Gold."

The 507th was sent from Shaw AFB, South Carolina to Tan Son Nhut Air Base, outside of Saigon, South Vietnam to set up a Control and Reporting Post (CRP) there, and was, in fact, the first U.S. unit in Vietnam in January of 1962.

> **Dick Kennedy**: *You need to go back to 1964, when the 1st MOB, USAF, from P.I. arrived and set up a mobile tower for Air Traffic Control. The only group there was one HH-43 that was flying out to pick up any downed pilots in Laos. There were maybe 10 people (that included air crew and support) and our group of 10 and we were the only GIs at NKP.*

THEY CALLED IT NAKED FANNY

But let's give it to the Seabees! They were the first in and built the runway. Dick Kennedy USAF 1960—1964, 1st MOB.

Skip Ward: *I was with the 507th Combat Control Squadron out of Shaw AFB, SC in 1964, when we were deployed to NKP. We had detachments from Myrtle Beach AFB, Pope AFB, Shaw AFB and Seymour Johnson AFB. I was in the 727th ACW squadron from Myrtle Beach. We left Shaw in September 1964, and after stops at Tinker, Travis, Hawaii, Wake, Guam, PI and Saigon, we finally arrived at Nakhon Phanom. We landed on PSP and set up a tent city that was the beginning of a full blown base. Even then, we had sappers trying to disrupt the operations of the base. Thai security and 507th personnel did our job in keeping the radar and communications van secure. Skip Ward, then-A1C, USAF.*

Herb Wild: *I originally started going to NKP around the end of '64, with "Invert." Left Ft. Bragg and flew to Seattle where we were given M-16s (no ammo) and didn't find out where we were headed until the flight crew opened an envelope and redirected. We landed on the PSP runway and helped set up the radar installation. Started out living in the village while the hooches were being built and still remember breakfast of goose eggs and water buffalo; mmm-mmm good, especially after a night of Singha and that whiskey with formaldehyde in it. Also remember sitting in a bar on the Mekong (bamboo tubes for urinals) and watching the war going on in Laos (right across from the Ho Chi Minh clock tower). Stayed for about seven months that time and went back to Bragg. Returned for a while in '67-'68, and saw how much the place had grown. Was working out of the P.I. then in Radar and also got to work at Green Hill, Phitsanulok and Dong Ha (Waterboy) during Tet of '68. Actually took the train from Bangkok to Phitsanulok (great ride). Returned again in 1971-72, as an Air Ops Specialist and worked with the 1st Special Ops Squadron for a year until it closed down. Many memories.*

On 4 January 1965, the 5th Tactical Control Group began deploying personnel to Nakhon Phanom, Thailand, to relieve the 507th TCG TDY personnel who were then manning Invert, the CRP there. On 21 January, the 5th TCG assumed all operational control and responsibility for the site. The 5th Tactical Control Group exercised command jurisdiction until May of 1965, when the 6235th Air Base Squadron was formed. In those early days the base housed the Search and Rescue detachment, a communications team, a CRP (radar operations/Invert Control) and the base support unit.

While the base grew to over 6,000 personnel and the missions originating from NKP expanded as the war progressed; that is a story for another day and is well detailed on various Internet websites as well as in other books on the subject.

Our story deals with the "early days" when there were no procedures or guidelines to conduct the missions at hand…especially for the conduct of rescue missions. Everything was considered "hush, hush," including the fact that we Americans were there. Again, this was during the time of what is referred to as the "Quiet War," or the "Secret War." The rescue missions conducted were at the time TOP SECRET; so much so that declassified documents were years behind what actually took place regarding the placement of U.S. Air Force helicopter aircraft at NKP. Never was an order given to the men who braved the unknown to attempt a rescue of a downed pilot. All that was asked was "could you attempt a rescue?" Always, the answer was "yes"—100% down the line for all personnel.

Today, the installation known simply as NKP, or Naked Fanny, is gone although identifiable remnants remain. The site is now the location of the airport for the town of Nakhon Phanom, Thailand.

This, then, is the story of the men who, from time to time, made up what ultimately would become Detachment 1, 38th ARS. The book covers that part of their lives from 1964 through 1965, with much of it told in their own words and from their recollections. Many missions are further detailed by those who were rescued by the pilots and crew members who laid their lives on the line to pluck them from behind enemy lines. For most, the written story begins with the day they received the orders that would start them on the way to an assignment they never anticipated.

Official reports of the missions remained classified and were buried for years in boxes at Maxwell Air Force Base, Alabama. Now, after having been declassified and released, they are enhanced by the memories recalled from nearly fifty years ago. While the primary focus will be on the fourth TDY group at NKP and their commander, Joe Ballinger, the stories of others who preceded them as well as memories of others who also spent time at NKP are included.

I was privileged to be there as a weapons controller—part of the 5th Tactical Control Group's Invert Control CRP (Combat Reporting Post) contingent for four months of that time. These brave men were my comrades in arms and some have become dear friends. I am honored to help tell their story, which is an important part of U.S. Air Force and American aviation history.

Because the blades of the HH-43B Huskie helicopters were hollow, laminated spruce covered with neoprene rubber, it has often been said about the Huskies and the men who flew and supported them that they were "Blades of Wood—Men of Steel."

The very early days, so far as Search and Rescue crews at NKP were described in the book *United States Air Force, Search and Rescue in Southeast Asia* by Capt. Earl H. Tilford, Jr. His writing came during the time he was assigned to the Office of Air Force History and was published by the Office of Air Force History, United States Air Force, Washington, D.C., 1980. The material is in the public domain. We begin at page 51:

> *Meanwhile, in accordance with the Joint Chiefs of Staff directive in May, directing the Air Force to send search and rescue units to Southeast Asia, two ARS HH-43Bs, their crews and mechanics, were sent from the 33rd Air Rescue Squadron at Naha Air Station, Okinawa, to Bien Hoa. Because of the Yankee Team*

rescue requirements, they were diverted and rerouted to Nakhon Phanom Royal Thai Air Force Base on the Thai-Laos border. Arrangements also were made to have two U.S. Marine H-34s placed on alert at Khe Sanh in northern South Vietnam whenever a Yankee Team mission flew over Laos. Simultaneously, the 33rd Air Rescue Squadron at Naha sent two HU-16Bs to Korat Royal Thai Air Force Base to perform as airborne rescue control ships during search and rescue missions. During this same period, the 31st Air Rescue Squadron, Clark Air Base Philippines, sent three HU 16Bs to Da Nang for rescue duties in the Gulf of Tonkin.

Since the 6,000-foot pierced-steel planking runway at Nakhon Phanom could not handle loaded C-97 cargo planes, the plan was to land the unit at Udorn, have the helicopters unloaded, assembled, and then fly them to their final destination. Major Saunders (Major Alan W. Saunders, Commander, Detachment 3, Pacific Air Rescue Center) flew up to Udorn to make final arrangements and to greet the men. Unfortunately, he failed to obtain the necessary support items such as JP-4 fuel, bedding and rations for the men at either Udorn or Nakhon Phanom. Consequently, when the rescue unit reached Udorn on June 17, and began unloading and assembling their choppers, Saunders discovered there were no facilities to accommodate the men for that night. Saunders had the men flown to Nakhon Phanom for the night where he assumed there were suitable facilities. Only a few rickety open-sided sheds awaited the tired crewmen when they reached the dusty, riverside base. The exhausted party made a campfire, barbecued their C-rations, and slept under the stars. At dawn most of the men returned to Udorn where they continued assembling their choppers. By the following morning the helicopters were ready to fly to Nakhon Phanom, then the crews discovered that the fuel had not arrived. Another day was spent in securing fuel, but finally, late on the afternoon of June 20, the HH-43Bs reached Nakhon Phanom.

THEY CALLED IT NAKED FANNY

During the next few weeks, barely livable conditions continued at Nakhon Phanom. Officers and enlisted men endured a lack of suitable latrine facilities, electric power, and even potable water. On June 27, an Air Force electrician arrived from Bangkok and installed a generator and some wiring for light. Three days later four Thai carpenters began refurbishing the sheds and building a kitchen. Meanwhile, the rescue personnel worked at putting in a latrine and constructing a shower. Such as it was, Nakhon Phanom was the only base in the world with an Air Rescue Service officer as its American commander. Substantial problems remained, but at last Air Rescue Service helicopters were entrenched in Southeast Asia. Pilots who flew over Laos had trained Air Rescue Service forces to support their mission. (In reality this training didn't happen until the fourth unit had been on scene at Nakhon Phanom for at least a month.)

The effect on morale was favorable, though not entirely warranted. The HH-43B was limited to a relatively small radius of action that varied between 125 to 140 miles. Due to this range limitation, the Nakhon Phanom based Huskies were not able to provide search and rescue services for the Plain of Jars or areas southeast of Pakse in the Laotian panhandle. An aircraft damaged by enemy fire over the center of the Plain of Jars had to be flown at least fifty miles south to be within range of any Nakhon Phanom based Air Force rescue choppers.

6

AS IT WAS IN THE BEGINNING

THE INTRODUCTION TO THE BOOK LISTS FIVE SEPARATE TDY or temporary duty helicopter rescue groups that served at Nakhon Phanom in 1964 and 1965. This chapter focuses on the first of those groups. While it has been possible to identify most of those whose boots daily walked across the PSP, pierced steel planking, it was Captain Leonard Fialko and Lt. Ken Franzel of that first Search and Rescue TDY group who first told their story about their foray into the jungle airbase called NKP.

Their story is reprinted with permission of the *Pedro News*, Stephen Mock, Editor:

> **Len Fialko**: *The 36th ARSq (we were the Air Rescue Service Squadron in those days) provided two pilots to augment the 33rd ARSq HH-43B unit at Naha, Okinawa. I came from Det. 1, 36th ARSq at Misawa, Japan and 1st Lt. Kenneth C. Franzel came from Det. 4, 36th ARSq, which I believe was at Osan, Korea. The Medical technicians for the crew were provided by the Base Hospital at Naha. We were the first rescue helicopters sent to Southeast Asia and the only Americans at NKP.*

THEY CALLED IT NAKED FANNY

I arrived at Naha on June 15, 1964. The next two days were spent preparing the two aircraft for air shipment and assembling mobility gear. We arrived at NKP on June 17. Some of us went to Udorn to assemble the aircraft. A T-28 unit of American advisors was stationed there and provided quarters and facilities for us. We flew the aircraft back to NKP on 21 June.

I remember the living and operating conditions best. We had always had support units, which provided meals, quarters and specialized maintenance. NKP was, when we arrived, just a PSP runway. There were three tin roofed huts and an outhouse, which the Seabees left when they built the runway. Someone had dumped some cases of C-rations, some bunks and 55-gallon drums of JP-4 on the ramp. We were on our own for everything else.

Shortly after we arrived, two communications NCOs were sent to set up a mobile radio station. This was our only link to the rest of the world. All traffic had to be manually coded and decoded, so we learned to use words sparingly. Operational control was provided by the Command Post at Saigon. Administrative support was provided from Bangkok. (Just one more example of the absence of direct organizational channels.)

No one in the unit had any combat experience (from World War II or the Korean War), nor did we receive any briefing on what to expect. We did a lot of guessing and hoped the bad guys were as dumb as we were. Fortunately, we had no rescue missions while I was there.

We did, however, make some modifications to the aircraft. Much of the area we were to cover was at the maximum range of the HH-43 and at high altitude. We removed all doors for weight and carried two 55-gallon drums of JP-4 in a wood rack in the cabin. I believe we intended to land and hand-pump the fuel into the aircraft tank. We also traded for two BARs (Browning Automatic Rifles), which we mounted on ropes firing aft from the cabin.

We were replaced by another TDY crew in the middle of August. I believe they were from the States, and they stayed until a PCS crew arrived. (Actually, there would be three more TDY groups after their replacements.)

The only other name that I can remember is then-Captain Michael C. Tennery. He stayed a month or so longer than I did and came from Naha.

Ken Franzel: *I'm happy to see some recognition of Air Rescue and the HH-43Bs in the early days of the Southeast Asia conflict.*

My part in Air Rescue in SEA actually began when I was assigned to Det. 4, 36th ARS in Osan, Korea. In April 1964, I had just arrived when Det. 4 was tasked to provide a pilot for the H-19 unit in Itazuke, Japan. Since I had H-19 (helicopter) experience and was not checked out in Korea, I was the one selected. After a month or more in Japan, Itazuke closed down and I was to return to Osan. However, Det. 4 had now been tasked to send an HH-43B pilot to the 33rd ARS at Naha AB, Okinawa. I was already TDY again so I was selected for this trip. From this point my orders were only verbal orders of the commander (VOCO).

Upon arrival in Naha, I checked into the BOQ and had a message waiting for me from the squadron commander (I think Col. Dyberg was the 33rd CO, but am not sure). The note said, "Don't unpack, we're moving out." The squadron had a meeting that evening and as I remember we were not told more than that we were going to SEA. The move, of course, was classified and kept as quiet as possible.

An aside: A couple of interesting incidents as we prepared for what, we knew not. During briefing a list of personal items required for the deployment was read. One item was the radiation dosimeter (the Cold War item for detecting an individual's radiation exposure). I raised my hand and said I didn't have one. The briefer (who was not being deployed) took his off from around his neck, tossed it to me and said, "Now you can go."

THEY CALLED IT NAKED FANNY

Another item was the issue of weapons. Aircrews were issued the .38 revolver and shoulder holster and all were issued the AR-15. The only AR-15s on base had arrived for the APs (Air Police). These were transferred to the 33rd and in turn to us. The AR-15s were still in plastic bags with the factory operating manual. None of us had ever seen one before.

The teardown of the HH-43Bs started that night. It must have been at least 24 hours later when the C-130s were loaded and ready to go.

We first landed at Da Nang AB to refuel, etc. Da Nang at that time had a rotation squadron of F-100s sitting out in the open on the ramp.

The only difference from an ordinary base, other than the old buildings was the sight of everyone armed all the time. The C-130 made a steep approach into Da Nang and a tactical takeoff in order to avoid the possibility of ground fire.

After a short flight over jungle terrain our C-130 made a short field landing on a PSP runway, which turned out to be Nakhon Phanom. Welcome to Naked Fanny! 5,000 feet of PSP runway, a PSP ramp and a couple of old Thai-occupied metal buildings left over from when the USN Seabees constructed the base sometime earlier.

The C-130 crew would not shut down the engines for off-load as they were unsure of the security of the airfield. On the ramp were stacks of metal cots, mattresses, bedding, C-rations and 55-gallon drums of JP-4. That was the beginning! We off-loaded except for the helicopters and some of the pilots went back onboard for the flight to Udorn. As I remember one C-130 with helicopters and mechanics had gone directly from Da Nang to Udorn to off-load and begin assembly of the HH-43s.

Leaving a skeleton crew composed of a couple of pilots, the unit CO and mostly medics behind, the other pilots including myself and mechanics left for Udorn. Note: We started out with medics, not PJs.

When we arrived at Udorn the other C-130 had been off-loaded. We off-loaded the pieces, etc., from our C-130 and it departed. Udorn was a busy Air America-CIA installation with much better facilities than NKP. A push was on for us to have the 43s ready to cover a mission the next day. This was not to be as the mechanics had already had little sleep since the teardown began. It was evident we had to have more time. After the mechanics had tried for two hours to put one blade attaching bolt in place (normally a few minute job) we had to call it a day.

In the meantime the Air America pilots told us to do something with the 43 paint job. We had been deployed into a combat situation with silver and day-glow orange paint. It was another indication that a lot of people, including our unit, were really not aware of what we were getting into. Air America gave me five gallons of OD (olive drab) paint and some brushes. We at least got rid of the day-glow.

After assembling the 43s and test flying them we took off on a dark night, with virtually no aids other than a compass, across the jungle, low level, for NKP.

While we were assembling the 43s in Udorn the 1st MOB had arrived at NKP. The 1st MOB combat communications SOG 17 team from Clark AFB in the Philippines had continuous back to back six month TDY duty, with USAF SOG support from MAGTHAI (Military Advisory Group Thailand). They had a vehicle with a rotating beacon on top. This we used as guidance as we neared NKP. With our arrival "Rescue 2" was born. Rescue 1 was a Marine chopper unit, which was based at Da Nang but stayed daily near the North South border (between North and South Vietnam).

Our mission early on was to cover U.S. Navy flights over Laos, primarily the PDJ (Plain of Jars).

It readily became apparent that we were ill prepared for combat operations; the day-glow paint was only the beginning. We developed flying tactics consisting of flying two 43s in formation, in clouds as much as possible to reduce visual contact by ground forces. Perhaps one of the best known early problems was the hoist cable length of 100 ft. In a jungle of 300 ft. trees the hoist was useless. This was solved by adding 150 ft. of rope with a weight and collar onto the cable. A weight was necessary as the rope would fly around in the rotor without it. Now, with a hover in the treetops, we could reach ground but it was still necessary to leave the victim hanging 150 ft. below while flying to a safe landing area. It was still difficult for the flight mechanic/hoist operator to thread the collar through the jungle growth. The forest penetrator was later developed to reduce the problem. The 43s had no armor plate or protection of any kind for either the crew or critical aircraft components.

We did have WWII vintage flak vests and hip protectors. The hip protectors were folded and placed under the seat cushions; the vest was worn over a T-shirt, with locally custom made fatigue pants (individually purchased). Flight suits were unbearably hot. Helmets were bright white (good targets) which, one by one, were getting hand-painted black or green. The 43 was also not armed. This was partially solved by each crew member carrying his AR-15 and .38 aboard. In a trading deal with a classified unit in the area (I'm still not sure who they were) we were able to trade a case of insect repellent for a case of hand grenades, two BARs (Browning Automatic Rifles) and ammo. The grenades were to drop from the 43 by putting the grenade in a glass jar (after pulling the pin) and dropping it from a safe altitude. The BAR was tied in the 43 with ropes. There was, of course, nothing to keep one from shooting the tail off!

The operating range of the 43 was always a problem, however, since our original task was covering Laos operations. We had Air America establish secure fuel stashes at LIMA Sites for our use. As the mission expanded to North Vietnam the concept evolved for carrying 55-gallon drums on skids inside the 43 and feeding directly into the fuel system. As a drum was emptied it was pushed out the rear of the aircraft. This was developed after my departure.

Mission control was somewhat confusing. The 1st MOB unit monitored ongoing missions listening for code words indicating aircraft downed or bailouts. We were monitoring with 1st MOB so we were alerted at the same time. An airborne HU-16 then was to take over rescue control in conjunction with JSARC (Joint Service Air Rescue Center) in Saigon. Politics did get involved in mission control especially in an initial requirement for JSARC approval prior to crossing a border (a mission delay of hours or days could result). The HU-16 not only provided control but was our source of mail and personal supplies. We would put in a BX (Base Exchange) order with Center or the HU-16 by radio. Then on their next mission they would drop our order in with a spotter chute.

Back to the facilities: The first few days we spent living under an open shed. We then took over a couple of the former Seabees' metal buildings, which had been Thai occupied. One we used for officer barracks, the other for enlisted. A field kitchen was sent in after weeks of C-rations. An outside shower was built using 55-gallon drums (solar water heating). Drinking water was brought in from NKP (the nearby town of Nakhon Phanom), treated and tested by our medics. Latrine facilities were field outhouse type.

After some time of this type of living we were able to contract for quarters in NKP. The quarters were known as the Civilized Motel and were not much of an improvement but at least it had running water and no, or at least fewer, snakes and scorpions. It was later learned that the motel was supposedly operated by North Vietnamese VC sympathizers.

We had many of our original group return for later SEA assignments. Two of these that I know of, a Sgt. Black and one of our pilots were captured on later assignments. Sgt. Black was a POW for 6+ years and I think the pilot for 5+ years. [Ken is

THEY CALLED IT NAKED FANNY

obviously referring to Airman 2nd Class Arthur Neil Black and Captain Thomas J. Curtis. Both spent 7 ½ years as POWs as did Airman First Class William Robinson.] *Our CO's first name was Dave and he was a captain.* [Probably Captain Robert W. Davis.] *He kept a daily log at NKP, which would really help the NKP story.*

During my second tour (May 71-72), after the HH-53Cs of the 40th ARRS had moved from Udorn to NKP, the Pedros returned—to support the F-4s on strip alert at NKP.

Dan Galde, SMSgt. USAF, Ret., who would earn a Silver Star for his actions as a PJ, added that 1st MOB out of Clark AB, PI, provided the field kitchen, water and power for NKP during this early time.

DET PROVISIONAL 2 PARC
Nakhon Phanom RTAFB 20 Jun-16 Nov 1964

Capt. Robert W. Davis (P)	33 ARS Det. CO
Capt. Lucian A Gunter III (P)	33 ARS
Capt. Leonard Fialko (P)	Augment from 36 ARS, Det. 1, Misawa AB, Japan
Capt. Michael C. Tennery (P)	33 ARS
1st Lt. Kenneth Franzel (P)	Augment from 36 ARS, Det. 4, Osan AB, ROK
1Lt. James W. Crabb (P)	
TSgt. Alvin C. Reed (FE)	
SSgt. Albert B. Parker (FE)	33 ARS NCOIC
SSgt. Charles D. Severns (FE)	33 ARS
SSgt. John Willcox, Jr. (EM)	33 ARS
SSgt. David H. Blouin (MT)	51st USAF Dispensary
SSgt. Donald L. Watson (MT)	51st USAF Dispensary
SSgt. William J. McDougal	Augment from 36 ARS
A1C. James W. Burns (FE)	Augment from 31 ARS, Clark AB, PI

Scott Harrington

A1C Fred D. Scott (FE)   33 ARS
A1C David C. Black (MT)   51st USAF Dispensary
A1C Morris Johnson, Jr. (MT)   51st USAF Dispensary
A1C Dan Galde (PJ)   Augment from 36 ARS

THEY CALLED IT NAKED FANNY

Radar sail.

7

INVERT CONTROL

INVERT CONTROL WAS WELL ESTABLISHED BEFORE WE arrived, with the original TDY group having come from the 507th Tactical Control Squadron at Shaw AFB, South Carolina. They were replaced by personnel from the 5th TCG at Clark and I believe that we were the third group there.

The responsibility for the identification and control of aircraft is known as airspace management. Tactical and strategic attack, reconnaissance and airlift support aircraft are considered "weapons" in Air Force parlance and personnel skilled in maneuvering aircraft in a 3-D airspace environment for combat purposes are known as Weapons Controllers (officers), or Weapons Techs (enlisted). The overall job title encompasses various specialized sub-tasks, but the essential difference between Tactical Air Control and what is commonly understood as Air Traffic Control, is that Weapons Controllers bring aircraft together (under normal intercept operations), whereas Air Traffic Controllers try to keep aircraft apart.

Our responsibilities were to manage aircraft missions that included fighter-bomber ground attack, search and rescue, cargo transport airlift, and in-flight refueling operations in, through or over our assigned airspace. Coordinating U.S. Air Force missions with Army and Navy aviation—mixing aircraft of all types and flight capabilities—was a constant and dynamic twenty-four-hour mission. Everything from piston-engine Korean War era A-1 Skyraiders; to supersonic fighter-bombers with KC-135 Stratotankers always available to refuel them; to the HH-43B, and later, CH-3C helicopters were airborne at the same time.

The radar network at Invert was operated and maintained by USAF crews working twenty-four hours a day, seven days a week, for eleven years. Radar operations personnel were scheduled to work shifts with three crews switching between three days, three nights and three days break.

Radar and radio maintenance sections worked a single day shift with one or two technicians on duty at night. Nighttime non-routine maintenance events were attended to on a call-out basis. Radar and radio maintenance was performed on twelve-hour "days," with twelve-hour night shifts performing scheduled preventive maintenance inspection routines (PMIs) around air mission tasking to avoid conflicts. Maintenance technicians accessed the Crypto vault with the shift account custodian, signed for and set up the daily "frag" keys, reprogrammed and tested the radar and radio cryptographic equipment each night.

The Radar Operations darkroom area was originally located next to the aircraft parking ramp on a similar foundation of PSP metal planking. The darkroom itself was originally a World War II-vintage design sectional canvas enclosure known as an S-80 shelter. The flooring was assembled from the wooden packing boxes that the canvas sections were transported in. The structural support for the canvas was provided by half-circles of metal-hinged, and pin-locked wooden hoops with lateral wooden braces, assembled to produce a large canvas version of a Quonset hut, with wooden doors fronting canvas alcoves at the sides and ends.

In 1965, the radar facility was relocated farther away from the flight line on a higher point of land. The canvas S-80 shelter was replaced by a more permanent metal-roofed wooden structure.

When we arrived, construction was underway on the new CRP Operations Center on the hill. Along with that construction, a second search radar was brought in and made operational while the initial radar handled the daily load during the transition.

Original Radar Operations darkroom housed in a WWII design S-80 shelter.

In 1965, the radar facility moved to a permanent wooden structure with a metal roof.

THEY CALLED IT NAKED FANNY

A height-finder radar that would show us the altitude at which aircraft were flying was also relocated to the hill location.

The new facilities sure beat working in the canvas-covered Quonset hut. There was a separate office for administrative personnel, an office area for Major Douthit, the site commander; and the operations officer, Captain Swenson; a briefing room and our CRP dark room where our scopes were located.

It was built on high ground with the road from the living area to radar operations raised several feet high with drainage ditches on either side. This allowed access during the Monsoon season and its torrential rains.

Entrance to the building was through the telephone room and a security combination door. The switchboard was the old drop and plug type.

The photo on Page 53 shows a typical dark room. They were built on three levels with planned position indicator (PPI) scopes on two levels. One level contained two PPIs and a heightfinder scope for the Weapons Controllers and Weapons Techs. The lower level scope was associated with the plotting board at the front of the room, which consisted of backlighted Plexiglas mounted on a wooden frame, and was manned by enlisted personnel. On it were numbered tracks and information about the various aircraft that appeared on the radar scopes. An airman would watch the scope and then, over a microphone and headphone set, relay the information to plotters who used grease pencils to mark the locations on the big board. All of their lettering and number markings would be written backwards so they could be read from the front. The grease pencil marks would be made iridescent on the lighted Plexiglas.

> **Joe Ballinger:** *I can't say enough about the working relationship between our guys and the troops at Invert. I assume the guys just before us must have made some sort of agreement for joint use of the facility on the hill. There were elevation maps on the wall where we posted anti-aircraft and missile intel and the briefing room that we used for intel briefings. A desk with telephone, earphones and scope for us to follow the various strike missions:*

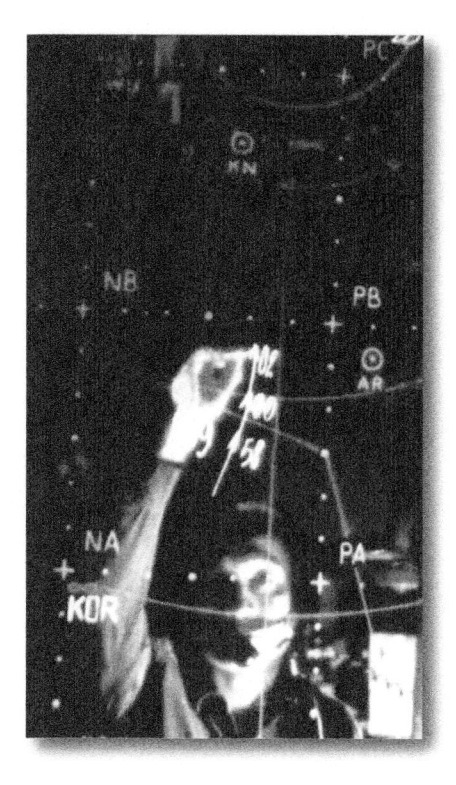

Top: A typical dark room, sometimes known as the Blue Room.

Left: The plotting board.

THEY CALLED IT NAKED FANNY

Operation Rolling Thunder and Operation Steel Tiger, where we had one of our alert crews posted during these missions. It was where I was when I got the call from ASOC, Udorn on 17 May to see if we would attempt the first mission. What Invert provided helped us immensely to keep our act together.

Bruce Hepp: *I would like to personally thank you and all the men at Invert for all they did to make our missions a success! I think that you and your great organization did not receive the praise that you deserved. Each and every mission you would skin paint us out to somewhere around 80 to 100 miles. Amazing, as I think back on our work at NKP and if it was not for your putting us on the pickup site or in a direct line with it, we could have burned up all our fuel wandering around in the clouds listening for a URT-21 beacon to home on.*

Curiously, in several official mission reports the air base at Nakhon Phanom is sometimes referred to as "Invert," as opposed to Nakhon Phanom or NKP. "Invert" was the call sign for the Control Reporting Post at the radar site at Nakhon Phanom. Each CRP had its own designation or call sign: "Paris," at Tan Son Nhut; "Panama," at Da Nang; "Paddy," at Can Tho; "Lion," at Ubon; and "Brigham," at Udorn, to name a few.

8

DOWNTOWN NKP: JIM BURNS'S STORY

A IRMAN FIRST CLASS JIM BURNS AND SSGT. CHUCK SEVERNS arrived about the same time as the HH-43s arrived. Story and pictures are shared courtesy of SMSgt. Jim Burns, USAF, Ret. and RotorheadsRUs.us website.

Jim Burns: *My first arrival at NKP, on a typical hot humid tropical day in June 1964, was loud as the C-123 "shuttle" slammed its tires onto the Pierced Steel Planking (PSP) runway. And it seemed that each plank "clanked" in a wave in front of the wheels as the bird rolled to a stop. We then taxied in to the PSP parking ramp and swung around and dropped the rear ramp.*

I helped the C-123 crew roll off some large fuel bladders full of JP-4 and then stepped off onto the ramp for the first time. This was definitely not the typical base that I was used to. I helped load some empty bladders onto the C-123 and she taxied out and was gone.

As I scanned the "base" I saw three HH-43B helicopters, three or four shacks, some more empty and full fuel bladders scattered around the edge of the ramp, some large diesel generators, three

THEY CALLED IT NAKED FANNY

Aerial view of NKP. (Photo by Jim Burns)

or four trucks, an outhouse and about twenty GI's. I began to introduce myself and meet the "base"—all twenty or so of them.

I arrived in mid-afternoon and after a short time I was told we had been released from alert for the day and we would be going into town. We all piled into the Air Force blue Dodge six passenger pickup trucks and headed into town to our hotel, about 10 miles or so to the east, leaving the base and helicopters guarded by the two Thai guards who lived in a small shack near the "front gate," with their wives and families.

The trip into town was like a parade, with all the kids and villagers along the way lining the edges of the road and waving to us like they had never seen a GI before. It was like this the whole four months I was there, both mornings and afternoons.

We arrived at the Civilized Hotel where I was assigned a room in the two-story part of the hotel. The two-story part had either six or eight rooms and the rest of the rooms were in a

The orginal bulidings, built by the Seabees, used by the Air Rescue unit along the south of the parking ramp, 1964. (Photo by Jim Burns)

one-story motel style building next to the two-story part. We bunked two to a room (I can't remember my roommate's name—for that matter I can't remember the names of most of the others either) and had GI beds in the rooms. These beds sagged so damned bad that after the first night, I had mine replaced with a Thai bed. It was hard as a board (as a matter of fact, it was a board) with a thin cotton mattress on it. It slept like a dream.

We would get up each day and head out to the base to stand rescue alert for the Navy photo-reconnaissance birds and other fighters flying into Laos and North Vietnam. About three or four days before I got to NKP the HH-43Bs were brought into Udorn on C-130s and re-assembled there for the flight to NKP. The HH-43Bs arrived in all their splendor, with their bright "day-glow orange" nose and tails and when the Air America types at Udorn saw this they volunteered to paint out the bright

THEY CALLED IT NAKED FANNY

The Ho Chi Minh Clock Tower in Nakhon Phanom. (Photo by Jim Burns)

orange colors. By the next morning it was done. (Conflicting stories about this attributed to long-term memory loss.)

The birds were flown to NKP where they began standing alert. The clam shell doors had been removed as unnecessary for our mission, and I remember that we "tweaked" the rotor blade flaps a little bit, to the point that when the engine was brought up to full power it only took a very, very small pull on the collective stick and the helicopter would be flying. I guess we thought we had more power and could get out of an area faster.

We had "traded" some rations or something to an Army group that had come through and obtained two Browning

Scott Harrington

Automatic Rifles with ammunition, which we mounted from cords in the rear cabin door opening. Now, I guess we thought we were AH-43Bs (the "A" stands for "attack" with regards to aircraft types and mission designations).

One day one of the rescue commanders dropped in on an HU-16 to pay us a visit and when he saw the BARs mounted in the HH-43Bs he got really upset that we had "armed" our helicopters. He ordered us to remove them from the helicopters and stated that "he did not ever want to see our helicopters 'armed' again." We removed them while he was there, but reinstalled them as soon as he left. As a result of his visit, and to prevent him or any other ARS higher-up from "seeing our helicopters armed again," we would remove and hide the BARs any time one of the HU-16s or HC-54s showed up.

We didn't have any "over the fence" missions (missions across the Mekong River into Laos or North Vietnam) while I was there, but we did go into Laos a few times to practice pickups in some tall trees. I also seem to remember pre-positioning some 55-gallon drums of JP-4 at some of the Air America sites in Laos so we could extend our range for rescue pickups. I remember that we were making plans to add a wooden rack in the HH-43B cabins that would hold three 55-gallon drums of fuel so that we could add fuel to the helicopter fuel tank through a hose hooked to a fuel tank "man-hole" cover in the cabin floor. After the drums were emptied, we could throw them out the back to free up cabin space for the rescue attempt. In no way was this an "authorized" modification, but we felt it would work and I believe some of the crews that came after I had rotated back to Clark AB, did install and use this system to extend their rescue range.

We extended our hoist cable pickup length by adding a rope (over 100' in length) to the 100' hoist cable, so that if we had a pickup in deep forest we could attach one end of the rope to the hoist cable, throw out the 100' of rope and lower the cable to its

THEY CALLED IT NAKED FANNY

maximum length and make a pickup in trees over 200' tall. We could then raise the survivor to within 100' of the bird with the hoist, hover straight up a 100' more to clear the trees and then fly the survivor, on the end of the 100' rope, to a clear area where we could let him down to the ground and either get him onboard using the regular 100' cable length or land and pick him up.

One day we had to do an engine change on one of the birds and we didn't have a hoist (we did have an engine cart) so we used a large limb on a tree. We pulled the helicopter under the large tree limb and raised the engine with a come-a-long winch or ropes. Then we pulled the bird out from under the tree, lowered the bad engine, picked up the new engine, raised it up and pulled the bird back under the tree to lower the new engine in place. Again, not exactly an authorized method, but, it worked like a charm and we accomplished the engine change.

The HH-43B had problems with the fabric peeling off the blades if you flew in the rain. One day we made a flight to Udorn for something, and on the way over we got caught in a rain shower. Right away you could hear the change in the sound of the blades as the fabric pealed back. Once on the ground, I used duct tape to fasten the fabric back down and wrapped the blade with it. Again, not according to the book, but we had a successful flight back to NKP. Once back at NKP we changed the blades.

Most of our flights were only training flights during my TDY; we would practice hoist pick-ups and we did a few PJ jumps at the downtown civilian airport to keep up their proficiency. We did not have any firefighters on our crews at this time, as local base rescue was not our mission. We flew with two pilots, one flight mechanic and one or two medics or PJs. We also used our helicopters in a few "self-help" projects, like hoisting a bigger water tank on top of our outdoor shaving station/shower.

Once we were released from alert each day we would head to our hotel, The Civilized, and spend the rest of the day in town as tourists or sit around the hotel and tell war stories and listen to Hanoi Hanna (she played American music). We were put on a higher alert status on August 2nd (the Gulf of Tonkin incident) but didn't know the reason for a couple of days. However, we still would get released from alert and head back to the hotel just like before, except that some of us now had to stay on the base at night to help guard our birds.

After we found out the reason for the higher alert status, I realized that we were not really getting any news from the "world," so I would scrounge around in the once a week C-123 shuttle and every other plane that landed looking for newspapers. Occasionally I would find one, usually a few days old, and devour it from front to back. One afternoon in town I saw a bus pull up to one of the local merchants and toss off a small bundle of the Bangkok newspaper that was published in English. I tried to buy one but was told that they were special ordered and were all spoken for. I then put in my special order for a copy and within three or four days I was getting my own newspaper (so what if it was two days old by the time it got to NKP by bus). Now I felt I had a reasonably reliable source of news (we didn't consider Hanoi Hanna's news and BS as reliable, but we did like her music).

While I was at NKP, my wife, back in Springfield, Missouri, was giving birth to our first baby, a girl, on Aug. 6, 1964. I would sometimes get messages relayed to me from Clark AB, when one of the 31st ARS (my home unit) HU-16s from Clark AB, P.I. was flying DUCKBUTT missions (a DUCKBUTT mission is a precautionary orbit mission designed to provide navigation, communications relay and on-the-spot rescue assistance for transoceanic deployment and attack missions along the coast).

On the 6th or 7th of August, we had already been released from alert and most of us had headed back to town, except for some of the communications guys. A few of us were sitting out

THEY CALLED IT NAKED FANNY

on the balcony of the hotel having a few beers and listening to Hanoi Hanna's music. After one of the songs Hanoi Hanna came on and said, "We want to congratulate Airman First Class James W. Burns, at Nakhon Phanom, Thailand, with the U.S. Air Force HH-43B helicopter unit, on the birth of your baby daughter. She was born on Aug. 6th (she gave the exact weight and length and time of birth), your wife Ann and the baby are doing fine." Well, I nearly fell off the balcony, and decided I had already had too much to drink. Of course we did not believe that she could possibly have known all this and been correct.

A short time later the communications guys came in from the base with a note that had been relayed by radio from the Red Cross at Clark AB, P.I., by one of the HU-16s to us at NKP. The note read "two birds, both o.k." Since twins run in my wife's family and although I didn't think we were expecting twins, I was not sure from the message they had brought me if we had twins or not. So at the time I didn't know what to think, except that the "Big Secret" that we were at NKP was sure out of the bag.

As it turned out, when I finally got a letter from my wife about two weeks later (all my mail had to be relayed to me from Clark AB), it turned out that Hanoi Hanna had it exactly correct, right down to the ounce and time of birth. The note that was sent to me from Clark was supposed to read "To Burns, a baby girl, mother and baby both OK."

One day we were in town and some Dutch and English guys showed up at our hotel. We got to talking with them and discovered that they worked for a Dutch road construction company (I think the name of it was Grove Jones Construction or something like that) and their crews were building roads in Laos. The Pathet Lao (Communist insurgents) had got too close to where they were working and they had to evacuate across the Mekong and into Thailand until things cooled down some in Laos.

They came in from their construction area, down the rivers to the Mekong, by speedboats and they were loaded down with booze. You could get almost any kind of booze you wanted in Laos, but on the Thai economy we could only get the Thai booze. Anyway, while they were temporarily run out of Laos, they had nothing to do but party, so they came prepared.

This Quonset hut served as the communications shack and was the first air-conditioned building on the base. (Photo by Jim Burns)

One day when we came back in from the base, they had dug a pit in the open driveway area of the hotel and had a pig roasting in it. Even though they had a good head start on us, we were working hard to catch up with them on the drinks. As we all approached a state of high "pollution," one of them decided that he wanted to go water skiing. They had the speedboats and ropes; the problem was they had no water skis. One of them came up with the idea of taking some boards (1" x 6"s or thereabouts) and nailing shower clogs to them. They thought that would make a great set of skis. I think the whole town was standing by the Mekong River, laughing their heads off, watching this bunch of drunken foreigners trying to water ski on 1" x 6" shower clog skis. One of them almost got up on the skis when the toe piece pulled out of the shower clog and he went tumbling head over heels into the river. After this circus was over, we all made our way back to the hotel. By then the roasted pig was done and we had a great meal.

On another day we were again drinking with the road construction crew and created our own little bit of mischief at the

THEY CALLED IT NAKED FANNY

hotel. The hotel owner, Mr. Wandee, had a small zoo at the back of his house in the hotel complex. He had some Mynah birds, which we had taught to cuss like a good GI, a couple of pigmy deer and a couple of monkeys. One of the monkeys was very tame and we would lead it around on its leash, feed and water it and play with it.

The entrance to Mr. Wandee's house had a little archway on the path leading in, and the monkey spent most of its time sitting on top of the arch (his leash was attached to a wire so he could move around).

This one evening someone began giving the monkey gin or vodka as we partied. I guess they got a little carried away and got the monkey plastered. The next morning, when I was leaving for the base, I saw the monkey sitting in a tight ball on top of the arch, with his arms wrapped around and over his head. I went over and shook the post of the arch to get his attention. I could not get him to move a hair.

When I got back to the hotel that evening from the base, the monkey was still sitting in the same position. So I again went over and shook the post to see if he was all right. After a bit of shaking, he finally lifted his arms and opened his eyes and looked at me. He had the worst set of "red road map" eyeballs I think I have ever seen; this was one sick, hung over monkey. The next day he had begun to move around some, but it was about three or four days before he seemed to get back to normal. Would you believe that from the day of the party until the time I left NKP, he never would take anything to drink (not even water) from any of us GI's. I guess he did have some smarts after all.

One weekend when I had the next day off duty, I rented a motorcycle and took Mr. Wandee's 14- or 15-year-old son (who spoke great English) with me and went riding up the road along the Mekong to the North. We spent the night in one of the villages and had a great time. When my commander found out about my

Mr. Wandee's monkey. (Photo by Jim Burns)

little trip, I got a butt chewing and was told that most of the area I had gone into was considered communist and that I was damn lucky I didn't get killed. They all seemed like real nice folks to me and I had a great time. But to prevent another chewing out for the same reason, the next time we went riding we went down the other way to Ubon for the weekend and visited with some Aussies there with an F-86 fighter unit. I really did have a great time while on this TDY and met a lot of fine Thai families while I was there.

Most of the time we ate our evening meal on the local economy and we had been eating at the restaurant just behind the Ho Chi Minh clock and testing our way through the food selections. I found that I liked "kao phat kung" (shrimp fried rice) a lot.

One evening we were eating, facing the street so we wouldn't see the chickens and pigs walking around in the "kitchen," when we saw two white "round eye" women walking down the street.

THEY CALLED IT NAKED FANNY

Being the gentlemen that we were we hopped up and introduced ourselves. They were with the Peace Corps and were assigned as teachers in one of the schools in NKP. They were not what you would call good looking, but they were nice girls and it was nice to talk with some American women.

They also shared their knowledge about Thai food and steered us to some really good dining delights. One that I remember was the "Thai Roti," the little pancake thing that was sold off a cart in the street.

We found a little restaurant across the street from the Civilized Hotel that had signs painted on the wall advertising "Hamburgers and French Fries." We asked the owner about the sign and he said that he used to make them for the "Seabees" crews that were building the base in 1962 and 1963. We convinced him to start making them again. Okay, so the "beef" was water buffalo, but they still were pretty good anyway. He also had the motorcycle rental business where I had rented my "rides."

Mr. Wandee found out about our dining habits and being the ever-smart businessman that he was, and not being able to stand our money being spent anywhere but with him, he hired a North Vietnamese cook that was trained as a French chef and opened his own restaurant at the hotel. This guy could really cook and made some fine meals.

The businessman in Mr. Wandee took over after he had us "hooked" on the great French cooking and he started raising the prices on the meals. In retaliation to this move we went back to the hamburgers, French fries and Thai food. He got the hint and lowered his prices, however this little game went on several times while I was there.

Once we were relieved of alert duty, we all scrambled to be on the first truck to leave for town. There was a practical reason for doing this because if you got back to the hotel first you got to take a shower with the water that had been in the small water tower, which had been heating all day in the sun. If you missed the first truck, the hot water would be used up and you were stuck with a cold shower. Brr!

We used to play basketball with the local town team a lot, and they would whip our butts. They would run us to death and we always had to send in subs. But we had a lot of fun and I think the Thais enjoyed whipping up on us as much as we enjoyed the fun of the game.

Had one experience where our samlor driver got drunk along with us and we decided he was too drunk to pedal so we threw him in the back and I hopped on to pedal. Did you know those things are tough to pedal and they don't turn worth a damn? Net result was that I turned us over in a ditch full of water (or sewerage from the way it smelled) beside the road and had to pull the driver out to keep him from drowning.

One of the memorable events that occurred at the base while I was there involved a C-124 from the unit at Hickam AFB, Hawaii. When it came in they landed long and ran off the overrun and into a ditch at the south end of the runway. This unit had flown a God-awful number of hours "accident free" and somehow they managed to classify it as an incident instead of an accident. It broke the nose gear scissors and bent up a couple of props and was stuck in the mud on the overrun.

This occurred in early August 1964, as the buildup of the base began after the Gulf of Tonkin incident. Another C-124 had brought in one of the large flight line fire trucks the day before. When this one went off the overrun and got stuck, the newly arrived fire truck and crew went charging down the overrun and tried to drive around to the front of the C-124 and it promptly got stuck in the mud as well. We had to hire a couple of local Caterpillars to drag the C-124 and the fire truck out of the mud and back onto the parking ramp. We tried to convince them to write the C-124 off and let us keep it for a "club," but instead they decided to repair it (no sense of adventure, I guess). I think it was still sitting there when I left in October 1964.

Another time we were shipping out one of the trucks, one of the big ones, I think they call it a deuce and a half, by a C-130. The C-130 had lowered its ramp and we were pushing the deuce and a half (which would not run) with one of the other trucks and got it up to a pretty good speed to try and roll it up the ramp and into the C-130. As this thing was lined up and headed for the ramp, whoever was steering it realized that when the engine was not running it didn't have any brakes. He swerved just in time to miss going up the ramp, and it was a good thing too, because as fast as we had it going, without brakes to stop it, it most likely would have come through the nose of the C-130 and out the front. Anyway, he rolled around in a few circles and finally came to a stop. We then slowly pushed him to the rear of the C-130's ramp and the loadmaster winched it inside with a cable.

There were not any other aircraft that were stationed there while I was on this TDY (not counting the stuck in the mud C-124, of course). But we did have a few types stop by for visits and also would have the Thuds (F-105s) buzz us on their way back after missions. We had no control tower, so the communications guys controlled everything. The Thuds liked to come at us without warning, low level, from all directions. They would check in with the communications guys, but the communications guys wouldn't tell us they were coming. All of a sudden there would be Thuds coming from all four directions, right on the deck, at what seemed like 500 or 600 miles per hour, and scare the hell out of us.

One day, I was working on the rotor head of my helicopter and they came over and almost scared the pants off of me. Then they made another pass, and I saw them coming this time, with one of them coming up the runway and across the ramp pointed

Jim Burns standing beside the "stuck" C-124.
(Photo courtesy Jim Burns)

right at my helicopter. He was so low that I thought he was going to hit me, causing me to jump off the top of the bird to the ramp. He had to get some altitude to miss me, but, as he "mushed" over me, trying to climb for altitude, the tail of the F-105 hit a tree at the south edge of the ramp and knocked a large limb through the roof of the new mess hall that was being constructed. He climbed on out and I guess he made it home okay.

Sometime, in October 1964, my first experience at NKP came to an end. I departed NKP to return to Clark AB on the

THEY CALLED IT NAKED FANNY

same, once a week C-123 shuttle that had brought me to NKP in June. The buildup of NKP had already started with tents, buildings and different kinds of antenna going up all along the edge of the PSP ramp. The next time I set foot on NKP was in February 1969 and what a shock it was to me to see a full-size base with people, buildings and aircraft everywhere in place of the jungle edged ramp and runway with three HH-43B helicopters that had been there when I left in October 1964.

I departed the same way I had come to NKP, on verbal orders of my commander, and headed back to Clark (minus one empty fly-a-way kit trunk…which is a whole story in itself) where my wife and new baby daughter joined me in November 1964. We lived off base in Angeles City until we rotated back to the States in January 1966. This TDY had been a great experience for me and I enjoyed my time at NKP in 1964, greatly.

As I have re-read this little tail, it kind of sounds like we were drunk all the time. That is not the case, we were mission-ready every day I was there, but we did take a few occasions to do a little partying; OK, OK, a lot of partying.

Chuck Severns: *June 17, 1964. I received Secret orders TDY 89 days to the Philippines. We never saw the PI. First stop was Da Nang AB, RVN. Next stop was Udorn RTAFB, Thailand. We assembled our HH-43s in Air America's hangar. Air America's painter painted out our day-glow and yellow rescue markings and we flew to our new home, NKP, Thailand. They augmented our unit with personnel from Japan; Jim Burns from PI; an electrician, instrument man, Security Police and 1st Mobility Communications—a grand total of 35 personnel.*

The chief flight engineer for Air America was an ex-Sgt that I knew from Stewart AFB. I told him we didn't have anything but M-16s for weapons. He came back in about 15 minutes with two BARs and several cases of ammunition. He told me to forget where I got them.

Jim Burns (*left*) and Chuck Severns. (Photo courtesy Jim Burns)

THEY CALLED IT NAKED FANNY

9

FRED, IZZY, JAY, JIM, NEIL AND WARREN

A S PART OF THE THIRD TDY HELICOPTER GROUP TO stand watch at Naked Fanny, these are the men who would fly the "Huskies" for the first four months of 1965. For the record their names are Fred Glover, Israel "Izzy" Freedman, Jay Strayer, Jim Rodenberg, Neil McCutchan and Warren K. Davis. This group of TDY rescue personnel was still at NKP when the 5th TAC contingent arrived.

> **Jay Strayer**: *In the first week of January 1965, Air Rescue and Recovery Service had a plan that called for periodic alert status where the entire detachment would be ready on a moment's notice to deploy via a C-124. When the Southeast Asia affair began, at least in our case, ARS decided to assign one pilot from six different detachments. Therefore, none of us knew each other and had never worked together before. It was a learning curve for all of us with considerable compromise to get going. Warren Davis was the Det. CO, only because he was the ranking officer. I do not specifically recall, but believe none of the enlisted folks came from the same detachment, either.*

THEY CALLED IT NAKED FANNY

Left to right: Jay Strayer, Fred Glover, Jim Rodenberg and Warren Davis.

Another pilot, a fellow named Fox, was with us initially, but left early for some reason. Cecil Boothby was one of our flight mechanics and Herbert Romish and E. J. Farmer were PJs.

Warren later died while attempting to rescue a B-52 crew from a burning crash site at Utapao, the SAC base in southern Thailand.

Major Diamond was the NKP overall commander and Bud Myers was one of the Weapons Controllers at Invert.

Neil McCutchan: *I was a replacement pilot that got to NKP after the January '65 date. Initially I went to Tahkli in January. Then perhaps in February or early March, I was reassigned to NKP.*

Without the official orders, it was difficult to identify the list of those in the third TDY group. Based on information from the three missions recorded by this group, we have been able to establish a partial list of those who were assigned to Det Provisional 2 during this time period.

DET PROVISIONAL 2 PARC
Nakhon Phanom Royal Thai Air Base, January-April 1965

    Det. CO Capt. Warren K. Davis, (RCC)
    Capt. Israel Freedman, (RCC)
    Capt. James C. Rodenberg, (RCC)
    Capt. Jay M. Strayer, (RCC)
    1st Lt. Fred Glover, (RCC)
    1st Lt. Neil McCutchan, (RCC)
    TSgt. John J. Kelly, (HM)
    SSgt. Enson J. "E-J" Farmer, (PJ)
    SSgt. Harold G. Stroud, (HM)
    A2C Eric A. Anderson, Jr., (PJ)
    A3C Frank P. Hanutke, (HM)
    A1C Herbert H. Romish, (PJ)
    A1C Cecil A. Boothby, (HM)

THEY CALLED IT NAKED FANNY

10

FIRST NVN HH-43 RESCUES AND FIRST NIGHT MISSION AT NKP

While U.S. bombing of the Ho Chi Minh Trail had begun on 14 December 1964, it was on 2 March 1965 that Operation "Rolling Thunder" began. This was the systematic bombing of North Vietnam starting at the DMZ and slowly progressing north. To keep the initiation of the "Rolling Thunder" Campaign secret, only the commander and intelligence officer at each detachment were notified. Rescue mission planners devised a SAR (Search and Rescue) plan and some Rescue assets (helicopters) were forward deployed.

Although "Rolling Thunder" kicked off fast and furious, the North Vietnamese responded with a vengeance against the U.S. invaders. The first report of an aircraft down occurred around 15:35 L (3:15 p.m.) on 2 March.

The following story, entitled "First to Go North," is excerpted from *PJs in Vietnam* by SMsgt. Robert LaPointe, USAF, Ret., and reprinted with his permission:

First to Go North
Two F-100s were over the downed pilot and they reported that they had him in sight. He appeared to be OK and in his life raft,

but numerous North Vietnamese fishing boats were nearby. The Hun (nickname for the F-100) pilots stated that they would remain on scene and keep the boats away from the pilot.

In rapid succession, five additional aircraft were shot down. One bailout took place in Thailand; another in Laos and the remaining four in North Vietnam. The JRCC (Joint Rescue Command Center) at Tan Son Nhut AB (RVN) directed Adman 63 (an HU-16 Albatross amphibious aircraft) to proceed to the pilot being capped (CAP or Combat Air Patrol) by the F-100s. Adman 63 headed north towards the pilot floating in the Gulf of Tonkin. Adman 63's Command Pilot, Major Ladou, radioed Adman 66 transferring On-Scene Command for the "Feet Dry" (missions over land) SARs in North Vietnam.

At 15:38 L, two HH-43s that were at a FOL (Forwarding Operating Location) in Quang Tri were scrambled. They headed northbound, flying a course a mile or so off shore. This over water flight would keep the crews safe from enemy ground fire until they recrossed the NVN coastline. Major Waechter, Adman 66's Command Pilot and the designated On-Scene Commander, radioed the Huskies and advised them that their objective was an F-100 pilot shot down near Dong Hoi. A few minutes later the HH-43 crews learned of another F-100 down near Xom Bang and almost immediately an F-105 Thud was reported down in the same area.

The rescue crews had plenty of time to think about what they were getting into. The North Vietnamese were shooting down high performance jets out of the sky at an alarming rate. What chance would a slow moving, unarmed helicopter have in this threat environment? The HH-43 crewmembers kept their thoughts to themselves. They knew that the only chance these downed pilots had was their helicopters and they were going in regardless of the enemy threat.

As the Huskies passed between Tiger Island and the NVN

coastline, several crewmembers simultaneously sighted red smoke coming from their two o'clock position. This was unexpected, but the choppers changed course to check things out.

Flying towards the smoke, they soon flew over someone in a U.S. military style life raft. In Brandy 95, (RCC) Lt. (Joe) Phelan entered a low hover over the raft. (PJ) Sergeant Young (Jon "Combat" Young) was lowered into the water to recover the pilot. During the rescue, Brandy 95 monitored a call to be on the lookout for a VNAF (Republic of Vietnam Air Force) pilot who had ditched his A-1H Skyraider in the Gulf of Tonkin. In just a few minutes, Sergeant Young and a slightly injured pilot were hoisted on board.

With one survivor rescued, both HH-43s headed north again, flying at an altitude of 100 feet to avoid enemy radar. Undoubtedly, the VNAF pilot was very happy to be picked up, but he certainly could not have been thrilled to learn that his Rescue Helicopter was now going to take him back into North Vietnam, in an attempt to rescue a downed American pilot. As the helicopters penetrated the enemy coastline, they came under heavy ground fire. This was to continue throughout their mission into NVN.

For the first 15 miles from the coast to the downed pilots' reported positions, the terrain was lowland vegetation. The HH-43s were being escorted by four USN A-1 Skyraiders, call signs "Fortress 5, 6, 7 and 8."

Fortress 5 had gone ahead, reconnoitered the area and found a parachute hung in some trees. He orbited this position awaiting arrival of the rescue choppers. Fortress 6 flew in front of the HH-43s radioing back vectors allowing the Huskies to avoid enemy antiaircraft positions. Because of the threat from these weapons, the flight was done at low level, just above the tree tops. Low level flight minimized the time that enemy gunners could track their target before it passed from view. This was not going to be an easy rescue. With utter disregard for their own safety these brave crews pressed on with their mission.

Fortress 7 reported that each area over flown by the Huskies was "lit up" like a 4th of July fireworks display with the antiaircraft shells air-bursting high above the ingressing helicopters. Pulse rates were elevated and "puckers" were tight.

The HH-43s then came upon some foothills, finally finding the parachute spotted by Fortress 5. As warned, it was entangled in the trees. Brandy 95 entered into a hover and (FE) SSgt. Regan stated that he thought he could see the pilot, but he appeared immobile. The (RCC) Lt. Phelan instructed (PJ) Sergeant Jon Young to ride the Forest Penetrator down and retrieve the pilot. Jon momentarily thought to himself that this might not be a good idea, but climbed onto the Penetrator anyway. After reaching the forest floor, he discovered what SSgt. Regan had seen was only a helmet, a parachute harness and some miscellaneous survival gear. The missing pilot was nowhere to be seen. Sergeant Young suspected that the pilot had either been captured or evaded away from the immediate area.

About this time, the hovering helicopter came under small arms fire. Major (Ron) Ingraham (RCC) in Brandy 96 radioed their High RESCAP (Rescue Combat Air Patrol) requesting suppressive fire to protect Brandy 95. The orbiting F-105s and F-100s rained down 20mm high explosive "hate and discontent" to protect their little friends.

Lieutenant Phelan continued maintaining his hover despite the enemy ground fire and the nervously close suppressive fire, until Sgt. Young was safely back onboard. On his way back up on the hoist, Jon Young wondered if the fighter planes might shoot them down in their zeal to provide close air support? With Sgt. Young back onboard, both Huskies proceeded further inland to the area where the F-105 pilot was reported down.

The third SAR objective was about five more miles inland in

the mountainous terrain that was mostly dense jungle. At 17:15 L, it was Brandy 96's turn to make the pickup. Major Ingraham's crew spotted a parachute hung in the tall trees. While in a descending circle, they saw faint smoke coming from a stream bed at the bottom of the valley. The survivor was burning the classified documents he was carrying. To get the helicopters' attention, he fired 3 tracer rounds from his pistol. The unusual combination of signaling techniques worked. Brandy 96 came to a hover above the 125 foot tall trees. Because of the dense foliage, the rescue crew could not see through to the jungle floor below. While Major Ingraham contemplated his next move, (FE) Sgt. Henderson and (PJ) A1C (John) Moore shouted on the intercom that someone was standing in a nearby clearing and frantically waiving a white cloth.

When the helicopter hovered above the clearing, they could see that the man on the ground was wearing a flight suit. Sgt. Henderson lowered the horse collar and reeled in Capt. Robert Baird. It was extremely important that the downed pilot found this opening. He had lost all of his survival gear when he climbed down from the tree in which his parachute had become entangled. A white handkerchief and his pistol were the only two signaling items he retained.

With the second survivor rescued, the two HH-43s egressed the area for the relative safety of the Gulf of Tonkin. Having more than earned their pay for the day, the Huskies proceeded back to South Vietnam. On board Brandy 95, the crew could hear a continuous loud whistling sound, but no one could figure where it was coming from.

Both HH-43s landed at Quang Tri at 18:15L. They had just completed the first "Feet Dry" SAR in North Vietnam. The two lucky survivors and 8 lucky Rescuemen were glad to be back at a friendly base. It was a 2 hour and 45 minute flight that they would remember for the rest of their lives. After refueling, the

THEY CALLED IT NAKED FANNY

crew of Brandy 95 discovered a bullet hole in one of the wooden rotor blades. This is what caused the whistling sound. After talking it over with the pilots, SSgt. Regan wrapped Duct Tape around the rotor to cover the hole and both aircraft departed for their home base at Da Nang. About half way back, Lt. Phelan reported a severe vibration. Landing at Hue, it was discovered that the duct tape had wadded itself into a large clump near the leading edge of the blade. Leaving the HH-43 there overnight, Phelan's crew accepted a ride back to Da Nang aboard a Marine H-34.

Then-Major Ron Ingraham, pilot of Brandy 96, was the Commander of the Da Nang Detachment at that time. He retired as a Lt. Col. Lieutenant Phelan—Joe Phelan—and "Red" Lempke were the pilot and co-pilot, respectively, during this mission.

The downed pilot, whose helmet and miscellaneous survival gear along with a parachute harness, was Hayden Lockhart. He was captured and was a prisoner until the POW release in 1973. Later correspondence between Ron Ingraham and Lockhart indicated that Lockhart moved away from his chute immediately because he heard troops coming to look for him.

"We didn't see any," Ingraham says. "Lockhart also said that he had no radio and that his beeper didn't work. Also, that he heard us at one point, but didn't remember the F-100s or 105s attacking the hut down the hill from us from which we figured the gunfire that hit Joe (his helicopter) had come. Anyway, he evaded for seven or eight days before being captured as he approached the DMZ."

Adman 63, the HU-16, with the help of the orbiting F-100s and seven A-1 Skyraiders from a nearby aircraft carrier, effected the rescue of 1st Lt. James Cullen.

While the day's work was done for the Da Nang "Huskie" crews, it was just beginning for two HH-43 crews at NKP.

Captain Israel "Izzy" Freedman: *Nakhon Phanom, Thailand, 2 March 1965. There was a lull in the bombing up north and we were doing nothing but a little training. It seemed like the perfect time for someone to take a little R&R (rest and recuperation leave) and Jay Strayer, who drew the lucky straw, departed for Bangkok. With five pilots on site and a max of four required for a normal mission we felt we were in fine shape. While Jay was away they resumed bombing. But still, with five pilots we saw no problem.*

On the morning of the second, for some reason I cannot remember, we were tasked to dispatch one of our choppers to Ubon and so Fred Glover and Neil McCutchan took one of the aircraft and departed. We thought nothing about it; in fact it was the first thing we had been asked to do since our arrival in NKP. We still had three pilots on site and nothing happening.

Later in the day things started to change. We were notified that an F-105 pilot had ejected in the Tchepone (Laos) area but for whatever reason the Air Force planned to use other resources to attempt the rescue. The only other resource, of course, was Air America who had until a few months prior been the only thing available. They also figured wrongly that Air America had H-34s at Savannakhet, Laos, which would have been well positioned to attempt the rescue. I think for some reason they just did not think we were ready or that we had the equipment to do the job and of course we were a little unproven.

We prepared for the mission anyway. We were briefed by the radar people (Invert) who were involved and had a good idea of where the downed pilot was. I was the Rescue Crew Commander for the day with Jim Rodenberg assigned as the co-pilot and it was decided that if we had to go Warren K. Davis would fly the cover bird and bring along the Flight Surgeon in the co-pilot seat (PARC policy required two aircraft with a fully qualified crew for all Combat Search and Rescue Missions). Not

Izzy Freedman talking to a group of children.

wanting to be disqualified by being a pilot short, we used a bit of G.I. ingenuity. At this time we still had plenty of time to make the pick-up in daylight and return before darkness and with the extended range provided by Fred Glover's brilliant range extension system, the mission was well within our capability.

As it got later, darkness fell with no response from Air America. The Air Force people who were supposed to be controlling the mission finally figured out that Air America did not have any H-34s at Savannakhet and, in fact, that crews and H-34s had been dispatched from Udorn to Savannakhet; about two and a half to three hours flying time away. On arrival in

Savannakhet the aircraft would have to be refueled before they could do anything. It was only then, well into the evening, we were asked if it was possible for us to attempt the rescue. Of course we had been ready to launch for hours and departed minutes after being given the word to go. (The two Huskies used the call signs Bandy 41 for the low bird and Bandy 21 for the high bird.)

It was very dark and we were in the middle of the smoky season, which made matters worse, especially for the crew of the second aircraft who was trying to keep us in sight.

Additionally, we had been at NKP for two months and still had never been issued maps of Laos or for that matter much else to help us in planning for the mission. The only thing we knew is what we could see across the river and that there were Karsts rising about 1500 feet above sea level. With no knowledge of terrain en route I thought that 4500 feet would give us plenty of ground clearance and tried to cruise at that altitude. We had heading information from Naked Fanny and were also advised there was an HU-16 in the area with flares.

Trying to fly VFR (visually, without depending on instruments) in the dark and thick smoke made our altitude control terrible. How Warren ever kept us in sight I will never know. At one point Warren thought we should turn around. As we were double crewed we wanted to continue and Warren decided to hang around a little longer. Also by this time we heard an Air America bird airborne out of Savannakhet trying to make contact and I wanted to be sure we made the pickup just to prove a point.

I radioed the HU-16 who advised us that they had contact with and were over the downed pilot. We felt we had to be getting very near the area and asked them to drop a flare. In fact we were very close and as we got closer we were totally blinded by the brightness of the flares in the thick smoke and had to ask them to hold the flares. They advised that the pilot's position was being marked by two small lights on the ground and looking down we found ourselves directly overhead.

As I said before, we had no knowledge of the terrain and I was thinking the ground could not be much higher than 1500 feet above sea level. We were briefed that the downed pilot's position was very close to the trail so I started down leaving the search and landing lights off not wanting to give away our position.

After descending about 1,000 feet, I suddenly felt that the lights on the ground that were supposed to be marking the downed pilot looked too close and threw on the search light.

We were almost in the trees and could see large limbs. I pulled a lot of pitch and our lovely little HH-43 responded, stopping the descent and in doing so we passed directly over the lights, which were in a clearing that looked large enough to land the Huskie. We immediately circled and set up a very steep approach into the clearing.

It is hard to believe that until we were on the ground I never even thought about the possibility of the enemy holding the position or what it was doing there. As we touched down some guys came running into the clearing wearing what looked like American fatigues and carrying U.S. carbines. As soon as they saw we were Americans they immediately brought the downed pilot, Major George Panas, out of the jungle and loaded him aboard the aircraft. (Panas had not radioed the HH-43s because his Survival Radio was broken and he had run out of flares signaling the HU-16.)

After a long very steep vertical takeoff we finally cleared the trees and with Warren in tow headed for home. There is no question that we were glad it was over and happy that the pickup was successful.

Despite darkness and smoke, no radio communications with the survivor, no prior visual identification of the pilot and an uncertain intelligence estimate, the SAR had found and recovered

Major Panas. Having rescued another "satisfied" customer, it was a risky way to conduct a combat SAR.

We thought at the time it might have been the first Air Force pickup of a downed pilot in Laos and for sure the first night pickup. In a conversation with General Heine Aderholt many years later he told me that the Air Force would not fly at night and that the first night pickup of a downed airman in Laos was in November of 1966, by a SOG helicopter under his command flying out of Vietnam. I had to tell him, "No, we did fly at night and did make a night rescue more than a year and a half earlier."

A couple of things, which I did not understand that night, were eventually cleared up. I left the Air Force at the end of 1967, and joined Air America in early '68. Once I got to Laos I finally figured out that a "Road Watch Team," most likely Thais working for the Agency, saw the pilot leave his aircraft and managed to get to him before the enemy had a chance to. They brought him to a clearing that had been cut in the jungle to allow Air America aircraft to night drop supplies to them. Good workers, it was big enough for a 43 to land in. One final thing, the pilot who was flying the H-34 that night for Air America was Bob Hitchman, a very senior Air America pilot and former Marine. I later worked with Bob in both Bells and H-34s while with Air America.

Captain Jim Rodenberg, Izzy Freedman's co-pilot that night, after reading the story, later wrote Freedman. Here are his comments:

Dear Izzy,
I received your message/story and got a kick out of reliving the experience. I remember the flight quite well; though I had forgotten some of the details you mentioned surrounding the mission. There is nothing I would add or correct.

What I most remember are the flying conditions of that night. You did most of the flying, but I remember taking the controls on a few occasions and having to fight vertigo. I felt I was flying with the left "wing low" the whole time I was at the controls.

I also remember that our pickup was mentioned in a Time magazine article following the event. The article indicated that we had "zipped into Tchepone" and made the pickup. I remember we laughed about the reference to zipping into Tchepone. While Tchepone may have been the closest town or city of any size, we were actually some distance from the town. At the time, Tchepone was very well defended with all kinds of antiaircraft weapons. The spot was too hot for the fighter jocks, and we would never have attempted to penetrate the airspace.

Captains Rodenberg, Freedman and Davis, as well as the Flight Surgeon, all received the Air Medal for their rescue mission, as did SSgt. Stroud, A1C Boothby, A1C Romisch, A2C Anderson and A3C Hanutke.

11

A PICKUP THAT DIDN'T COUNT

THE NORTH AMERICAN AVIATION T-28 TROJAN WAS A piston-engined military trainer aircraft used by the United States Air Force and United States Navy beginning in the 1950s. Besides its use as a trainer, the T-28 was successfully employed as a Counter-insurgency (COIN) aircraft, primarily during the Vietnam War. Both the Royal Thai Air Force and the Royal Laotian Air Force flew the T-28s.

What follows is the story of the "Pickup that didn't count":

> **Jay Strayer**: *We received a call from someone at Udorn AB asking if we could help recover this T-28 that had crashed not far across the bordering Mekong River in Laos. They had removed the engine so there were two trips to make. I asked Jim Rodenberg which one he wanted to pick up and he took the engine, which we estimated weighed in at 800 pounds. He flew his sortie first...*

> **Jim Rodenberg**: *When I tried to lift the engine, it became exceedingly clear that the engine was still attached in some way to the fuselage. I pulled in full power and couldn't lift the engine. Being tethered to a non-moving object was a bit disconcerting to say the least.*

THEY CALLED IT NAKED FANNY

This is the original picture of Flight Mechanic Cecil Boothby, lying prone on the floor, and Pilot Jay Strayer recovering a Thai T-28 from across the Mekong River.

Finally, I managed to reduce power and lower the HH-43 and the mechanics managed to free the engine.

Jay Strayer: *I wanted the fuel to be as low as we could safely get it for my lift because we didn't know how much the fuselage weighed. The Udorn folks estimated it at 2,800 pounds and the HH-43 pintle hook was limited to 3,000 pounds.*

When I had it hooked on, I had a difficult time lifting it though we had checked the Tech Order for what power might be required.

Obviously, to me, it was somewhat heavier than estimated, but how much? I started to edge forward to get translational lift, but it was a struggle to get the fuselage clear of the ground. (Note: If the helicopter can attain an early speed of about 15-20 miles-per-hour of wind thru the rotor system, it takes about 15 percent less power to fly.) I skipped the T-28 across the ground as I slowly tried attaining this translational lift speed which I finally did. As I gained speed, I looked outside to my left and saw that the T-28 was flying formation with me—as it, in and of itself, possessed aerodynamic characteristics. It wanted to fly on its own, which was quite dangerous as I had no control over its flight path. So I had to keep the speed as slow as possible but above translational lift speed and I didn't want it to touch the ground or the river's water either for obvious reasons. Anyway, I managed to nurse it across the river and set it down as soon as I had a good place to do so. As far as I know, this was the first and final time an HH-43 was used in such a recovery effort.

And that's my story...and I'm sticking to it.

As a post script, Cecil and I worked the operational chart backwards to see how much weight we were really carrying and it computed out to about 3,800 pounds. Whew, we made it!

THEY CALLED IT NAKED FANNY

12

FIRST RESCUE OF A "HUN" PILOT IN S.E. ASIA

SEARCH AND RESCUE (SAR) STORIES HAVE ALWAYS HAD a warm place in the hearts of aviators. This one will be a special story for F-100 pilots because it's about the first successful combat SAR for a "Hun"—short for F-100—driver at the beginning of the Vietnam era. The tale is told by two eyewitnesses—the downed F-100 pilot, Ron Bigoness, and the rescue chopper pilot, Jay Strayer, both captains at the time. The story will also find a warm place in the hearts of HH-43 pilots, especially those that share a Naked Fanny heritage, since Jay Strayer was in the third TDY group at NKP. The following was written by Ron Bigoness and Jay Strayer, and reprinted with permission from Jim Burns and www.rotorheadsrus.us:

> **Ron Bigoness**: *My squadron, the 615th of the 401st Tactical Fighter Wing (TFW) out of England AFB, Louisiana, was the first Tactical Fighter Squadron (TFS) to operate in North Vietnam (NVN) and Laos. We were TDY to the Philippines in June, 1964, when LTJG Everett Alvarez, the USN pilot, was shot down in Laos; thereafter becoming the very first U.S. aviator POW in SEA. Shortly after that event, several of us flew "retaliatory"*

THEY CALLED IT NAKED FANNY

strikes in Laos near the Plain-of-Jars. That '64 TDY provided most of us with our first taste of combat.

The 615th returned to SEA in March, 1965. This TDY sent us to Da Nang, South Vietnam. On March 31, 1965, I found myself leading one of the very early "Operation Rolling Thunder" missions headed up North. My two-ship flight's mission that morning (call signs Panther 10/11) was a weather recce for the strike flights scheduled for that afternoon. The target for the strike package was on the border between NVN and Laos at the northern end of the infamous Ho Chi Minh Trail—a place called Mu Gia Pass. When we arrived at altitude in the target area, there were multiple layers of clouds below. Descending through the layers we finally got under the broken ceiling at about 1,500 feet. We set up our weaving recce formation headed toward the pass, individually jinking like crazy. But as fate would have it, I was immediately nailed in the tail section by automatic weapons fire.

"I'm hit!" I called out to my wingman, Lawrence "Dutch" Holland.

"Yeah, you're on fire, Lead! You better get out!" Dutch replied.

"I ain't getting out of here yet. This thing is still flying!" My immediate concern was maintaining aircraft control. Somehow; I was able to get the nose headed up before the flight controls froze, and the good old Hun eventually climbed to about thirteen grand. I still had trim control, but soon all systems failed, and every red light in the cockpit was flashing. The heading remained between 200–220 degrees, sending me toward the nearest friendlies. The right wing was on fire, and there were small explosions in the aft section; but that J-57 just kept on churning!

As we topped out, the airspeed fell off, and the nose dropped below the horizon as the old bird tried to maintain the "trimmed-for" airspeed of around 400 knots. About then, with frozen controls and throttle, I was just a passenger riding a roller coaster. But as long as I was getting further and further away from Mu Gia Pass, I was more than willing to go along for the ride…with good ol' Dutch in chase.

As we descended through about 8,000 feet, the speed and lift increased, the nose rose, and we climbed back to about ten grand. However, as the next descent began, the aircraft started a slow roll toward the inverted. Either rolling or upside down, I knew the nose would never come above the horizon again. It was time to leave. But I knew the leaving wouldn't be easy because I was doing about 450 knots, nose down, and upside down—well out of the safe ejection envelope. I raised the ejection handles which blew the canopy and ejected. Upon hitting the slipstream, my helmet was torn off along with my kneepad and other unsecured objects; and, worse yet, my right arm was jerked out of its socket. Then came the chute deployment. It looked like a streamer because of the high speed, and I just knew that was gonna be the end. But suddenly, the streamer ballooned into a "good chute," albeit one with two adjacent panels blown out. Those missing panels compounded my concern about my impending penetration of the rapidly approaching, triple-canopy jungle.

Meanwhile, Dutch had watched my ejection, seen the apparent streamer, and noted the two blown panels. He also saw the stricken bird go in, leaving a long flaming scar on the ground. Dutch circled until he saw me disappear into the vast jungle, and wisely marked the range and bearing of that spot in reference to the wreckage, having figured out rough coordinates for both. Then he climbed for maximum endurance altitude and got on the horn with the initial "May Day" call. The SAR effort was about to begin.

The Aircraft Commander (AC) of the HH-43B helicopter that eventually found and rescued Panther 10 was Jay Strayer. In the letter he wrote to Ron years later, he described the SAR situation he encountered upon his arrival at NKP.

> JAY STRAYER: *I was stationed at George AFB at the time, and arrived, TDY, to the then-unheard-of-place called NKP. The red dust was terrible in the heat of summer. There were six of us "heli" (helicopter) pilots assigned to the new Pacific Air Rescue Center's Provisional Detachment 2, located there. None of us had served together before, so we suffered a bit of conflict as we struggled to come up with operational plans and tactics to conduct combat rescues. Good personal equipment (PE) for our aircrews was woefully lacking and the venerable HH-43B "Huskie" was way out of its design environment in the new combat SAR role.*
>
> *The new Det 2 didn't even have any survival vests. Luckily, I had brought with me the WWII survival vest that had been issued to me back at Kincheloe AFB. In a former life I had been stationed there supporting the F-106 ADC mission. For about $6 U.S. apiece, we got a Thai lady to make very serviceable copies for each aircrew member. GI weapons were also scarce, so most of us carried our own handguns. My weapon was a Ruger Blackhawk 357.*
>
> *The "Huskie" was originally designed to respond to aircraft crashes fairly near airports (air bases) where a rescue unit was stationed, carrying a 1,000 pound bottle containing fire retardant and a couple of firefighters dressed in silver fire-proof suits. So, its operational range was very limited—about 75 miles. But thanks to Yankee ingenuity, one of our pilots (Fred Glover) came up with a way to use up to three 55-gallon drums as "jettisonable" auxiliary fuel tanks. You don't want to hear about the plumbing, but needless to say, the smoking lamp was never lit when that configuration was installed. Each drum extended our normal sortie time by about 35 minutes and 30 miles. We cleverly named this jury-rig the Range Extension Fuel System (REFS).*

Our tactics always included flying with two rescue helicopters if assets were available. We dubbed the two choppers "low bird" and "high bird." The low bird was the lead and the first to attempt rescue when the downed aircrew was located. The high bird would set up in trail about a mile or two away as a radio relay and spare in case "lead" aborted or its crew became "rescuees" themselves. Once launched, we were on our own because the sophisticated SAR "system," which subsequently developed from our early and hard-learned lessons, was yet to come. Hell, we didn't even know to call for fighter cover! All of us were fresh from the States, and none had any combat time or even knew how to spell the words. We were just hell bent to rescue fellow Americans who were in deep trouble.

The Main Event

RON BIGONESS: *After Dutch Holland put out the initial "May Day" call on Guard (the emergency frequency) about 1000 hours local, he contacted the airborne alert HU-16 "Albatross" (Call sign Basil 66, playing the later-to-be developed role of the C-130 "King" bird) on a secondary SAR frequency and told them his lead was down about 65 miles from NKP in Laos. (The later-to-be developed role of the C-130 was preceded by the C-54 in that role and referred to as "Crown.")*

He gave them my coordinate information and reported that he was unable to contact me via my handheld UHF survival radio. The proto-King bird asked him to orbit the area, conserve fuel, continue trying to contact me on the UHF, and stay as long as he could. Dutch did just that until he had to RTB (Return to Base) at BINGO fuel...but he never heard from me on the ground.

JAY STRAYER: *At NKP, two Huskies were rapidly prepped to include installation of the REFS on both birds. They launched at 1050L as "Alban 21 and 41," climbed to 4,000 feet, and headed*

THEY CALLED IT NAKED FANNY

Capt. Ron Bigoness after his right arm and shoulder had been immobilized by an NKP flight surgeon. (Photo courtesy of Neil McCutchan and Jim Burns)

northeast into Laos—with no fighter escort. Based on the estimated 65 mile distance to the downed F-100 and with our REFS, this should have been an easy rescue. But I screwed up and got the outbound heading wrong. So we wound up spending lots of valuable time searching in the wrong area about 25 miles north of the actual crash site's location. By the time we realized our error, we had already gone through all of our aux fuel. Very frustrated, we finally corrected our initial error and moved south to intersect the right (correct) radial off of INVERT, the NKP TACAN.

Ron Bigoness: *While the SAR was mounted and the Huskies launched, I was taking stock of my situation. As I descended toward the ground...I was concerned about further injury to my arm and shoulder as I crashed into the jungle canopy. Luckily, my arm didn't catch any limbs as I passed through the branches. The chute hung up in the treetops leaving me suspended about ten feet above the jungle floor. I got out of my harness and managed to drop to the ground with only minor further injuries. I could hear my wingman, Dutch, circling helplessly overhead, but I couldn't see him through the thick jungle canopy. As I moved about in the dim light below it, my shoulder was very painful. I tried to raise Dutch on my handheld UHF survival radio, but the radio wouldn't work. I guessed that the battery was dead. Our entire supply of PE (personal equipment) came directly from our TDY kits which, obviously, were not well maintained.*

It was a little after 1030L when the noise from Dutch's plane disappeared, and it suddenly got real lonely. After that, I heard nothing…except for screaming monkeys!

Jay Strayer: *We arrived in the vicinity of the downed F-100 about 1150L and searched diligently and frantically for what seemed the longest time with no useful results. We had heard a few beeps from Panther 10's URT-21 radio beacon, but the signal was faint and neither of us (the two Huskies) could home in on it. At 1230L, we were almost bingo fuel when one of my crewmembers caught a glimpse of a flashing, bright glint of metal and steered me to it. It was the still smoking wreckage of Panther 10's plane, so we knew we were getting close. We circled it at 3,500 feet four or five times. Suddenly, the URT-21 signal strengthened and we were able to home in on it with the ADF. At 1250L, we spotted a parachute in the trees and dropped a smoke grenade to mark it. Shortly after the visual on the chute, the two PJs ("Parajumpers" —SSgts. Enson J. "EJ" Farmer and Herbert Romisch)* on my low bird spotted some smoke coming up from a small (really tiny) clearing near the chute. Upon closer approach, the PJs saw Panther 10 beside his smoking fire below, wildly waving one arm. Wasting no time, we went to hover directly above him and practically in the 100 foot treetops because our hoist cable was only 100 feet long!

Ron Bigoness: *After about two hours on the ground listening to the monkeys, and starting a fire hoping to create a smoke beacon since my UHF radio was useless; I heard the noise of the circling SAR flight. When I heard the choppers, my dismal thoughts soared with hope. I tried to position myself in a spot where I could see through one of the few small openings in the jungle canopy. One brief moment in time which I vividly remember was when I looked up through one of those small breaks and saw a PJ (Sgt. Farmer) looking out the back of a Husky and staring straight at me. I'll never forget it. I was the proverbial needle in the haystack of the jungle! And, they had found me! I wildly waved my one good arm and he waved back. I could almost taste a cool one in the Club. But Jay and his crew's pick-up work was just beginning.*

Jay Strayer: *All we had at that time, for lowering a PJ or bringing up a survivor with our power hoist cable was the ancient "horse collar." Unlike the tree penetrators that would come later and could carry both a PJ and a survivor, this one person device was not very sophisticated. So, Sgt. Farmer donned the horse collar and Sgt. Romisch lowered him into the dimness below. Upon reaching the ground, his first words were, "Don't worry, Captain, we've got you now."*

When Sgt. Farmer discovered the pilot's arm and shoulder injuries, he told the captain that it would hurt like hell, but that he'd have to put the horse collar under both his arms. This he did, *and up went the captain, screaming in agony. He was still screaming when Sgt. Romisch pulled him in. And he kept screaming as Romisch began lowering the horse collar to Sgt. Farmer, still on the ground. When the cable was about 20 feet down, I told Sgt. Romisch to stop and give the pilot something for his pain—it was tough enough holding the hover in the tops of the trees without this distraction, and I really did "feel his pain."*

On the ground, Sgt. Farmer became concerned that the hoist had stopped. What was going on? His concern was growing because he had removed his survival vest to get into the horse collar easier (unbeknown at the time to me, the AC), and he realized that he'd be in deep trouble if we had to suddenly depart the area for some reason - and leave him with no survival equipment, particularly a radio to help us find him again. (Rescue men too, as well as fighter jocks, were learning their lessons at the "school of hard knocks.")

In a couple of minutes, the morphine administered to the injured pilot took effect, and Sgt. Romisch resumed and completed the retrieval of Sgt. Farmer. We proceeded to RTB (return to base) to NKP as fast as we could go, all of 85 knots, and landed long after the fuel low light came on. We logged 3½ hours on that sortie, which established a time-in-flight record for the HH-43B. And…we had saved our first F-100 pilot who happened to be the first Hun driver successfully rescued in the long, difficult conflict; just beginning…way back then.

Jay's official mission report stressed the importance of two things that were critical to the success of the mission. First, the makeshift HH-43B Range Extension Fuel System, or REFS, that allowed an extra thirty-five minutes, as he called it, "stay" time over the survivor. And second was the survivor's possession of an operating URT-21 radio beacon that allowed them to pinpoint the location of the downed pilot.

The crews for the mission consisted of the following personnel:

Low A/C (Alban 21)
Captain Jay M. Strayer, 65501A (P), Captain James C. Rodenberg, 66754A (CP), A1C Cecil A. Boothby (HM), SSgt. Ensign J. Farmer (PJ), A1C Herbert H. Romisch (PJ)

High A/C (Alban 41)
Captain Israel Freedman, 72104A (P), Captain Warren K. Davis, AO3043721 (CP), A3C Frank P. Hanutke (HM), SSgt. Harold G. Stroud (PJ), A2C Eric A. Anderson, Jr. (PJ)

Epilogue

Ron Bigoness*: An HU-16 flew me from bare base NKP to Ubon where U.S. Army doctors put my arm back in its socket and pronounced me fit for further travel. (Also, it turned out that my upper arm bone was fractured, but we didn't know that at the time.)*

The following day I was returned to my squadron at Da Nang where I remained for about a week before departing for the States. After five months rehabilitation at Wilford Hall Hospital in San Antonio, I was discharged and returned to flying status. I managed to get back to Nam in 1968 by volunteering to complete my tour, flying another 220 combat missions before being reassigned to USAFE HQ (U.S. Air Forces Europe Headquarters).

Jay Strayer*: After surviving the steep learning curve of my TDY introduction to combat SAR operations, I managed to get back to SEA two more times. Strangely, I never "got"—meaning was never credited with—another successful combat rescue. I did, however, participate in the planning for the November 21, 1970 raid on the Son Tay Prison Camp, 21 miles northeast of Hanoi. I also flew one of the Jolly Green's trying to rescue some of our POW friends. I was bitterly disappointed to find they had been moved. But, that's another story…*

[Note: According to an item in the *Intake: Journal of the Super Sabre Society (www.supersabresociety.com)* in the Fall of 2012, there should be a change in the title of this chapter. As reported to the Super Sabre Society by member Norm Turner:

> *The first Hun pilot shot down and picked up was 1st Lt. Arnie Clarke, who was in my squadron (the 522nd TFS, TDY out of Cannon AFB, NM) when we deployed to SEA in 1964. I was there when he was shot down on 18 Aug 1964. He was hit while supporting a SAR for a shot down UH-34 in Laos but he made it into Thailand before bailing out. He was picked up by an **Air America** chopper.*

The editor/publisher of *The Intake: Journal of the Super Sabre Society*, Medley Gatewood, gave his blessing to include the item here.

No doubt the circumstances surrounding the Clarke rescue were responsible for limited knowledge of the rescue; i.e., the fact that the mission he was supporting was likely an Air America aircraft (UH-34) also, that he was rescued by an Air America chopper. This was early on in the Secret War where little to no information was shared regarding any kind of U.S. presence in Laos.

Because his rescue occurred on March 31, 1965, more than seven months later, Ron Bigoness's claim to fame should be entitled: "First Rescue of a Hun Pilot in S. E. Asia by USAF SAR Forces."]

In another incident, on 27 April 1965, Navy LTJG S. B. Wilkes, flying an A-1H off the USS *Hancock*, was hit by ground fire while on his way to the target on a strike mission near the Mu Gia Pass. His Skyraider's left wing caught on fire, but he managed to fly the aircraft across Laos and into Thailand and was within about two miles of the runway at Nakhon Phanom when he was forced to bail out. An HH-43B flown by Captain Jim Rodenberg, RCC, followed the chute as it drifted earthward and made the pickup of LTJG Wilkes. Others aboard the Huskie were Captain Strayer, co-pilot; Airman Boothby, helicopter mechanic; and SSgt. Farmer, PJ.

THEY CALLED IT NAKED FANNY

LTJG S. B. Wilkes's bailout two miles from the runway was the shortest rescue mission from NKP during the early years. (Photo courtesy Neil McCutchan)

13

5TH TCG AND 605TH TCS ROADRUNNERS

A IRCRAFT, WHETHER IN A WAR ZONE OR FLYING IN civilian skies must be monitored and controlled. In civilian skies the Air Traffic Controller's job is to keep all aircraft separated from one another. In the military, for the most part, the Weapons Controller's job was, at least Stateside, to bring aircraft together, especially when running intercept missions. Because most all encounters with enemy aircraft occurred beyond the range of our radar and primarily over North Vietnam, we, at Invert Control were not involved. Our mission at our Combat Reporting Post was more of a potpourri—bringing aircraft together for refueling, counting noses of flights of fighter bombers crossing the Mekong River and taking good care of our helicopter rescue guys to get them where they were needed for a rescue, and back home again.

I was a 1st lieutenant at the time, assigned to the 605th Tactical Control Squadron, 5th Tactical Control Group, Clark Air Base, Philippines.

> **Scott Harrington:** *Just before Easter of 1965, I got orders to go TDY to Nakhon Phanom. I had been rooming with 1st Lt. Al (Allen) Childress in an off-base apartment near Clark AB, PI. Al*

5th Tactical Control Group patch.

had been in Thailand prior to my arriving at Clark and had been stationed TDY with Major Howard Douthit at Udorn.

Major Douthit was to head up a contingent headed for NKP. Al was to go along and he had convinced Major Douthit that I would be a good one to be part of the team. Howie, I say Howie because that was what we called him behind his back, was a wild sort—the kind who would have been right at home with the Air America guys. He loved his booze and was very casual around his house, which was located not too far from where Al and I lived. In fact, we were to pick him up on our way to the base the night of our scheduled departure for NKP. We stopped by his house in the early evening to tell him we'd be by to pick him up about 10 o'clock. He came to the door in his underwear (his attitude was that if you didn't like the way he dressed at home, you didn't have to stick around). He extended an invitation to us to come on in since he'd just made a fresh batch of margaritas.

Scott Harrington

Lieutenant Allen Childress.

We politely declined saying that we still had to finish packing and that we'd pick him up at 10. We left and finished our packing and at the stroke of 10 o'clock we drove up in front of his house. His wife, Jean, came to the door and said, "He's drunk."

We gathered his gear and got him in the car and headed for the base. As the rest of the contingent proceeded to get aboard the several C-130 aircraft, we managed to pour Howie on the plane (without anyone being the wiser about his condition). He climbed up into one of the crew bunk beds on the flight deck and slept through the entire flight across the South China Sea to Bangkok.

Our group was actually a replacement contingent that would relieve the current group of weapons controllers, communications and radar types who had also been at NKP TDY. Our orders were for a four-month tour and I was to be the Senior Director of my own radar operations crew. But before all of that could take place, we had to get there.

The author, Scott Harrington, then a 1st Lt., at Nakhon Phanom Royal Thai Air Force Base during the summer of 1965.

When we landed in Bangkok in the bright light of day, Howie (Major Douthit) had slept off his margarita-induced drunk and was now sober. Despite a pounding headache he managed to inform me that not all of the aircraft could continue on to NKP. I was to be in charge of all of the officers, NCOs and enlisted men who would have to RON (remain overnight) in Bangkok. He gave me the name of a major I was to meet up with at Don Muong Air Base, which was nearby the main airport. Air Force buses at the flight line were to pick us up and take us to our interim destination.

So here I was in a strange country; didn't speak the language; being sent to meet someone I'd never laid eyes on and charged with feeding and housing 30 or 40 guys and having them back to meet an aircraft that would fly us on to NKP the next day.

Everyone boarded the buses and we were taken to the proper squadron building on Don Muong Air Base. Carrying our M-16 (AR-15) rifles, we made our way inside. An Airman 1st Class (three-striper) was on duty in the day room. The guys all took seats as I headed up the stairs to meet with the major. Although I can't remember his name, I do recall that he was very pleasant and put my mind at ease about feeding and housing our guys and making it back to the flight line the next day.

Now, part of the agreement with the Thai government allowing us to conduct operations out of Thailand was that we were not supposed to carry any weapons on our person. I didn't find out that the following incident had taken place until sometime later, but while I was upstairs talking with the major, the Airman 1st said to the ranking NCO with our group, "Hey, Sarge. How about bringing all of your troops back to the weapons room and we'll get all of your weapons checked in?"

The NCO, a master sergeant, told the A1C in no uncertain terms, "Airman, did you see that lieutenant that just went up those stairs? Well, I'm not doing anything or going anywhere until he comes back down here and tells me to."

Needless to say, I was honored when I learned what had happened. It validated some great advice I had received when I was finishing up OTS (Officer Training School). "Listen to your senior NCOs. They can make you or break you." Apparently I had done some things right during our training at Clark, both in the squadron area and up at Lilly Hill, that earned his respect.

We got everyone fed and billeted for the night; up and fed the next morning and on the buses in time to catch our flights to NKP.

Nakhon Phanom Royal Thai Air Base certainly wasn't what we had come to expect air bases to be. It was located about 10 miles from Nakhon Phanom, the town, out in the middle of nowhere in northeast Thailand. The runway was not poured concrete or even tarmac. This runway, as well as the entire ramp area, was made of something called PSP or pierced steel planking. It had coffee cup-sized holes in it and each metal plank was 10 feet long and 16-inches wide. The planks interlocked to form a firm steel runway. It was used during World War II to create air bases on the Pacific islands and worked fine there, so it was used to build the initial runway at NKP. When the aircraft touched down, there wasn't the same familiar sound that you hear when the tires touch concrete. To say the least, it was a rude welcome to NKP.

We would live in what we called "hooches" with one room on each end for officers. Enlisted "hooches" were like open bay barracks. They were made of wood with galvanized metal roofs. Our rooms had screens across the front and sides from about waist high to the ceiling. The weather was so hot and humid that you really needed to have as much circulation as possible to be able to sleep. Hinged shutters could be dropped down in the event of rain. There was a single bed in the room and the window ledges served as our shelves.

With the exception of those clothing items that we had to hang, all of our clothes stayed in travel trunks. While on the base we wore short-sleeved olive drab fatigues. Our last names were embroidered onto Air Force blue cloth tapes and the tapes were sewn above our right shirt pockets and, as officers, our rank was embroidered into our collars. We had acquired hats—called "go to hell" hats—that resembled cowboy hats, but the sides could be snapped up or tied up with the chin strap. Our rank was embroidered into the front of the hat. And since we weren't out in the jungles, we wore black Air Force-issue boots or brogans as opposed to jungle boots. If we were to fly to another base, we had to wear either 505s or 1505s—tan short-sleeved uniforms.

View from the ramp area showing search radar at left, below rotor blade. Height-finder radar is at far right. (Courtesy of Jim Burns)

The 505s were cotton and had to be starched and pressed, while the 150Ss were a nicer material that required dry cleaning. Needless to say, the 150Ss stayed at Clark.

In the Philippines, we had grown accustomed to having our houseboy do our laundry. He would take the laundry one day and the next day it would come back to us—the uniforms all starched and on hangers and the other items washed and ironed. We had the same sort of service at NKP, only it was Thai women from the nearby town that did the laundry. Young men, just as in the Philippines, would shine our shoes and boots overnight. Many of us had purchased laced-in zippers for our boots to give a quick on and off.

Mike Sweet, a 2nd lieutenant, was assigned as the other Weapons Controller on my crew. Having been TDY with him in

THEY CALLED IT NAKED FANNY

Saigon, I was convinced that Mike eventually would get into trouble. He had earned a commission and was sent overseas just days after he had been married. But he didn't conduct himself like a married guy when in Saigon, and he seemed to think that everything was a joke. The night before one of our off days, he and Staff Sgt. Ogle went into Nakhon Phanom (the town) and apparently did some serious drinking. On the way back to the base—and I guess they had stumbled most of the way—they fell into a ditch alongside the road. They got a couple of scratches on them and told guys around the base they had been jumped by some Thai thugs and had been beaten up. I usually slept in on my days off and was rudely awakened with the information that they had been attacked and beaten. I talked to both of them and finally got the true story. With the major's blessing, I restricted them both to the base for the remainder of our four months. Mike just didn't understand what all of the fuss was about. But I think I finally made him understand that we had to have everyone available for duty all the time because we were, after all, dealing with people's lives.

Tech Sgt. Pitzer was my NCO Crew Chief. Pitzer was a good man and very loyal. He was there through thick and thin with me, and was a great help. Sadly, he was one of the guys who received a "Dear John" letter from his wife while we were TDY. It tore him up and he was given emergency leave and was sent home.

Initially, we worked lots of nose-counting missions, checking in flights of fighter/bombers going "over the fence" out of Thailand and into Laos and North Vietnam. We also began working refueling missions. This would involve having radio contact with KC-135 tanker aircraft when they arrived over an orbiting point and guiding the fighter/bomber aircraft to them to top off their tanks on the way out and to make sure they had enough fuel to make it back to their home bases on the way back. We would always want to make the hook-ups in the direction the F-4s or F-105s were heading, otherwise we would waste valuable flight time as well as valuable fuel. Some of the aircraft were equipped with a probe that would fit into what was called a drogue—a web-like basket attached to a fuel line from the tanker. Other aircraft had to be refueled using a boom that was extended from the tanker and would enter the refueling port on the fighter aircraft.

Tech Sergeant Wade Ketron was the crew chief for Lt. Childress's Invert Radar Operations Crew.

Wade Ketron: *My orders, dated 13 April 1965, stated that I would proceed on 25 April, 1965, from the P.I. to support PACAF Ops Plan (Contingency Operations) for approximately 120 days. Weapons were to be hand carried and returned the same way. Eighteen of us were taken by bus to the Manila Airport and flew on a C-54 to Nakhon Phanom, Thailand. We landed on a pierced steel planking (PSP) runway. The apron for parking aircraft was also constructed of PSP.*

I had noticed the radar site during landing—it was just an area cut out of a jungle with a lot of tents and a few buildings. I had also seen a radar antenna turning.

After arriving and being assigned to my tent, with a bed and footlocker, I went to the Doctor's tent with a blocked eardrum. I had tried many ways to unblock it, but was not successful. When I walked into the tent, he asked, in a grumpy tone, "What's the matter with you?" I told him about being on flying status for five years and yet had an ear I couldn't get unblocked. He perked up and said it was nice to treat something other than VD, and quickly got my ear fixed.

That evening I was met by Lt. Scott Harrington and Lt. Harvey Childress, who went by Al. (His given name was Harvey

Allen Childress). *They quickly told me that I would be assigned as crew chief to a crew that had a bunch of troublemakers and misfits. They mentioned some of the names and I had known some of them from the P.I. Lieutenant Childress was to be the Officer in Charge of my crew. Two other TSgts, Parker and Pitzer, came on the same plane as I, and would be crew chiefs, too.*

The base, when I arrived, had several rough constructed wood buildings: Dining Hall, NCO Club, Officers' Club, and Latrine.

The radar operations area was located in a wood framed-canvas covered Quonset hut at that time. The living quarters were six-man tents stretched over wooden frames. The frames allowed us to roll the sides of the tents to get some ventilation. We also had a recreational area with a softball field and basketball court. There were some wooden walkways to prevent muddy trails due to rain in Monsoon season and avoid Krait snakes. (Krait snakes bite with poisonous venom so strong in attacking nerve endings that a person can die of suffocation.)

We had two alternating outhouses for human waste (which went into 55-gallon drums cut in half). Charcoal was used to burn the waste from one while the other was in use. The outhouses were a distance from the living area, but the aroma was unbearable at times, especially when the waste was being burned. (The barrel burning process was affectionately named the "Texas Barbecue.") We had mirrors in the latrine and wash basins were used for shaving; the showers were sufficient and kept us clean.

I don't believe there was ever a day that we could call normal operations starting from the first time I got on a scope. NKP's TACAN (Navigational Aid) was used by almost all aircraft operating in the area. Regardless of where I was stationed, I would always familiarize myself with the surrounding areas so I could assist pilots who were lost or needed information. I could

1st Lt. Al (Allen) Childress (*right*) shown with some of his crew. Crew Chief TSgt. Wade Ketron is in the center.

tell pilots or the weapons controllers where a radio tower, railroad tracks, lake or other landmark was to gain a pilot's confidence if pointed out to them. However, I made an error the first day. I had a slow flight over Laos and knew it was an Air America bird. The scope showed what I thought was an isolated thunderstorm. On the radio I said, "Aircraft on a bearing of...and so many miles from Invert..." They replied and I advised them of the storm and vectored them around it. It so happened that it was a mountain range, but they never told me I was in error. However, knowing where the mountains were on the scope came in handy. Whenever the paint (radar return) from that location grew weak on the scope, I would request a tune-up on the radar. We had

Left to right: SSgt. Ogle, unknown, TSgt. Pitzer.

some of the greatest radar techs and they never questioned me anytime I notified them of a weak signal.

Scott Harrington: *First Lieutenant Phillip Hamilton was in charge of the third Invert Operations crew with Chief Warrant Officer George Wolfram the second controller on that crew if memory serves me correctly. Their crew chief was TSgt. Barney Parker.*

14

MEET JOE BALLINGER, CAPT. USAF

JOE BALLINGER, WHO PROVIDED A GREAT DEAL OF MATERIAL for the writing of this book, would be the Commanding Officer of the fourth TDY helicopter group to come to Naked Fanny. The following chapter will give you, the reader, the opportunity to meet Joe before his duties to oversee a Combat Search and Rescue detachment brought him to the land across the Mekong River.

Portions of the following are from an article about Joe Ballinger entitled "Local man lived life of his dreams." It was written by Mary Kay Woodyard for the June 28, 2013 issue of the *Norton (Kansas) Telegram*. She has graciously given her permission to use the material.

To Joe Ballinger, being an officer in the United States Air Force and flying as a helicopter pilot in the Air Rescue Service (ARS) was one terrific job. Their motto was simple: "These things we do, that others may live!"

Joe loved flying helicopters, and felt strongly that saving lives was one of the best things a man could do while in the service to his country.

Needless to say, every man and woman in the Air Rescue Service is dedicated to this. While there were those who didn't actually go out on the lifesaving missions, it took their full support to do every mission, and saving lives was what it was all about.

THEY CALLED IT NAKED FANNY

Joe Ballinger, Captain USAF.

The history of the Air Rescue Service is full of heroes and headlines, but there are many whose stories were never told. Ordinary men who became heroes because when their time came to do—as in "These things we do, that others may live,"—they laid their lives on the line and did it in spite of the odds. They were the only group in the military that was granted, in regulations, the option to prosecute a mission on "Calculated Risk." This meant that in the field they could make the decision to risk their lives and their machines, if they thought they could get away with it and save a life. This book is about five groups of these men who were stationed at "Naked Fanny" during five separate TDY (temporary duty) tours. Joe Ballinger was the commander of one of those groups.

Scott Harrington

All wars start somewhere for everyone. Pearl Harbor, as everyone remembers, was the beginning of the United States involvement in World War II. And growing up during WWII, Joe's heroes were soldiers. They provided a bigger-than-life image, especially the aviators.

Joe was commissioned through the Aviation Cadet program and became a rated navigator.

But being a navigator was not his dream. Those aviators of WWII still were at the center of his aspirations and in 1958, he was accepted for Jet Pilot Training. Further training and testing in 1959 resulted in his becoming a helicopter pilot. It may have been a career move determined by circumstances, but for the lad from Kansas it was the culmination of a dream. He was now one of them: his heroes.

After a tour in Newfoundland, Joe was stationed at Kirtland AFB, New Mexico, with an ARS Local Base Rescue (LBR) detachment flying HH-43B helicopters in support of special weapons testing and base rescue when the "Gulf of Tonkin Incident" occurred in August 1964. One of the first things he did was change his life insurance from twenty-year pay life to several term policies before they could put in a "War Clause." Little did he know then what fate had in store.

In 1964, fighter units were sent into Southeast Asia on temporary duty for strikes against North Vietnam. Composite rescue units of highly experienced personnel were made up and sent every place a fighter unit was based. It was all on a volunteer basis so we could keep our Continental United States (CONUS) units operational. Joe was thirty-one, happily married, and had the attitude of "let some other crazy guy go and wait until I was ordered to go." Since there were five pilots in the Kirtland detachment, one of them was sent TDY to fill in at one of the undermanned CONUS units.

In March of 1965, Joe was at Webb AFB, Big Spring, Texas, when the call came that the whole detachment at Kirtland had orders to go to Southeast Asia at the end of April. He was ordered back home to get his affairs in order for the move. When he got back, everyone was busy preparing to shut down the unit and ferry their helicopters to other units for use while they were gone. They learned that they would be going to Thailand, but not exactly where. Just the fact of going to Thailand was classified information, so they couldn't tell their wives why they were not that concerned about the assignment. There was no combat in Thailand as far as they knew. It looked like they had lucked out and had an LBR crash fire mission at one of the fighter bases.

Still, because they were to take their weapons with them, they got themselves upgraded in the care and firing of the new M-16 carbines. They also tried out some combat flying tactics before losing their helicopters. No one in the detachment had been in combat, nor had anyone even trained for such a possibility, so everything they knew was from hangar flying and reading about others' experiences. Joe had read and heard about combat pickups in Korea, and the techniques used to minimize the time for a hoist rescue of a survivor. But reading and reality are two different things. You've heard that a little knowledge can be a dangerous thing? Joe's "little knowledge" nearly led to disaster!

"I really wasn't thinking that day when I got Bruce Hepp and went out to try it," Joe said.

The HH-43 was a powerful helicopter, but at Kirtland the altitude is 5,300 feet above sea level with the density altitude sometimes getting to 8,000 feet, making even hovering marginal depending on the gross weight of the aircraft.

> **Joe Ballinger:** *Bruce and I went out by ourselves on a training flight after I had briefed him that we would simulate a combat pick-up the way they had done it using the H-19 helicopters during the Korean War. I told Bruce that I would fly towards the training pad on the dead crossed runway at 100 feet and 60 knots; flare the helicopter; simulate putting the hoist out and slow to a 50 foot hover over the pad. I would hold the hover for ten seconds, and then rotate to forward flight getting out of there in minimum time. That is what I attempted. Thank God we were light!*
>
> *I gave the helicopter an abrupt flare to slow over the spot, then*

leveled pulling in the collective to hover at 50 feet. The HH-43 came out of the sky and settled onto the runway hitting level, but so hard we bounced back into the air. I had the throttle twisted on and the beep switch full forward just barely keeping it in the air and not hitting the ground again as the engine came back to full rpm. I had forgotten that not only can high density altitude kill you if you're not careful, but so can other things. Like the fact that the automatic fuel control reduces engine rpm when the rotor speeds up and there is a three to five second lag in a turbine engine response. That's far too long for the maneuver I had just tried. The H-19 with a reciprocating engine gave you instant power to the rotor as you applied the twist grip throttle.

Feeling dumb, but lucky, with a lot of adrenaline running thru us, we took the HH-43 back and had it checked for any damage. Also, confessing (privately) to the other pilots what I had done. In our business, it's better to own up to your mistakes so others can learn from them and, you never pass on a machine that has had its limits exceeded without inspection. Very fortunately, there was no damage and we learned. If we had attempted this later in combat, we would have never returned. Later, at NKP, we discussed autorotative combat penetrations and threw that idea out too. And just the thing that happens if you roll the throttle to flight idle and it sticks there has happened. Far better to do a bottom beep and you can still fly the machine home if there is a failure of the control.

All kinds of things led up to the actual deployment and many of them would be the reasons for survival and sanity later. One of the things that would help a lot later on was that everyone had a good sense of humor, despite the presence of some practical jokers, and they hung together as a unit. Little did they know how much that "Crazy Sense of Humor" would mean in breaking tension and relieving stress later on.

THEY CALLED IT NAKED FANNY

15

PREPARING FOR TDY: THE KIRTLAND STORY

I N THE SMALL, TWO HELICOPTER RESCUE DETACHMENTS, such as the one at Kirtland AFB, all personnel in the detachment—officers, NCOs and enlisted men—had additional duties other than flying and maintaining the helicopters.

Joe Ballinger was the Administrative Officer and had plenty of paperwork to do to get ready for the deployment and close out the unit's records and reports.

The Detachment Commander, Ken Baliles, was on hold for assignment to Air Command and Staff College. That made Joe, as the senior ranking officer, the TDY Commander. While Ken remained in command for the shutting down of the detachment and getting the two helicopters farmed out to other detachments to use while the unit was gone, Joe picked up command on things having to do with travel and required equipment needed for SEA duty.

> **Joe Ballinger:** *When the first rescue units were deployed TDY to SEA in 1964, they took their own helicopters and supplies. But, because we were to replace just the personnel whose TDY time (120 days) was running out, we were to take uniforms and our personal flight gear.*

THEY CALLED IT NAKED FANNY

Usually, even with your personal survival kit, PRC handheld radio, knife and helmet, you can get this into a B-4 bag and an A-3 bag. But our deployment orders also specified that we would have to carry the mechanics' tool kits and weapons for the aircrews. Each pilot and flight mechanic was issued a new M-16 automatic rifle and a Colt .38 revolver; plus 300 rounds of .223 and 50 rounds of .38 ammunition to be broken down and carried in our bags. To be able to do all of this, we asked for and got a travel authorization for an additional baggage allowance of 250 pounds for each individual, all to be broken down and stowed in our individual luggage.

Walt Turk doesn't recall having the M-16s and associated ammo issued at Kirtland.

Walt Turk: *Seems to me the M-16s came to us via a Klong Bird (C-123 shuttle) and were covered with Cosmoline, which the PJs cleaned off using JP-4 as solvent, but there was no ammo for them. The container with the ammo arrived a couple of days later.*

Joe Ballinger: *Walt was right about also getting more weapons there. We needed more weapons for those who didn't bring any. And later, after we got the CH-3s with more aircrews, we needed more weapons.*

Getting to war in 1965, was a bit different from past wars. They were to fly on commercial airlines from Albuquerque to San Francisco, and then by military transport to Thailand.

Usually military personnel on official duty traveled in Class A uniforms, but Joe decided his troops would travel in civilian clothes to San Francisco then change into their uniforms when they got to Travis. At that time of the year, in New Mexico, they were still in the period of winter uniform, i.e., heavy blues.

Joe Ballinger: *It didn't make sense to me that we should travel to the tropics in Class A Blues. Probably taking more authority than I had, I directed that we would carry one set of Class A Blues, but report into the Travis Military Airlift Command (MAC) Aviation Transportation Coordination Office (ATCO) wearing Class B tan 505s. I figured that if we reported in as a unit wearing the wrong uniform, ATCO could have a piece of me as the commander, or not send us. I knew the last wouldn't happen, but the first was a possibility. But you don't boss a unit, no matter how small, without some hazards.*

After saying goodbye to their families and friends at the airport, four pilots, four mechanics, and one admin type got on Continental Airlines in civilian clothes with seven automatic rifles (Joe's recollection), seven pistols and ammunition in their luggage. This would have been on April 29, 1965. Fast forward to today with TSA and all their sophisticated search gear—it would have been a whole different story.

Joe Ballinger: *At San Francisco International Airport (SFO), we knew that we would have to take a bus to Travis AFB. Even though we were dressed in civvies, it was obvious who we were with our piles of military bags and heavy tool boxes. And since military types aren't known for heavy tipping, the Red Caps, or Porters, didn't want a thing to do with us. So, as the guys lugged our stuff out to the curb, a couple of us got on the airport shuttle bus to find where the bus stop for Travis was located. We found it on the opposite side of the terminal, about a quarter mile away. Also, a small problem, the shuttle bus was not allowed to stop at the commercial bus location. Lugging about 2,500 pounds of gear a quarter mile didn't seem like good logistics to me. So, after a little discussion with the shuttle bus driver and some green stuff, he agreed to take us, stopping at the last terminal arrival area that* was just short of the unauthorized drop we needed to get to. Another small problem in being commander is sometimes you pay for it out of your own pocket. Later, my other three officers coughed up, too.

After four baggage drills, loading and unloading, the group managed to get to the MAC terminal at Travis. There, after changing into their Class B uniforms, they reported in as a unit without any more problems. They then learned they would not be flying on military aircraft, but on a contract civilian airline in a DC-8 with refueling stops at Wake Island and Tan Son Nhut Airport, Saigon, South Vietnam.

Joe Ballinger: *About the only thing I remember about going over was it was a damned long flight, and I had the shortest birthday (May 1st) in my life. Because of the International Date Line, my 32nd birthday was only seven hours long.*

At Tan Son Nhut, Captain Bill Hays from the Joint Air Search and Rescue Center met the group and took the four officers (Joe, Bruce Hepp, Stan Schaetzle and Walt Turk) up to the Airport Café for a briefing. It didn't take long, after looking around and seeing all of the new windows that had been installed, for them to realize that they were in the very same café that had been bombed out about six months before.

Joe Ballinger: *All of a sudden you became very conscious of all natives with a bag. Captain Hays told us that we were being assigned to Det Provisional 2 at Nakhon Phanom, Thailand. He also told us that this unit was not an LBR as we thought, but ACR (Aircrew Combat Recovery). LBR (Local Base Rescue) units like the one we just left at Kirtland, normally do local bailouts and crash fire rescue with FSKs and firefighters. ACR was something new to us! Our job would be to recover fighter aircrew that had bailed out on the way back from missions over North Vietnam,* *wherever we could get them. In our minds, that was Thailand, and a pretty good mission.*

These are the nine men from Kirtland AFB who would make up half of the "Naked Fanny" team for the next 120 days:

Capt. Joe E. Ballinger, RCC—Kirtland AFB, NM
Capt. Bruce C. Hepp, RCC
Capt. Stanley O. Schaetzle, RCC
1st Lt. Walter F. Turk, RCC
TSgt. Chester E. Rainey, HMFE
A1C Harry L. Hart, Jr., Admin. Clerk
A1C John H. Stewart, Engine Mech.
A2C David M. Cutillo, HMFE
A3C Darwin L. Devers. HMFE

Joe Ballinger: *So then it was on to Don Muang RTAFB/Airport, Bangkok, Thailand, where we unloaded again to await transport to NKP. There, while I went to the MAC ATCO to arrange for transportation for our unit, the guys got the baggage outside the terminal. The ATCO NCO told me that we needed an in-country briefing before we could proceed on. It took over an hour to find the briefing officer, a Captain West. This was mostly useless to us as we had already been provided with the Thailand Customs and Courtesies Booklet. To make it more frustrating, the guys had already found a hotel with cabs waiting at the curb.*

We stayed in the new Rex Hotel with a nice outside pool; did sightseeing and had a beer or two at the Bangkok Enlisted Club for the next two days. What a way to go to war!

The reason for the delay getting out was two-fold. One was that the in-country transport (C-123) traveled around the USAF bases every two days, rotating direction each time. The other was that I refused to send our guys in, piecemeal, two or three at a time. We came as a unit and we were going in as a unit. Finally, I suspect because of the men at NKP wanting to get out and go home, ATCO got us on a C-47 and on to NKP.

The Gooney Bird, that is what the C-47 was nicknamed, touched down on the PSP runway at Nakhon Phanom at 7:40 in the evening on May 3, 1965. There, we met the rest of our unit:

Captain Thomas J. Curtis, RCC
Captain Richard Laine, RCC
SSgt. Roberto Rodriguez, HMFE
A1C Francisco Alverado, HMFE
A1C William A. Robinson, HMFE
A1C Richard A. Wallace, PJ
A2C Arthur N. Black, PJ
A2C Marvin Brenamen, PJ
A2C Michael T. Henebry, PJ

The nine men—two officers, an NCO and six airmen—unlike the group from Kirtland were from individual units and, as with the group that preceded them, had never been stationed together. Both officers were pilots, the NCO and two of the enlisted men were helicopter mechanics and the remaining four were pararescue jumpers, or PJs.

Tom Curtis had been Detachment CO at England AFB, Louisiana prior to deploying, while Dick Laine was stationed at Grand Forks AFB, North Dakota where, although he was flying helicopter missions in support of some radar sites, his assignment was to an Air Rescue detachment. He was only at Grand Forks for a short time after finishing Bootstrap at the University of Omaha.

As mentioned earlier, Dick was the only pilot from his detachment deployed TDY to NKP in May 1965. He flew to Bangkok and after a few days hopped a C-123 to NKP.

Joe Ballinger: *We also met the current TDY pilots (Warren Davis, Jay Strayer, Izzy Freedman, Jim Rodenberg, Fred Glover and Neil McCutchan) who gave us a very thorough briefing and mission training before they departed and left Det Provisional 2, PARC to us.*

The mission training was on Aircrew Recovery in the Thailand area and a classified operational plan for ACR in Laos, ASOC (Air Support Operations Center), Air America, Lima Sites and other safe areas! That was quite a lot more than we had planned on. To do this we had three peacetime HH-43Bs (60-0279, 60-0280, 62-4510) with no armor or self-sealing fuel cells. For defense we had the M-16s and .38s that we brought with us, and a mix of weapons (Thompsons, Swiss Ks, Grease Guns and BARs) their group had scrounged from the local CIA unit in downtown NKP.

The briefing also included the Low Bird/High Bird concept to be used in Laos during combat recoveries. Low Bird was to be the pick-up bird with the High Bird flying counter-clockwise around the Low Bird, defending it. The High Bird co-pilot was to fly the chopper while the pilot, mechanic and PJ fired out the right side doors and the back. (Unlike a fixed wing aircraft, in a helicopter the pilot sits in the right-hand seat while the co-pilot is in the left-hand seat.) Here I should mention that the rear clamshell doors had been removed from all three of the helicopters for that purpose, leaving only the safety net covering the rear exit. The High Bird was to recover the Low Bird's crew if it was shot down. They had also developed a range extension rig using three fifty-five gallon barrels of jet fuel in the helicopter cabin. The normal range of the HH-43 was 75 miles out, 30 minutes on site, 75 miles back with 20 minutes of fuel reserve. This apparatus (illegal, but better than nothing) extended the range to 105 miles out and back with the barrels to be thrown out the back before a pickup. They had used this concept when they made the pickup of Major Panas out of Laos in March.

The HH-43 stateside detachments had been using the Pedro call sign along with the last two digits of the aircraft tail number, but here we would use classified AFSAL call signs (Armed Forces Security Agency List). They would change every seven to ten days, but each helicopter would carry a permanent two-digit tail number - - 21 for 60-0279, 22 for 60-0280 and 41 for 62-4510. This made for some confusion later as no one knew who we were. The past TDY personnel had come up with "Naked Fanny" as the unit identity, like the fighter units (Wolfpack, etc.) with a spray on stencil, too. It was a corruption of Nakhon Phanom, and also a reference to the fact that they flew with the rear clamshells off, letting their asses hang out!

For support there was a very small airbase group consisting of cooks, Air Police, refueling, etc., commanded by Major Ercy B. Carver. No hanger, and open air hooches for offices, mess hall and living quarters with boardwalks connecting each. Two hooches had been converted into an officer's lounge and an NCO Club. There was also a small unofficial PX run by Lt. Scott Harrington, an Invert controller, which had small items on hand for nonprofit sale. The Invert radar unit was in an air-conditioned Quonset tent on the ramp when we got there. Shortly thereafter, it was moved up on a little hill about a quarter of a mile from the runway.

I became Det. Commander by one day of rank over Tom Curtis, with Tom taking the Intelligence Officer duties—a slot we never had in a detachment before, but definitely needed now. I appointed Bruce—Operations Officer; Stan—Safety Officer; Dick—Admin Officer; and Walt—Maintenance Officer. Since the pilots were all RCC (Rescue Crew Commander) qualified, we formed up three aircrews at first: Tom and Dick; Bruce and Stan and Walt and me along with the HMFEs and PJs. We stood

The Ballinger Det. Group. *Front row, left to right*: SSgt. Roberto Rodriguez, CMSgt. Tom Luty, TSgt. Chester E. Rainey, Capt. Tom Curtis, Capt. Joe Ballinger, Capt. Bruce Hepp, 1st Lt. Walt Turk, Capt. Dick Laine, Capt. Stan Schaetzle. *Back row*: A1C Francisco Alverado, A1C William Robinson, A2C Robert Evans, A2C Michael T. Henebry, A2C David M. Cutillo, A3C Darwin L. Devers, A1C John H. Stewart, A2C Arthur N. Black, A1C Richard A. Wallace, A2C Marvin Brenaman, A1C Harry L. Hart, Jr.

alert for ACR with two birds and their crews as High Bird, Low Bird and one bird "Off." The Off bird, if available, was used for training and "Cats and Dogs" flights. More on those as I come to them.

Finding that there was very little in guidance (no Det policy letters) and very few AF regulations, except for maintenance, I conducted a short Commander's Policy briefing for all of our guys...That no matter where we came from TDY, we were now one unit and I expected us to work together to get the job done! That my door was always open for their problems. I had an office but probably wouldn't be there! Come find me and discuss it! That laziness and hangovers were no excuse for not being on the job. And, that I wanted everyone to show up for breakfast every morning, even when off duty. I hated breakfast, but I'd be there with them. And last, there were no 'the N word' in my outfit no matter what color they were. I then turned it over to Walt for a briefing of the maintenance guys, and he said, "I go along with the Captain!" Policy briefing was then concluded.

We had an armory with all our weapons in it, but with the huge orange fire hazard sign on the door, I didn't think it best to keep them there. So I had the aircrews take their personal weapons out and keep them secured in their lockers.

16

NKP ARRIVAL: THE WORK BEGINS

THE KIRTLAND DETACHMENT ARRIVED AT NKP May 3, 1965, and joined up with the other TDY pilots, mechanics and PJs.

As briefed, their job (mission) as Detachment Provisional 2, PARC, was to pick up pilots who bailed out in Thailand, and, under special conditions and with permission, in highly classified Laos. But the boys were in for a big surprise!

They had three HH-43Bs, no armor, no self-sealing fuel tanks; only the .38s and M-16s brought from the States along with the BARs, Thompsons, and Swiss K-31s left over from the previous TDY guys.

Their first mission, on May 12th, held true to form—at least the Thailand part. It was an in-country pickup of an F-105D driver en route to a strike mission whose aircraft experienced engine failure. The pilot ejected south of NKP. Joe, Walt Turk, TSgt. Rainey and A2C Cutillo scrambled to recover him. The pilot, Capt. Ralph E. Schneider, had his parachute spread out in a rice paddy where they landed and picked him up uninjured.

"We told him to give his parachute to the Thai's who had helped him and brought him back to NKP," said Joe.

As fate would have it, the mission would change in less than a week

THEY CALLED IT NAKED FANNY

when Air Force Captain James L. Taliaferro, Jr.* was shot down while on an armed reconnaissance mission on 17 May, over North Vietnam. He ejected from his F-105D fighter/bomber over Khe Bo, North Vietnam, on Route 7 near Laos after his aircraft was hit by 37 mm AAA. Khe Bo is approximately 105 nautical miles slightly northwest of Nakhon Phanom.

Bruce Hepp was pilot and Stan Schaetzle co-pilot on the Low Bird on this mission, with SSgt. Rodriguez as crew chief and A1C Wallace as PJ. Walt Turk was pilot and Joe Ballinger co-pilot on the High Bird. A1C Robinson was their crew chief and Airman Brenaman, the PJ.

> **Joe Ballinger:** *We were asked if we could make it. Quite frankly, I came up with one helluva lot of reasons, excuses, etc., in my mind why to say no! But the old story is there is an American down and we were the only ones available to help. After being assured that if we didn't have enough fuel to return to NKP (and God forbid, other reasons) that we could land at a Lima Site; and that we could leave the birds behind and Air America would evacuate the crews, I committed us to trying it!*
>
> *After deciding to attempt the rescue of Captain Taliaferro, who was down on the Black River in North Vietnam, I came down from INVERT and took my place in the barrel as CP on the High Bird with Walt and we took off across the Mekong into Laos. After crossing it, some of the crew members, who hadn't fired the M-16, were cleared to fire a few rounds to become familiar with the weapon.*
>
> *On the way across Laos at 10,000 feet, the weather deteriorated, so we had very little to navigate by except mag compass heading to the downed location 105 miles out on the Black River, NVN. Then, with us in loose trail with the Low Bird, we went inadvertently*

---

*Captain Taliaferro is identified in the Air Force press release as James L. Taliaferro, Jr. Other sources list him as J. J. Taliaferro or J. U. Taliaferro.

The pilots in Joe Ballinger's group (*left to right*): Capt. Joe Ballinger, Capt. Tom Curtis, Capt. Bruce Hepp, Capt. Stan Schaetzle, Capt. Dick Laine, and 1st Lt. Walt Turk.

IFR. Not a great experience in helicopters as close formation is extremely difficult, and we weren't trained for it. But there was inadvertent IFR procedure that had been sort of practiced. Lead holds altitude, airspeed and heading, while the trailing helo breaks right 30 degrees and climbs 500 feet to separate them. That we did! Now, not only are we sort of lost over enemy territory, we are separated and hopefully not going to hit each other until we could get a break in the soup. We got that break and using our ADF vectored back together again. And about the same time we came into radio communication with the U.S. Navy A-1s covering the downed pilot. One came out and escorted us to the site as we drained the barrel fuel into our main tank and jettisoned the three fifty-five gallon barrels out the back. [Note: A-1 single engine propeller-driven aircraft were flown by both the Navy and the Air Force in support of the Combat SAR missions with the Air Force A-1s using the call sign Sandy. They were often referred to as "Spads" after the French World War I aircraft. The first A-1 aircraft was delivered in 1946 and were designated as AD aircraft. In 1951, when the Navy, Marine Corps and Air Force numbering systems were merged, the Skyraiders were redesignated as "A" series aircraft.]

As we descended down through the cloud cover, we saw a hill next to a river in a green valley. When the Low Bird spotted the parachute in the trees and smoke, they went in for the pickup.

Bruce Hepp: *The RESCAP fighters continued trying to suppress the ground fire with 20mm cannon as we descended to make the pickup. As we got lower, Captain Schaetzle, Sgt. Rodriguez and Airman Wallace began answering enemy fire with their M-16 rifles. It was impossible to move the chopper nearer than about 20 feet from Captain Taliaferro's position. Our blades were clearing trees by five feet or less and undergrowth was brushing underneath us. (The bamboo at the site was almost 100 feet high.)*

We ran out 100 feet of hoist cable and waited for Captain Taliaferro to reach the hoist sling so we could pull him up.

Joe Ballinger: *At the same time, I took the controls to circle the site, counter-clockwise, so that Turk, Robinson and Brenaman could concentrate suppression fire from the right side and tail of our chopper. We descended to two to three hundred feet AGL (above ground level) to fly around the hill as the Low Bird made the pickup. While in this defending circle, I saw Walt jerk in his seat, and thought he had been hit! At the same time a load of rockets came under the helicopter from right to left into the* hillside below me. And next came an A-1 under me! I had heard of close-air support, but that was my first experience with it!

It doesn't seem to me that I made a complete circle before the Low Bird called that they had the pilot and were departing from the site. As we quickly climbed back out of the area with the A-1s escorting us, I asked Walt if he was okay. He told me, "yeah," but when he saw eight feet of prop out the door heading straight for us, he thought he was dead. Then, when the A-1 unloaded the rockets, he knew for sure, until they and the A-1 flew under us.

By then, I'm sure all of us were on adrenalin high beyond imagination; but after finding out that all were okay and we got the pilot, it was one helluva great feeling! However, as our weapons were cleared, we got one more jolt! When Walt seated his M-16 in the window well, a round went off, and I believe we both looked up to see if there was a hole in the upper bubble! And, that we may have just shot ourselves down! An even better feeling came when we found no hole and that the PJ had cleared his weapon at the exact same time Walt's went into the well!

When we got back to 10,000 feet, we found that we had enough fuel to make it all the way back to NKP. The weather had cleared a lot and at the North Vietnam/Laos border, there was an Air America Caribou circling to direct us to a Lima Site, if needed. After releasing him, we made it all the way home in the clear with fuel to spare and no one hurt. Don't remember if the A-1s came with us or departed when we crossed into Laos.

Immediately following the mission, General Harris sent the following message:

"My personal congratulations are extended for your noteworthy pilot pickup of 17 May 65. The professionalism displayed by all who participated in this mission, plus the outstanding teamwork by all who participated in this mission, plus the outstanding teamwork under heavy ground fire, was noted with pride. For all who participated, a well done."

THEY CALLED IT NAKED FANNY

Joe Ballinger: *The next day we received a lot of congratulatory messages for the rescue along with one that wasn't so good! It was this message that simply said, "What you did yesterday is your new mission! Plan and find a way to do it!" I called the unit together and told them this! So we all pitched in and brainstormed all kinds of ideas for this new mission. One of the things not to do was send the High Bird down with the Low Bird like we did, but hold it back high until needed! From this session, Tom and I wrote up a sort of dream sheet and sent it to Saigon! We wanted two-engine helicopters, armored with self-sealing tanks and machine guns for defensive protection! Fully instrumented for all weather capability! And most definitely A-1s for close support, rather than fast-movers! We had no idea of how all that could be done.*

Eight Silver Stars for Valor were awarded for that mission. Captains Joe Ballinger and Bruce Hepp, 1st Lieutenant Walt Turk and SSgt. Roberto Rodriguez were presented their medals in Saigon (actually at NKP, but reported to be at Saigon to keep our cover) by General Hunter Harris, commander of Pacific Air Forces. At the time of the presentation, Capt. Stan Schaetzle had returned to the U.S. and was stationed at Hamilton AFB, California, as was A2C Richard A. Wallace. Also at Hamilton was A2C Marvin F. Brenaman. A1C William A. Robinson was listed as missing in action at that point and later confirmed to be held by the North Vietnamese as a POW.

The official citation accompanying the Silver Stars noted that the mission flown by the Air Rescue Service airmen "required a flight of more than 200 miles" over hostile territory.

General Hunter Harris presents the Silver Star to (*left to right*) Capt. Joe Ballinger, Capt. Bruce Hepp, 1st Lt. Walt Turk and SSgt. Roberto Rodriguez.

THEY CALLED IT NAKED FANNY

17

A REBUFF, THEN A BUFF

As a Detachment Commander, for the good of the mission, you sometimes have to make unpleasant decisions.

Joe Ballinger: *It was about the 26th of May that I sent one of our PJs home—A2C Brenaman. I believe it was Gordon Thayer who replaced him.*

The Rebuff

Joe Ballinger: *Sometime in late May or early June, Tom Curtis led a mission where they could neither find nor confirm the pilot and returned to base against Crown's orders. (The Crown, and later the King, call sign was used by the HU-16 aircraft, and later by the C-54s and C-130s, that carried mission coordinators whose job it was to assemble and manage the Search and Rescue Task Force [SARTF].) The Crown aircraft landed at NKP and complained. I told the Crown that as far as I was concerned, Crown was no longer Mission Control as they weren't over the North with us. And that we (our on-site crews) were the only ones who could prosecute or deny a mission. Didn't set well with them, but it established our position from then on, as Saigon concurred with us.*

THEY CALLED IT NAKED FANNY

The Buff

It was on June 8 that the call came to pick up a "Thud" (F-105) pilot who had been shot down just south of Vinh, NVN. Vinh is approximately ninety-five miles northeast of NKP. The pilot was Captain Harold "Buff" Rademacher. It was on his second TDY to Vietnam in 1965 when his aircraft was shot down and he was wounded.

Captain Rademacher: *On June 8, 1965, I was flight leader for four aircraft that were on a mission over North Vietnam. At about 4:30 p.m. we were all set to hit a target of opportunity, a bridge protected with air defense guns. I made a pass, drew fire and my F-105 took a single hit, but that one hit was all it took. The plane was on fire and I had to eject. My parachute came down in difficult terrain. I was fairly well beaten up with facial cuts and some other injuries, and found myself on the floor of a deep ravine with high peaks on every side. The area was densely forested; nothing could be seen but hundred foot tall trees in all directions. I was in big trouble and I knew it, having gone down in North Vietnam at that early time in the war, my chances of being picked up and gotten out of there were really slim. The remaining three planes of the flight watched as I went down and kept that location on the ground in view. As they circled the area, my second in command called for air rescue.*

Unknown to me at the time, when air rescue was on the way they asked for an estimate of how long it would be before enemy troops could get to the downed pilot (me). Looking down at the really bad spot where I was located, (the best way I can describe it, I was down in the bottom of a deep hole with trees all around), my second in command was only half joking when he replied that it would take enemy troops about three weeks, at the earliest, to reach where I was on the ground. He knew air rescue would not have to contend with enemy interference, but they were going to have a tough time getting me out due to the limitations of the

Buff Rademacher (*center*) being assisted by PJ Richard Wallace (*right*).

rescue helicopter and its equipment in making a pickup, and especially so from my unfortunate place on the ground.

In those early days the big long range H-53 "Jolly Green Giants" were not yet available. Air rescue was equipped with small jet engine helicopters of the type in use at that time for emergencies at major civilian airports in the United States. They had limited range and were very ill-suited for air rescue service in our environment, but that's what we had in 1965. Two of those, each carrying an extra 55-gallon barrel of fuel inboard, had launched and they set down together and refueled well inside North Vietnam, en route to my crash site. One took on just enough fuel to return to base, while the other refueled with most of what was in both barrels, and it continued on north.

THEY CALLED IT NAKED FANNY

While not wanting to detract from Captain Rademacher's story, but to set the record straight: 1) The HH-43B was never used at civilian airports, only at military facilities; 2) The HH-43s from Nakhon Phanom used three fifty-five gallon barrels cradled in a pyramid and connected with PVC pipes to the main cell tank with a shutoff valve. After they were drained, the barrels were thrown out the back of the aircraft. 3) At no time on a rescue mission did the NKP HH-43s land and refuel anywhere, although JP-4 jet fuel was available at LS-36 in Laos for the CH-3s and the HH-43s to use.

Captain Rademacher: *That helicopter arrived over my location less than two hours after my plane went down. But, I was still in plenty of trouble. There were no open areas anywhere near me and the helicopter had limited loiter time. They either had to get me out of there quick, or they had to leave without me. There was no open space for the helicopter to descend safely below the tree tops, and the hoist cable was not as long as the trees were tall. The helicopter came to a hover above me and lowered the penetrator, but it was still suspended above me after the cable was fully paid out. Without hesitation, the helicopter slowly descended, bending down the tree tops, until finally I could reach the penetrator. By 6:30, they had me out of there and on the way home. That pilot and crew had just set a new record, making the northern-most rescue ever from North Vietnam at that time in the war. They took a tremendous risk to save me and I owe them my life.*

Joe Ballinger: *While waiting for a transport plane to pick up Buff, he had an Afterburner with us at the O Club hooch. It was then when he told us that we had to be the craziest bastards in the world to fly over the North in a peacetime unarmed helicopter to pick him up. In answer to that, Walt Turk looked up at Buff and told him, "If it wasn't for you crazy bastards, we wouldn't have to do it!" Damned funny retort, but the truest statement ever made about CSAR.*

After treatment for his injuries, Captain Rademacher was returned to the

United States for five days to be re-equipped with a new individually configured helmet and other items replacing those lost when his plane was shot down. Shortly after his return, the entire 357th Squadron sent pilots, including Buff Rademacher, to different bases, providing combat training for other F-105 units. Buff was an instructor pilot for the F-105s at Takhli Air Base in Thailand, but he also continued to fly bombing missions to North Vietnam himself, working on his 100 missions. His unit, the 357th Squadron, had been the last unit to deploy where the pilots had their choice of serving temporary duty for four months, or until they had been credited with having flown 100 combat missions. Buff opted for and completed 100 missions.

> **Joe Ballinger:** *I was the Rescue Detachment Commander at McConnell AFB, Kansas in 1966, where the F-105 combat mission training was being done. When Buff completed his 100 missions and returned there, I had a few drinks with him and his wife at the O Club. And after the lights were turned out, we had Afterburners together. When I said, "Damn, I burned my mouth on that one," he laughed and slapped me on the back saying, "Serves you right! That was the only injury I got after your guys picked me up!"*

Tom Curtis and Bruce Hepp flew the Low Bird on that mission with David Cutillo as Crew Chief and Richard Wallace was the PJ. All four received the Distinguished Flying Cross for their efforts.

The crew of the High Bird, piloted by Stan Schaetzle and Walt Turk with Francisco Alverado as Crew Chief and Michael Henebry as the PJ, all received Air Medals for the mission.

> **Joe Ballinger:** *I believe that it was after the Rademacher pickup that his squadron sent us parachutes. If memory serves me correctly, I think we got Jungle Penetrators from the Army shortly before this mission. A short time later our maintenance guys also got HH-43F hoist spools with 250 foot cables and installed them on our birds.*

THEY CALLED IT NAKED FANNY

18

HECK OF A WAY TO SPEND A RAINY DAY

T HE FOLLOWING CHAPTER DEALS WITH ONE OF THOSE missions that never should have happened. And it shows the frustrations of an unfavorable mission result that came so close to having a positive result.

Scott Harrington: *Most of the aircraft activity having to do with fighter/bombers originated in Thailand. Korat and Ubon, to the west and south of NKP, served as home bases for the F-4C Phantoms. Korat and Tahkli were home bases for the F-105D Thunderchiefs or "Thuds." Most of the aircraft would fly north-northeast on the way out and south-southwest on their return and the KC-135 tankers would maintain orbits oriented in the same directions, as well.*

Working with tanker aircraft was always a ticklish task. While they maintained their orbit, there was always the presence of good ol' Murphy (as in Murphy's Law) to deal with. Just as soon as you thought you had everything all lined up in good order to take care of the birds you knew would soon be coming back, somebody else's immediate need would throw a monkey wrench into the operation. A clear case in point happened June 9, 1965, a dreary, rainy, overcast day when very few aircraft were flying. We had many dreary, rainy, overcast days during what is known as the Monsoon season in Southeast Asia. Monsoons were usually the result of typhoons—the same thing as our hurricanes. Of course we didn't have the likes of the Weather Channel back then to keep us abreast of weather conditions.

On this particular day, our crew was on duty at Invert Control and we got a call from an F-4C pilot flying towards Thailand across Laos. We confirmed that we had picked him up on our radar and heard him make a request for a tanker as he was running low on fuel. As we scrambled to locate an available tanker aircraft, we learned that his target area had been over SOUTH Vietnam and he'd been told to make one pass over his target, release his ordnance and return to base. Unfortunately, some of his ordnance didn't release so he made some additional passes over the target with no success. When he came on our radio frequency—our call sign was Invert—he was running low on fuel, with hung ordnance and flying in pea soup weather. We thought we would have him in good shape soon since we had been able to free a tanker from orbit and point him in the direction of our friend.

Again, over the radio came "Mr. Wayward" requesting permission to jettison his ordnance. Why he didn't do as much over the target, I'll never know, but I denied him permission to do so, even though it would have lightened his load considerably. It seems that in recent days there had been some problems with aircraft dropping bombs on friendly troops as they overflew Laos and General Thao Ma, the Laotian General in charge of the Royal Laotian Air Force, had vowed to cut off U.S. bombing privileges over all of Laos, even into hostile areas where the Pathet Lao forces were situated, if there were any more bombings of friendlies. This message had come across our teletype wire in the form of a dispatch from the U. S. Air Attaché Laos. Needless to say, our friend was not happy with the answer I gave him.

General Ma with Air Attaché Bill Keeler.

In the interim, I was obtaining information from the tanker pilot and got both aircraft at the same altitude, heading toward each other. Because the weather was so bad, the pilot of the tanker wanted to make sure that I turned him in plenty of time to avoid the chance of a collision. I reassured him and kept the two aircraft on course. When they finally reached what I thought was adequate distance apart, I instructed the KC-135 pilot to make a 180 degree turn and began calling off the distance between the F-4C and the tanker to the fighter pilot. He didn't seem to be able to locate him, even on his radar, so I continued to call off the distance between the two aircraft. And once again he made an impassioned plea to jettison his ammo. Once again I just as firmly denied his request.

THEY CALLED IT NAKED FANNY

Shortly thereafter the two aircraft broke out into clearing skies and the F-4C moved in for a hookup only to hit another patch of bad weather. Again they broke out in the clear and were just finally able to hook up when the F-4C pilot radioed, "Oh, oh. I think I just flamed out." The tanker pilot immediately began descending to try to keep the fighter hooked up and perhaps give him the opportunity to get an "air start." Despite all efforts, it just didn't happen and the pilot of the F-4C and his backseat guy ejected from the plane once they had crossed the Mekong River and were over Thailand. My only mistake, I learned after talking to the tanker pilot, was that I had turned him too soon in an effort to avoid any chance of a collision. All of our missions were recorded on audiotape and the only question the board that investigated the incident had after hearing the tape was why I had denied permission to jettison ordnance. When they heard the reason was the memo from the Air Attaché Laos, they had no more questions. Apparently, the Phantom pilot was reprimanded for his screw-up, which resulted in the loss of a $3.8 million aircraft—a healthy chunk of change back then.

I later learned that the aircraft was part of the first USAF F-4 Phantom unit to arrive in Southeast Asia, belonging to the 45th Tactical Fighter Squadron, 15th Tactical Fighter Wing, which had deployed to Ubon in April. The pilot was Captain Carroll D. Keeter and his RO was Captain G. L. Getman. Not only was this the first aircraft lost from Ubon, but it was also the first USAF Phantom lost in the war. The "list of ejections" states only that "The aircraft had to be abandoned when it ran out of fuel after a strike in South Vietnam."

That was a sorry way to lose an aircraft.

Joe Ballinger: *We scrambled out so fast on this mission that we forgot to take the Pitot tube cover off. We only took one bird, but we flew by power setting and at DSAS (Directional Stability Augmentation System) when it turned on and off at 80 KIAS. I*

Scott Harrington

pulled the cover off when we landed in a dry area to pick up Keeter and Getman. While we were gathering up the pilots, Dick (Laine) got a call on the UHF radio that we were to wait until the Ubon LBR Det chopper got there to take them back to Ubon. We waited for over an hour for them to get there and the two F-4C crew members, who had not been injured, were not too happy about that. Interesting note; this incident was listed on a USAF shoot down list as the first F-4 combat loss and since the Ubon chopper picked up the two crew members, Saigon gave them credit for the save.

THEY CALLED IT NAKED FANNY

19

"THUD DRIVER" IN A TREE

Virtually every aircraft had, in addition to its nomenclature identifier, a nickname. For example the F-89J, a 1950s jet fighter, had limited ability to glide should it lose its engine. So it was referred to as the "lead sled." The Vietnam era F-105 was called the Thunderchief, but it was commonly known as a "Thud." Hence, the pilot of an F-105 would be a "Thud driver."

It made the day a special one for all of us at Naked Fanny when the rescue crews were able to bring back a pilot. It was even more special when a pilot or aircrew from another aircraft involved in the rescue would accompany the 43s back home.

Such was the case on June 23, 1965, when Maj. Robert Wilson's F-105 was hit by ground fire while on a mission over southwestern North Vietnam, some twenty to thirty miles north of the DMZ. Wilson could not fly his damaged Thunderchief over a ridgeline, so he ejected.

After a normal descent, he found himself suspended upside down in a tree 150 feet above the jungle floor. Wilson managed to swing into a crotch of the tree where he wiggled out of his parachute harness. He then took out his survival knife and cut a small branch from the tree. Wilson used the branch to snag his seat pack, which contained all of his survival equipment. After drawing the pack over to where he stood, he retrieved

THEY CALLED IT NAKED FANNY

his URC-11 survival radio. Wilson contacted the HC-54 airborne rescue command post called "Crown" which, in response to his "Mayday" call, had moved off its orbit along the Thai-Laotian border and now flew nearby.

Half an hour later four Air Force A-1 Skyraiders droned into view and contacted the survivor.* Soon the pilots spotted Wilson's chute and after radioing the downed pilot's exact position to Crown, flew to an orbit several miles away so as not to reveal Wilson's location to any enemy troops.

Ninety minutes after Wilson's ejection, an HH-43, from NKP showed up. Wilson fired off a small flare that was part of his survival equipment. The "Huskie" pilots spotted it and moved their chopper directly overhead while the PJ lowered the penetrator through the foliage.

A few hours later, safe at the Nakhon Phanom officers' club, Wilson set up drinks for the chopper pilots. The next day he returned to Korat.

The description of this mission is credited to Major Michael A. Wormley, from his Thesis entitled "Combat Search and Rescue: Searching the History; Rescuing the Doctrine," which was presented to the faculty for completion of graduate requirements, School of Advanced Air and Space Studies, Maxwell AFB, Alabama, June 2003. Approved for public release, the document's distribution was unlimited.

The pictures that follow were taken both before and after the pickup of F-105D pilot Major Robert W. Wilson, who ejected about twenty to thirty miles north of the DMZ and landed in a tree. When the choppers located him, they lowered a jungle penetrator—the first use of the device where the pilot didn't know what to do with it. He just held on to it for dear life and had to be pried off of it once he was in the chopper.

Wilson became the only pilot to have ejected over North Vietnam and be rescued from North Vietnam without ever putting his feet on the ground in North Vietnam.

---

*The USAF A-1s are questionable, since a Navy A-1 pilot came back to NKP with the 43s and rescued pilot.

HH-43B crew preparing to board chopper before heading out to rescue Major Bob Wilson. A2C Arthur Neil Black (*center, with M-16*) would later be on a chopper shot down near the border of North Vietnam and Laos.

Left to right: Captains Stan Schaetzle, Bruce Hepp, and Tom Curtis, along with CWO George Wolfram of Invert Control, check time and maps before departing to pick up Major Bob Wilson.

Left to right: Capt. Tom Curtis, Major Wilson, A-1E pilot (with back to camera), and Major Howie Douthit.

Major Bob Wilson (*left*) shakes hands with Capt. Bruce Hepp after Wilson was plucked from a tree in North Vietnam.

Left to right: Major Bob Wilson, Major Howie Douthit and Navy A-1E pilot share a laugh back at NKP after Wilson's rescue from North Vietnam.

Major Bob Wilson thanks 1st Lt. Walt Turk for his rescue efforts. In background is A2C Neil Black, PJ.

THEY CALLED IT NAKED FANNY

Bruce Hepp and Tom Curtis were on the Low Bird with Francisco Alverado as Crew Chief and James Poole as PJ. Stan Schaetzle and Walt Turk flew the High Bird. A2C Black was their PJ.

> **Bruce Hepp:** *When we arrived on site the CAP aircraft gave us the heading and distance to his location. As I recall they said, "You can see his orange chute ahead of you." And I replied, "But it's in the top of a tree. Where's the pilot?" Their reply was, "He's in the tree, too."*
>
> *We came to a hover over the chute and moved it around a little bit with our rotor wash. The tree was a very large cap tree with a huge flat top. I think that one of our two crew members in the cabin reported that they thought that they could see him in the branches below us. The chute seemed to be pretty well entangled in the tree and it did not appear to be a problem with the pickup. The high bird stayed above us and relayed information to the others on scene.*
>
> *We started the hoist down into the top of the tree. It took a little work to get it in a position where Major Wilson could climb on the penetrator. After all of these years, I now realize the problem he had with the forest penetrator—he never did get on it properly.*
>
> *After our crew got him in the AC, we started our climb and headed home along with the high bird. I don't recall any other particular happenings during our trip back. It was a fairly routine mission as I remember, short of the fact that he was in the top of a very large cap tree. I don't recall any hostile fire.*

It was a treat for all of the guys at Naked Fanny to see the A-1E come back with the Huskies as well as for the pilot to spend some time with Major Wilson and the rescue crews before heading back to his carrier off the Vietnam coast.

20

AIR AMERICA AND LIMA SITES

JOE BALLINGER: *WHEN WE WERE BRIEFED BY THE DEPARTING group that shared our duties, they showed us a book that covered all of the Lima Sites in Laos used by Air America and other contractors. It gave the coordinates, and a description of the runway and fuel available. L-sites were runways for larger fixed wing aircraft. LS-sites were for V-STOL and helicopters. But we called them all "Lima Sites.*

Covert activities by the CIA were underway in Laos from the early 1950s.

According to William Leary in his book *Supporting the Secret War*: "In August 1950, the Agency secretly purchased the assets of Civil Air Transport (CAT), an airline that had been started in China after World War II by Gen. Claire L. Chennault and Whiting Willauer. CAT would continue to fly commercial routes throughout Asia, acting in every way as a privately owned commercial airline. At the same time, under the corporate guise of CAT Incorporated, it provided airplanes and crews for secret intelligence operations."

Consequently, small bases were scattered throughout Laos and their locations could make the difference between helicopters running out of fuel and having refueling points on the way back to NKP.

THEY CALLED IT NAKED FANNY

Joe Ballinger: *The day after the Wilson rescue we were again scrambled, this time to a Lima Site just below the Plain of Jars (PDJ) to await a possible pickup. But we came home with the same folks in the birds as when we left.*

Two days later I got a direct order from ASOC—one of the only times—to bring two HH-43s and my best crews to Udorn, packed and ready for one week, Destination: Unknown, Mission: Classified. I elected to send Tom and Stan in one bird with Turk, myself and David Cutillo in the other. Two days earlier, Stan had put in his resignation and it was laying on my desk for me to decide what to do about it. After receiving the order from ASOC, I called Stan in and told him I had ten days to review his resignation and that I needed him and what was happening! Then I got Tom and Walt and told them the news; to pack and that we were going to Udorn on a special mission. The purpose of the mission was to learn about Air America operations and survey some Lima Sites for forward rescue use. We were to go no closer to Vientiane than 50 miles.

When we arrived at Udorn, we were introduced to an unshaven guy in old khakis wearing a beat-up Marine drill hat and were told that he would be our guide through Laos. That was our introduction to the legendary Tony Poe, a contract officer for the "Company"—the CIA—who some called "Lawrence of Laos." It would be the first time an American, officially and in uniform, would be allowed in Laos since the signing of the 1961 Peace Agreement.

With Tony on board, on June 27, 1965, we took off from Udorn and went north across the Mekong River into Laos heading for Long Tieng, and Lima Site 98; sometimes called Alternate for its other designation 20A. There was another Lima Site just north of Alternate designated as Site 20, which was used mainly as a cover site to confuse the media, etc. Alternate was the in-country base for Air America and Laotian Lieutenant General Vang Pao's Meo (Hmong) Army.

The weather was lousy and without any reliable navigation aids, we were quickly finding out that our guide, Tony, was not a great map reader from the air. Hearing us calling into "Alternate" somewhat lost, an Air America H-34 came along and led us in to the site. Upon arrival we were introduced to General Vang Pao, got our helicopters blessed from evil spirits and were treated to an impromptu "lunch" of corn on the cob doused in a gallon can of butter with Johnnie Walker to drive away the buttery aftertaste. We stayed overnight in the Air America hooch on a hill at the end of the runway and in a notch through the mountain karst.

The next day, again with Tony on board, but following two Air America H-34s this time, we left "Alternate" and dropped down into the Nam Ngum River canyon with sheer walls and maybe 700 feet deep. We had a cloud layer above us and a ground fog layer below us and were warned to fly the right side. For good reason, too, as suddenly an AA Caribou flew by us from the opposite direction and told the one behind him, "Look out! Here come two single motor, dual rotor flyin' purple people pluckers!"

As we flew out of the canyon and past Site 20, we were warned not to fly any further north up the river as it ran underground and was covered by a massive wall of rock.

As we made our way around the west side of the Plain of Jars (PDJ) we were shown some of the other Lima Sites, all unbelievable for fixed wing landings except for Lima Site 105. That site had a long conventional runway that ran east and west along the highway that went across the PDJ. On the way east across the top of the PDJ, we saw a C-47 dropping supplies on the PDJ, but were told by Tony that it was an IL-2, the Russian copy of our C-47.

At LS-36, we found another screwy runway with a dip on one end and then up and over a hill on the other. After landing we were met by a grungy, skinny, unshaven kid in jeans and a white shirt who was introduced to us as Jack, as many "Company" and Air America guys were called by only one name. Come to find out, he was an Air Force captain named Jack Teague, who was up there calling air strikes on the PDJ. Having seen a Newsweek Periscope *comment* made by Texas Congressman Olin Teague, who was now fully supporting the new GI Bill, as his son was in the military, I asked the obvious question, "Does your dad know where you are?" Jack admitted that he didn't at that time! As he showed us around the site, I saw a lot of small, young boys carrying M-1 carbines and asked if they were gun bearers. He told me, "No. They are some of the best soldiers we have. At 12 they have no knowledge of fear. And when Tony had been shot in the gut on the PDJ, two of them went in at night and carried him out, saving his life!"

After having lunch in their military mess—shooing away the flies and digging into the big bowls of sticky rice and whatever meat was available; and not asking any questions there—we flew back east across the top of the PDJ on our way back to "Alternate." When we got to the notch above LS-20, it was socked in. The Air America H-34 driver we were following told us to dive through the notch and make an immediate descending 90 degree left turn into the Nam Ngum canyon. Thinking about the options, I did what he told us to do with Tom and Stan close behind me. We made it and got back to "Alternate" together in one piece—happy as hell to call it a day.

That night we were honored with a dinner by General Vang Pao and two other visiting Laotian generals from Vientiane who sat on either side of him. As the senior officer, I was offered the first plate. I should mention that there were no chopsticks, just a fork and a tablespoon as eating utensils. Tony had informed me that they used the spoon as a knife to cut, just as we sometimes cut things with a fork. On the plate before me was a cube of steak

Lima Site 36. Note the CH-3C at far right. Two other helicopters are at left of fixed-wing aircraft.

about three inches square and an inch thick. And just before I stuck my fork in it to pull it onto my plate, Tony whispered in my ear, "That's all the meat there is! Slice off a small piece and pass the meat to General Vang Pao." So I did and I don't know to this day if all the guys got any of it.

From there the dinner went as usual with sticky rice, vegetables and some other meat. That was, until the toasting. We had already been warned to sip the Lao-Lao, a native booze fermented from rice, similar to Tequila. It was served in shot glasses and as soon as it was emptied, it was immediately refilled. Now, to the toasting: Before General Vang Pao raised his glass to me, he took a spoon full of red "jello" from a bowl in front of us and put it in his glass and then offered me the spoon. So I did the same with mine and then we tossed the shots down together. Unfortunately, I sometimes read too much about native customs, and as the concoction went down my throat, I remembered the custom for bravery done with coagulated pig blood in some societies. It hit bottom, came partway back up and I choked it down all the way. I grunted and held my glass up to the General again. WRONG—as now it was time for the senior general on Vang Pao's right to toast me. After I got through three of these, General Vang Pao toasted the man on my right, which I believe was Walt. And the same toasting went through all of us with a lot of bravery on their parts, too!

Next came the blessing in combat conducted by a Buddhist priest (monk). I had seen the rope of strings that General Vang Pao had on his wrist and now we found out what it was all about. You kneeled before the priest and he offered you an orange and a cookie while others gripped your elbows behind you. Thus the blessing was passed through me to them also as the cotton strings were tied on my wrist. We all got six to eight strings before the ceremony was finished. The custom was to wear the strings until they came off! (Walt and I did! Tom tore his off just before he was captured and I don't know about Stan's.)

After the blessing, there were dancing girls and Laotian music. No touching and a lot of use of hands in the air. Also, Tony had us split up and standing around with the other generals so no favoritism could be claimed. As the night went on I got the other guys to fade out of there, one at a time, while I stayed to the last. Also, that was the last I remembered until I woke up the next morning, naked, and Tom handed me some needed coffee. Then he told me "the rest of the story!"

When I didn't show up at the hooch, Tom went back down the hill looking for me. It had been raining a lot that day and the laterite mud was slippery as hell on that hill. As he got down near

This is a three-photo composite of LS 20. The CH-3s are at the far right (*inside circle*). The black karst hill at the right edge of the middle third sits on the end of the runway.

the bottom, the "Bear" waved him over. The "Bear" was a huge guy with a wooden plug in his nose. The story was that he killed a bear with his bare hands, but got clawed in the nose by the bear. The "Bear" was Vang Pao's bodyguard and assassin, as needed. Anyway, the "Bear" pointed me out to Tom. I was down in this pig pen among the hogs, sleeping. The "Bear" and Tom carried me back up the hill and threw me in the shower and then Tom put me to bed. The red laterite mud never did come out of that flight suit. And I was told later that the "Bear," who was like a stone around anyone, would get a slight smile on his face when he saw me. I guess I made a lot of face at "Alternate" that night.

In Asia, causing someone to "lose face"—even if done by accident—is an infraction rarely forgiven. Particularly in Laos, people go to elaborate lengths to give "face" to others and prevent them from losing it.

Joe Ballinger: *We tried to get out and back to Udorn on the 30th, but the weather was too bad. Even Air America quit flying that*

THEY CALLED IT NAKED FANNY

day. When some of the guys wanted to keep going, the message was sent out on the radio, "Okay, but flight pay stops at four!" I guess they were all on the ground at four o'clock.

That night I was invited up to Tony's hooch for a drink with him and there I saw some strings of what looked like dried chili peppers hanging on his porch. When I asked what they were, he told me that to confirm the Lao soldiers' kills he gave them 500 Kip (about 6 cents in 2016) for a pair of ears. Later, I heard that when he found some young boys with no ears, he stopped that practice.

Finally, on the 1st of July, we flew back to Udorn between cloud layers with Tom and Stan's flight instruments mostly out. We had to find a hole for them to get down VFR. The next day we were back at NKP where we received orders that activated us as Det 1, 38th ARS as of 1 July 65.

After that, I personally only went back to the Lima Sites three more times, not counting Savannakhet, which was General Ma's Air Force Base with C-47s and T-28s.

As the CH-3 guys arrived shortly after our initial trip, we took turns, starting with Tom, then Walt and then me, last with Freddie (Liebert), getting them familiarized with Laotian operations and Lima Sites. It was on that trip that we overflew LS-36 and on over to the Sam Neua area, stopping at what I thought to be LS-85 to lighten the load on the CH-3 by dropping off three 55-gallon drums of JP-4. This site had a runway that ran up the hill at about 30 to 40 degrees with a flat turn around spot on top among some buildings. There was a small village at the bottom of the hill. A Pilatus PC-6 Porter, a single-engine Short Take-Off and Landing (STOL) utility aircraft designed by Pilatus Aircraft of Switzerland, was unloading in the flat spot, so Freddie touched the nose gear down on the slope and we dropped off the barrels.

The third time in was by mistake. The CH-3s were being tasked daily to cover the deep north missions out of LS-36, while the HH-43s covered the lower Laos and North Vietnam panhandle areas. When the HH-43s were suddenly given a frag order to go to LS-36, I didn't question it as I figured that the CH-3s needed a break. By this time we had the internal fuel cells installed and we took two birds straight out of NKP and around the west side of the PDJ and across back east to LS-36. After getting there and setting up we reported in to Crown. That was when we found they had sent us the frag order by mistake, but to stay and cover that day. Nothing happened and we came back around the PDJ to NKP the same way that evening.

The last time was when we got a call to scramble north to, I believe LS-12, under the belly of the PDJ. A recce bird had been shot down and they were trying to locate the crew (the RF-101 Voodoo used for reconnaissance was a two-place aircraft). On the way up, Tom was lead and I followed several miles behind for some reason. By the time I caught up with him, Tom had done a 180 and told me that there was no flag flying and the site symbols had been torn up indicating to him the site was closed. So we headed north again and found the site we were looking for. Again, it was one that was cut out of the jungle with a small ville or farm, and a contingent of Laotian troops. There we set up and waited for the mission. It must have been really late in the day, as I remember when the Laotian troops lowered their flag. Seeing five or six ragged troops line up and march to the flagpole—a scraggly, skinny tree, I called all of us to attention and rendered a hand salute. It may not have been proper procedure, but I figured a little respect and courtesy was not out of line. Shortly after that the mission was aborted and we returned to NKP.

Interesting to note that in the book Air War in the Shadow of Vietnam, a Major Aderholt, out of the embassy, set up the Lima Sites in conjunction with the CIA in 1961. Upon reviewing his book Air Commando One, he makes comments about doing that.

THEY CALLED IT NAKED FANNY

General Vang Pao was born in the Laotian jungle in 1929 and died Jan. 6, 2011 in suburban Clovis, California. Along the way, Pao, son of Hmong farmers, became a key, if controversial, American ally and the symbolic father of a persecuted people.

General Pao, who was 81 when he died, is best known for his role in America's "secret war," a covert, CIA-backed campaign against Laos's Viet Cong-aligned leaders during the Vietnam War. In the lead-up to war, North Vietnamese forces cut tracks through the Laotian jungle, creating the supply route now known as the Ho Chi Minh Trail. Laos was also at war, split between the communist Pathet Lao and the Royal Lao forces. The Americans teamed up with the latter, working with Vang Pao and a band of guerrilla fighters to disrupt the North's network of trails. For Vang Pao's fifteen-year fight against Southeast Asia's communists, former CIA chief William Colby once called him "the biggest hero of the Vietnam War."

21

UDORN DET GETS A SAVE

JOE BALLINGER: *ON THE 3RD OF JULY, A PILOT BAILED OUT south of the PDJ in Laos and ended up hung up in a tree. An Air America H-34 crew had tried to get him, but snarled their hoist cable in the tree and somehow broke the pilot's arm. They had to shear the hoist cable and leave him there in the tree. The Udorn detachment was sent in and we were called on to assist and to bring a chain saw. Walt and I headed out from NKP.*

As noted earlier, HH-43 helicopters were stationed at other bases in Thailand. For the most part, their mission was of the Local Base Rescue variety. The detachment based at Udorn would often provide backup for the troops at NKP and would occasionally get the chance to pluck a fighter pilot from harm's way.

The official de-classified Combat Mission Narrative reads as follows:

> An F-105 pilot, Capt. Kenneth R. Johnston, discovered he had a severe shortage of fuel en route to a strike in North Vietnam. He immediately jettisoned his external stores and started heading for friendly territory. He contacted the HC-54 on precautionary orbit, which in turn advised the control center to scramble helicopters

from Udorn AB, Thailand. The F-105 ran out of fuel while over Laos, and the pilot made a successful bailout. He landed in high trees and was dangling in his harness 50 feet above the ground. He had suffered a broken arm. When the helicopters arrived on the scene a rescue from above was attempted. Due to heavy foliage the pararescue man was suspended in the horse collar 100 feet below the helicopter and for ten minutes tried to chop away the vines and branches above the survivor. It soon became apparent that this approach would not work. The helicopter then landed approximately ¼ of a mile from the survivor. The pararescue man walked to the site and the helicopter lowered the hoist to him. The pararescue man was hoisted up to the survivor, and tied the survivor to him utilizing nylon rope. He then cut the parachute shroud lines, and the helicopter climbed vertically for 150 feet, then flew at 20 knots to the clearing with the two men dangling 75 feet below the helicopter. After the recovery of the two into the helicopter an uneventful flight to home base followed. The helicopter aircraft commander was Capt. David E. Allen.

Not surprisingly, the official report mentions nothing about the Air America H-34 helicopter being the cause of the pilot's broken arm, nor is there even any mention of the AA aircraft having been on the scene.

Unable to remove the pilot from the tree, both Udorn birds landed in a clearing on a hill. Their initial plan was to access the pilot's location on foot and have the PJ climb the tree, cut the pilot out and lower him to the ground. But after finding the survivor deep in the rain-soaked jungle and the tree covered with moss making it slick like a barber pole; the initial plan was scrapped.

Plan B was for the PJ, Sgt. Free, to be hoisted up to the survivor; cut him free; and both would then be lowered to the ground. Captain Dave Allen, Udorn's CO, flew his copter over the pilot's position and lowered his hoist with a rope tied to the hook to reach the ground. Once Sgt. Free hooked the survivor to the rope and cut him free, he signaled to be lowered. But in reassessing the situation and realizing how difficult it had been to come into the valley through the jungle, the decision was made to lift both men to a clear location; set them and the helicopter down and then bring both the pilot and Sgt. Free aboard. The decision proved to be the right one as all involved were completely exhausted. Bill Wirstrom was flying with Dave Allen.

> **Bill Wirstrom**: *We delivered the pilot to Udorn with a dislocated shoulder which was caused by the H-34. (Note: the only award or decoration out of this mission was given to Sgt. Free who received the "Soldiers Medal.")*

> **Joe Ballinger**: *By the time we got there, Davey had the pilot and all we did was follow him back to Udorn, refuel and come back to NKP. Davey's crew was credited with the pickup.*

The Udorn Det was made up of pilots from different bases. First Lieutenant Bill Wirstrom was from Shaw AFB, SC. He received a copy of orders with no destination. He was to go through TAC mobility (the NKP group belonged to MAC), draw an M-16 and fifty rounds of ammo, a .38 revolver and fifty rounds, bring a mobility bag and report via commercial air to Griffis AFB, NY.

Upon arrival at Griffis, he was joined by the others. Bill says none of them knew exactly where they were going except it was to SEA and a briefing stop at Clark AB, Philippines. He later found out he was the only one to follow the orders and bring weapons!

> **Bill Wirstrom**: *Two HH-43B helicopters and supplies were loaded onto the lower deck of a C-124 with personnel on the upper deck for the long journey. Nicknamed "Old Shakey," the C-124 had a limited range requiring "island hopping" across the Pacific, landing at islands to refuel. Twelve days later we arrived*

THEY CALLED IT NAKED FANNY

at Clark; via Travis AFB, Hickam AFB, Wake Island and Anderson AFB, Guam. At Clark, during the in-brief, one of the first questions they asked was how many weapons did we have. When it was determined I was the only one that followed the orders, I was no longer the "butt" of jokes. It was then we were informed we were to be a Provisional Detachment at Udorn AB Thailand. We were to join four other detachments in Thailand for LBR Operations, but also to assist the unit at Nakhon Phanom (NKP) with rescue work in Laos and North Vietnam.

We arrived at Udorn unannounced. The local U.S. base commander had no idea we were inbound. The base was overflowing with aircraft and personnel as war buildup had begun. On-base quarters were not available. But because we were rescue air crews, he wanted us on base and temporarily put us into an office building until some officers were moved off base to the nearby city of Udorn. Our enlisted troops had a very difficult time as they were assigned quarters in old barracks built by the Marines in 1962. None of the buildings had air-conditioning. It was not a pleasant situation.

The only large flying unit there was an RF-101C Kodak (recce) squadron, which turned out to be from Shaw AFB, SC. The Flight Surgeon, Doctor (Capt.) Dave Hunter, was my neighbor at Shaw and a fellow graduate of LSU. From then on it was "scrounge, scrounge, scrounge." We received very little, if any, support, except for parts, from Pacific Air Rescue Center. I must also mention there was an Air Rescue SC-54D and an SA-16 at Udorn but the only time we spoke to them was on the UHF radio in the air. (Those aircraft would have served as Crown during rescue missions.)

After our rescue mission, we were joined by a detachment from Taiwan.

The Taiwan detachment's CO was a major and became the new

Detachment Commander because he was the SRO. Almost immediately, he refused to allow flying fifty-five-gallon fuel drums in the back of the HH-43s, so he was relieved by PARC and sent home, placing Capt. Dave Allen back in charge.

Bill Wirstrom: *Things then began to get hot and heavy. We started flying very far north in Laos, living at Lima Sites, with fuel delivered by Air America C-46s (yes 46s).*

The Udorn birds would fly to Lima Site 98 (also called 20 Alternate, and the primary CIA base) for refueling. They would then fly on to LS-36 or LS-85 to be near the daily air strikes, or to other places such as Paksan on the Mekong River. In the late afternoon they would fly to Lima Sites 20 or 98 to spend the night, or RTB. They often spent several nights up north but never at LS-36 or 85, which were not considered that safe.

Bill Wirstrom: *We would receive launch orders by HF radio from Saigon and there were many missions into North Vietnam. We sometimes landed at LS-36 near the North Vietnam border right in the middle of "Indian Country." I think we saw Hanoi from 10,000 feet about four different times.*

We met many unusual people at this site and LS-95. But, the guy I really remember is Edgar "Pop" Buell. He was the senior USAID official in Laos, an organization that provided help to the locals. A book was written about his activities.

There were also a large number of "Company" operatives. The Air America guys received about three or four times the amount of money we received but refused missions into North Vietnam. They would "Bank $100,000" in eighteen months and depart. That was a heck of a lot of money in the middle of the '60s.

In November I was allowed to return from my "60-day TDY" after about eight months only to find out five months later I was to be given a PCS assignment to Nha Trang AB, Vietnam for one year.

THEY CALLED IT NAKED FANNY

Joe Ballinger: *Somewhere in this time frame, a team of Air Force photographers showed up to fly with us and get a picture of an actual pickup. I argued with them and with their boss at Saigon that we didn't have the space and needed the extra fuel more than bodies. They took film of us scrambling, etc., and a simulated shot of a pickup (taken from the ground). That footage I swear I saw many times later representing an actual pickup. I mean, who in their right mind would get on the ground to make a shot in combat like that? Later, they also rigged a camera on the CH-3 hoist to get a picture.*

On the 4th of July, 1965, I wrote a letter to my folks that my mom kept. In that letter I told them that we were getting more helicopters and crews to augment our rescue work. Also that they were deactivating the Kirtland Detachment, and that we had Air Force photographers here to document our rescue work and that we may be on Walter Cronkite's "Twentieth Century" program sometime in the fall.

Udorn would get another rescue on 31 August 1965. The Combat Mission Narrative tells the story:

Captain William Henry Bollenger was making a bomb run on a target in North Vietnam when his F-105 was hit. He was able to fly over one mountain ridge and ejected. HH-43s were scrambled from a forward site in Laos upon notification of the downing. While the helicopters were on the way A-1E RESCAP aircraft had located the survivor's position in a heavily wooded area with trees 125 feet high. As the helicopter hovered and lowered the hoist several groups of people were seen running toward the pickup area. The A-1Es fired warning rockets which discouraged further approaches. Two men were also seen about 100 yards from the hovering helicopter. The copilot fired his M-16 almost continuously during the recovery to protect the survivor as he was being hoisted into the helicopter. The survivor was returned to Udorn AB, Thailand. He had slight lacerations which he incurred when his head struck a tree branch during landing. The HH-43 aircraft commander was Capt. David E. Allen."

And a third Udorn pickup occurred on September 6 when Captain Gary D. Barnhill ejected from his aircraft in the midst of a refueling mission. His F-105D developed a fuel leak and he disconnected when his aircraft caught fire. He was able to eject just before his aircraft exploded.

THEY CALLED IT NAKED FANNY

22

CH-3S: FROM EGLIN AFB, FL TO NKP

THE NEED FOR ADDITIONAL RESCUE AIRCRAFT MADE for drastic actions to be taken back in the U.S., as you will learn in this chapter. This next group of TDY personnel would make for strange bedfellows, so far as the types of helicopters that were being deployed was concerned.

Captain George Martin was what is known in the Air Force as a "short-timer" at Eglin AFB near Ft. Walton Beach, Florida, in late spring of 1965. He had served in World War II and Korea and was looking forward to retirement. But, there would be a delay in those plans. George would shepherd the first CH-3C unit to perform CSAR missions anywhere in the Laos-Vietnam theatre. This is his story.

> **George Martin**: *It was late May to mid-June 1965, when I first became aware of the efforts to pick a group of pilots and crew to leave for training concerning high-altitude operations and survival training after possible shoot-down, etc. It became apparent to me that I was not to be included in the group. Being curious as to why, I sought out the First Sergeant for answers. It appeared that at that time I did not have sufficient time available prior to scheduled retirement. Therefore, I sat back and quit wondering why I was not included.*

THEY CALLED IT NAKED FANNY

Since forming the group virtually decimated our squadron personnel-wise, no one was concerned about what would happen to the few officers who remained, qualified or not. Subsequently I found myself assigned as Staff Duty Officer to the group that was actually running the air war in Vietnam. I had a desk with several telephones, including a red one, and a sergeant to act as my assistant.

I remember it was Friday, the 27th of June (1965) when I looked up and noticed our squadron commander standing in the shadows, and apparently trying to get my attention. I called the sergeant's attention to the telephones and rose to go over and find out what the Colonel wanted. He handed me a telegram to the squadron from Headquarters USAF which read, and I quote: "Urgent immediate requirement exists for CH-3C type helicopters and qualified air crew in Southeast Asia."

At this point, I asked Colonel Blackburn why he was querying me. Didn't he know I had insufficient retainability and therefore couldn't go overseas? To which he replied, "Well George, sometimes we have to break the regulations..." and other words to the effect that I was one of the few remaining qualified officers available so, after exchanging a few other words with him, I realized his mind was made up and there were no other reasons I shouldn't go.

So I said to him, "When do I leave?"

His reply was, "How soon can you pack?"

Then I asked him how many officers and crew he had in mind to send. He said, Freddie Liebert, Phil Stambaugh, and myself along with two unqualified co-pilots, and he was sending two aircraft along with sufficient qualified air crew as yet unnamed. I then asked him who and how many ground crew were to go with me. He gave me about six names and said the squadron was identifying the rest. He said the squadron was busy cutting orders and assured me the tour was to be four months TDY. He then excused me from my Staff Duty Officer position and departed. I went back to the SDO's desk and picked up my hat.

Suddenly, it seemed I was besieged by various people reminding me of many things that had to be done. First and foremost I needed to get shots for all personnel, check the status of the aircraft to see if they were being made ready to depart, and check on the men to remind them of their financial status. Another man suggested I check on guns we would have to check out and carry over, etc.

Not knowing where to start, I ran into Freddie Liebert and Phil on the way home to tell my family and filled them in on all the information I had. I then went to the squadron to check on the orders and found them busily working on a list. I scanned it and realized I just barely knew the men by name except for one or two. The highest in rank was a tech sergeant that I barely knew by sight. I approached him and said, "You are now NCOIC of this group." Then I told him there would be a meeting of all men on the order at 0800 the following morning, a Saturday.

The next morning I arrived at the meeting amidst much grumbling and excuses from the men. It turned out the biggest complaints were the need to upgrade their shots and to receive partial payments. Their complaints centered on the fact that Finance was only going to give them $50 advance pay, so I spent much time and effort with the few people working that morning at Finance. It appeared the only one who could approve more than $50 advance pay was the Finance officer himself, and he was on the golf course. It was finally arranged to increase the amount paid to the men to $200.

So, after coping with these and several other delays, I managed to get time to go to base operations and check on our transportation. Base Ops assured me there were three aircraft inbound to handle our transport—two C-124s and one C-130—but it developed, due to the necessity for crew rest, they would not *be leaving Eglin until Sunday evening. The two helicopters had to be partially disassembled to fit on the two C-124s along with a starting unit and a large compressor.*

The personnel for the C-130 included my group of six officers, fifteen men, and one civilian tech rep from Sikorsky.

The orders were for a TDY of 125 days for six pilots and fifteen support personnel to APO 96233. (That APO was actually listed as a Camp Friendship located at Korat AFB, Thailand. NKP would eventually have its own APO of 96310.) The orders said: "To participate in classified mission."

The roster included the following:

    Capt. James P. Stambaugh—4488 Test Sq. (Heli)
    Capt. George C. Martin—4488 Test Sq. (Heli)
    Capt. Fred M. Liebert—4488 Test Sq. (Heli)
    1st Lt. George Warren—4488 Test Sq. (Heli)
    1st Lt. Orville N. Keese—4488 Test Sq. (Heli)
    SSgt. Eddie Walker—4485 A&E Maint. Sq.
    A1C Bing Gibson—4485 A&E Maint. Sq.
    A1C George R. Alston—4485 OM Sq.
    A1C Jerry H. Price—4485 A&E Maint. Sq.
    SSgt. Jim P. Byrd—4485 OM Sq.
    A1C Sheldon C. Tart—4485 OM Sq.
    A2C Harry W. Hylander, Jr.—4485 OM Sq.
    A2C Garold L. Isenhour—4485 OM Sq.
    A2C Bobbye J. Gonzales—4485 OM Sq.
    TSgt. Michael Hoffman—4485 OM Sq.
    SSgt. Francis L. Hill—4485 OM Sq.
    SSgt. Curtis W. Pert—4485 OM Sq.
    SSgt. Lee R. Diggs—4485 OM Sq.
    SSgt. George A. Johnson
    A1C James E. Armenia

Phil Stambaugh recalls that the tech rep, Rubin Hardy, did not have a passport. To remedy that situation he was flown in a T-33 to Washington and processed through on an emergency need basis, flown back to Eglin and was ready to depart with the group on Sunday.

George Martin: *The pilot's itinerary included the shortest flight over the Pacific and ending in Ubon, Thailand.*

The Situation Overseas

George Martin: *Ubon was some 50 miles south of Nakhon Phanom (NKP). Upon arrival at Ubon, all hands set to work reassembling the two aircraft, whereupon we discovered one final delay. A vital part for one of the helicopters was missing. It involved a tail rotor connector called a Thomas Coupling.*

There were six of these couplings used among the two aircraft, and they were identical. Each coupling consisted of 11 stainless steel flat washers. This lost coupling was searched for high and low and, in our desperation to find it, I ordered all the men's personal baggage be included in the search. When we finally decided it was not to be found, we turned our attention to solving the problem of the missing part. It was suggested that we should divide the remaining 22-odd washers by three. This would give us three weakened Thomas Couplings but would allow assembly. I checked with our tech rep, Rubin Hardy, to see if this idea would work. He agreed that way of doing the assembly would work, but didn't think Mr. Sikorsky would approve.

It was about this time that I appointed Freddie Liebert our test pilot. Each aircraft, of course, needed an acceptance test after being disassembled and reassembled. After the flights, he assured us he could tell no difference in control characteristics. I then appointed Phil as scheduling officer. I assumed overall operations control as well as OIC duties.

So we arrived at Nakhon Phanom ready for combat with two unarmed cargo helicopters, no armor plate, no self-sealing gas (fuel) tanks, and a cargo winch for a hoist. I picked up the phone and called Saigon and reported both aircraft checked and ready to go, to which the duty officer in Saigon replied, "Fine. I have a mission for you."

23

THE JOLLY GREENS ARRIVE

JOE BALLINGER: *ON JULY 5, 1965, THE FIRST CH-3Cs arrived out of the blue onto our ramp from Ubon with George Martin, Phil Stambaugh and Fred Liebert wondering what their mission was going to be. The CH-3s sure weren't what Tom and I had on our dream sheet. Yes, they had two engines, but no armor, no self-sealing fuel tanks, no guns and the 1250 shaft-horsepower engines were underpowered for our use. They also had a "Mickey Mouse" internal detachable hoist. And the mission was not what they were looking for, either. But they did it, too!*

The next day, I called Saigon—Lt. Colonel Krafka—to turn over the command of the detachment to George Martin. Liebert and Stambaugh also outranked me, but I was told that the CH-3Cs were transferred to MATS (Military Air Transport Service) and ARS (Air Rescue Service), but the TDY CH-3C crews remained under TAC (Tactical Air Command) where they came from. Since I was senior ARS officer, I would remain in command. I told this to George and George, being a helluva fine guy with two wars already under his belt said, "No sweat." Unofficially, we formed a composite unit with George in charge of his troops, and me Commander over all. Liebert was assigned Ops Officer duties; Stambaugh was the Maintenance Officer. We never had any problems.

THEY CALLED IT NAKED FANNY

The CH-3Cs at rest on the PSP ramp at Naked Fanny.

George Martin: *Let me say a word or two about the origin of the name "Jolly Green Giant." Each morning, prior to take-off from Nakhon Phanom, the aircraft commander was required to walk over to Invert headquarters and pick up a call sign. This call sign was changed every eighth day. (The reason we checked each morning was that we were too busy attending to all of our responsibilities that there wasn't all that much time to worry which day was the day to change call signs, so we would just check each day.)*

The changing of the call sign every eighth day led to increasing confusion for many reasons. We requested that Saigon solve this problem by giving us our own call sign for the CH-3C helicopters. But, to no avail. Many months earlier, during training in the CH-3 helicopter, because of its large size and, at one time its green color, it was off and on referred to as the Jolly Green Giant. Back at Nakhon Phanom, as our operations became ever more routine, the call sign confusion continued. Early on I was directed by headquarters in Saigon to call them and make a report of each day's activities. After the routine report, they always asked how things were going and what we needed, if anything. So I reported the confusion about the call sign and suggested we be assigned our own call sign. After many denials and after my persistent requests for a call sign change, to my surprise one afternoon Saigon replied, "What did you have in mind?" When I replied with the name Jolly Green, he abruptly said, "We'll get back to you," and hung up. It was the second or third night later that he stated we could go ahead and use "Jolly Green" as our permanent call sign along with the last two digits of the tail numbers—76 and 85.

Joe Ballinger: Using the CH-3C called for a different concept of recovery. They were going to be used for the deep missions. They would go as a single ship and would be staged out of Lima Site 36, but since ARS required two ships on a mission, the Udorn HH-43s would also stage out of Lima Site 36 as backups to the CH-3C. Meanwhile, we covered the panhandle with our HH-43s.

The first familiarization flights with the CH-3C began on July 11, when I flew to Udorn with George and Freddie to get a briefing at ASOC. After that, Tom, Walt and I took turns flying with them into Laos for familiarization with the Lima Sites.

On the 15th of July, on my turn up with Freddie, we got a mission to pick up two F-4 Recce (reconnaissance) pilots shot down the day before in the Sam Neua area in northeastern Laos. They were separated and on opposite sides of a village. An Air America H-34 got the first one just before we got there. Freddie, as pilot, was flying from the right seat, and Orville Keese was flying copilot from the left seat. That put A1C James Armenia and SSgt. Lee Diggs at the right cargo door with the hoist, and the PJ on the aft ramp in the stinger position. There was an emergency exit pullout window on the left side over the sponson. I pulled it out, so I could cover the left side with my M-16, if needed. Freddie and another Air America H-34 made a side-by-side approach to the ridge that the pilot was supposed to be on. The H-34 hovered right, as Fred hovered left, to find him in the dense jungle canopy while Laotian Air Force T-28s suppressed gun fire from the village. The H-34 got him and we left to go back to LS-36.

THEY CALLED IT NAKED FANNY

So I got my first combat time in a CH-3C. But for the fickle finger of fate, that would have been the first Jolly Green pickup.

At about this same time, the Air Force Rat Pack guys brought us some portable radios for testing at the Lima Sites in Laos. One of them was a Suitcase HF (high frequency) radio, on loan from the Secret Service. I still have a hand receipt for that one.

The Air Force Rat Pack was a special communications group that developed communications equipment to be used in planes and helos like that used by the Secret Service on Presidential duties.

Joe Ballinger: *With these radios you could talk to anybody in Washington, D.C., from almost anywhere in the world out of a suitcase unit! By 1965, they (Rat Pack) were involved in SEA. Someone pulled some heavy strings to get a unit delivered to me—maybe General Aderholt? When I signed a hand receipt for them, I was told to protect them with my life and destroy them before being captured.*

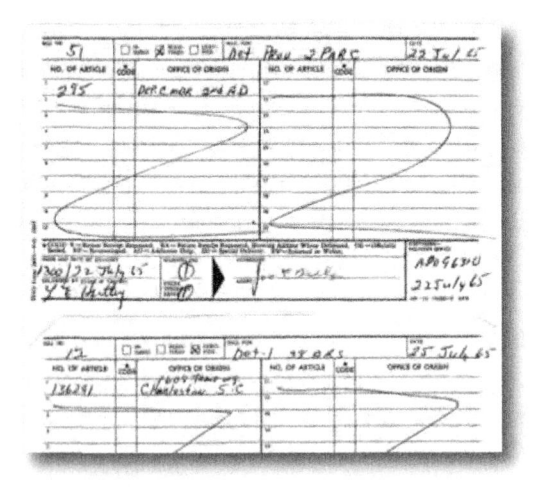

Hand receipts for "Rat Pack" Communication gear, signed for by Joe Ballinger.

24

TWICE IN, TWICE OUT: LEFT HIGH AND DRY

JOE BALLINGER: *RECALLING THE JULY 7TH MISSION THAT took us over to the south of Vinh, NVN, the Low Bird, with Bruce Hepp and Dick Laine, got a bad out of track situation (a condition of the helicopter rotor or the propeller of an aircraft in which the tips of the blade do not follow the same path in their rotation) and had to return to NKP, so Walt and I went in alone. We circled around as the cover aircraft were trying to find the downed pilot until we went bingo on our fuel and returned to NKP. While we were refueling, we got word that they had him spotted so we went back in again. One of the Udorn birds went in with us as High Bird. When we got there, he was supposed to be standing in a rice paddy waving at the passing aircraft, but no radio contact. It didn't sound right to me as the whole area was flat with rice paddies all the way to the beach.*

Walt Turk: *Of the few times we went out of country and didn't have any success with a pickup, this is probably the one that still gripes my ass. It was the first mission flown by Air Force A-1s—call sign Sandy—out of Udorn. We were almost to the bailout* site just south of the city of Vinh, when the Sandy flight showed up. The Navy A-4 that was capping the location told the Sandy flight of four not to go near the end of the small valley because there was a guy with a gun and he would shoot you. Well, as I remember it today, two of the Sandies came up to join us at 9,000 feet and the other two proceeded to fly down the valley and sure as hell one of them took a hit. He told everyone about it and the next thing we knew, all four of them took off for Da Nang!!! So here we are just south of Vinh, and all alone except for Crown who told us they would get us some rescap airplanes. They did after quite a while: two F105s with bombs still on the hardpoints.

And now what I really remember to this day, is the comment by the wingman, "Lead, don't run over the choppers." I looked out the bubble and all I could see was the radome and the air intakes. He missed us. Then to add to this sorry escapade, they had to cycle back and forth to a tanker and, after a while, they too departed.

That was when Joe's past training as a navigator came into play. As we neared our bingo fuel state it was time to head for NKP. Weather was a definite factor and in order to stay clear of the clouds we began a slow climb and pretty soon we were up around 12,000 feet—heading kind-of toward home plate. In the meantime Bruce is on our right wing and signals that his radio is inoperable. Joe sat there very calmly figuring how far we had come from the orbit and we were now getting to the point where fuel remaining could be a problem. It was then that he called in the blind for Invert and a steer, if they could hear us. They did and asked if we had any weather near us. Well we sure as hell did—SEA thunderstorms with tops up around 40,000 feet! They found us with the heightfinder radar, the one that had a red tag on it when it arrived at NKP, told us what heading etc., and we made it back with very little fuel in the tanks.

This has been a long "get it off my chest" tale but like I said, we were kind of left to fend for ourselves and we did. I still harbor a dislike for the AF A-1s that day—they sure weren't the Spads!

Joe Ballinger: *Coming back in lousy weather between layers, somewhat lost, I took a heading of 270 for Thailand. I called Invert and asked if they could help. We didn't have IFF on our birds so I told them we were between two of the biggest thunderstorms I had ever seen at 10,000 feet. Their answer was, "Roger! You are 78 miles out! Take up a heading of 279 degrees!" I did that and found a hole just before Thakhek and came on home. Later that evening I bought the controller a drink telling him that was a damned good skin paint assist. His reply was, "Hell, we didn't have you until about 50 miles! We just found the two big thunderstorms and gave you a heading from between them!"*

THEY CALLED IT NAKED FANNY

25

SAM HAS HIS SAY, AND A BAD WEATHER PICKUP

ON JULY 24, 1965, A NEW THREAT TO U.S. PILOTS reared its ugly head—the SAM, or Surface-to-Air Missile.

It was on that day that USAF Captain Richard Keirn was flying over North Vietnam with a flight of four F-4Cs on a "MiG combat air patrol (MIGCAP)," a free-ranging hunt for MiGs, when a Guideline popped up through the clouds and exploded. (The S-75 Guideline was a Soviet designed high altitude surface-to-air missile used extensively by the North Vietnamese to protect Hanoi and Haiphong. NATO countries call it the SA-2.) Keirn's aircraft was shot down and the other three Phantoms were damaged. Both Keirn and his RIO (radar intercept officer), Captain Roscoe Fobair, were listed as prisoners of war (POWs), although Keirn was the only one ultimately released. There were later reports that Fobair had died in prison.

This was the second time Keirn had been a POW. He was captured by the Germans in WWII at the age of nineteen when his B-17 was shot down.

This was the war's first loss to a SAM. Both USAF and Navy brass asked their political superiors for permission to hit SAM sites, and were refused, due to worries that there were Russian advisors at the sites. (We were still in the middle of the Cold War with Russia with the thought that any incident that killed Soviet personnel could trigger hostilities.)

On the night of the 11th and morning of the 12th of August, a Navy Douglas A-4 Skyhawk was shot down by an SA-2. The brass repeated their requests, and this time they were granted permission. However, the North Vietnamese moved the SAMs around, and in two days of strikes none was confirmed destroyed, while five aircraft were lost.

> **Scott Harrington:** *My crew was on duty on the July 24th night shift after Keirn was shot down and we expected to receive orders to attack SAM sites the next day. We always had to remove a code book from the safe to decipher the Top Secret fragmentary or "frag" orders we would receive by secure cryptographic messages each night. There, of course, were no such orders. And it wasn't until the night of August 12th and morning of the 13th that we finally got those long awaited orders. The reason for such shortsightedness, at least that's what we thought it to be at the time, was political. Fears were that since the SAMs were Russian-made and Soviet technicians were often on the ground at SAM sites, bombing and perhaps killing Soviet personnel might lead to all-out Russian support of the North Vietnamese effort. Night after night we expected to get "frag orders" to attack those sites and none came. I can't imagine how the pilots felt.*

Further research indicates that three days after the first shoot down by an SA-2; Air Force planes attacked two SAM sites. Six of the 46 F-105s conducting the raid were shot down and more were damaged from AAA. However, we at Invert never saw orders for retaliatory strikes until August 12th.

It was also on July 24th that a Navy A-6A was shot down over Laos with both crew members ejecting successfully. The Combat Mission Narrative identifies them as LCDR Richard P. Bordone and LTJG Peter F. Moffett:

An F-105 that was searching for the downed Navy crew developed engine trouble and had to bail out within 25 miles of the first incident. Marine helicopters that were prepositioned for search and rescue operations at Quang Tri, RVN and USAF HH-43 helicopters from Nakhon Phanom, Thailand were launched to effect recovery of survivors. In spite of low visibility and marginal reception of beacon signals all crew members were located and recovered. The Marine helicopters rescued the two Navy pilots. Capt. Thomas J. Curtis who was the pilot of the HH-43 helicopter picked up Major William J. McClelland, the F-105 pilot.

Tom was on the "low bird" and is shown as the recipient of a Distinguished Flying Cross with Combat "V"...for heroism while participating in aerial flight as Aircraft Commander of an unarmed and unarmored helicopter over North Vietnam on 24 July 1965. On that date, Captain Curtis's aircraft penetrated deep into hostile territory to recover a downed U.S. Air Force pilot. This rescue mission involved flight in excess of 260 miles over unfamiliar territory, under marginal weather conditions, and without navigational aids. It is believed that 1st Lt. Duane Martin was co-pilot on the "low bird."

Bruce Hepp and Walt Turk were pilot and co-pilot aboard the "high bird" on that mission.

THEY CALLED IT NAKED FANNY

26

FIRST HH-43/CH-3C COMBAT RESCUE UNIT IN SOUTHEAST ASIA

JOE BALLINGER: *JULY 25, 1965, THE DAY AFTER the first SAM shootdown, the guys who came over to form the HH-43B unit got some unwelcome news: we were being extended from 120 days TDY to 179 days.*

When the two CH-3Cs that were transferred from TAC arrived at NKP in July 1965, Det. 1, 38th ARS became what was a first, and probably the only, Combat Rescue Unit with both the HH-43B and the CH-3C aircraft.

With the original engines (T-58-GE-5 Turbo Shaft), the CH-3C wasn't able to pick up much and the HH-43B could outrun it at 10,000 feet, as the CH-3C would encounter blade stall at about 65 knots.

George Martin, Phil Stambaugh, George Warren, Orville Keese and Fred Liebert (now deceased) were the original "Jolly Greens" who flew missions along with the HH-43Bs. During the period of May through October 1965, eight pilots were picked up out of North Vietnam. The HH-43Bs recovered five and the CH-3Cs brought back three.

THEY CALLED IT NAKED FANNY

George Warren: *Our standard procedure was to send one bird out each day to stand alert at Lima Site 36 and then return. The other bird would only leave NKP if the designated rescue bird had been dispatched on an actual search/rescue. The NKP bird would head up to LS-36 as backup if there was enough daylight left to make it practical to depart.*

George Martin: *So we set up a routine flying back and forth between our home operating base at NKP and various sites in northern Laos just short of the North Vietnamese border. As soon as we landed there (Lima Site 36), we set up long-range radio contact with Saigon.*

Much as we would like to have copied the HH-43Bs' method of always responding to a call with two helicopters, when I had both of my CH-3Cs in commission, one was sent to the east and the other to monitor the western half of the front. So we pretty much operated alone.

In addition to Lima Site 36 being a staging site for the Jolly Greens, it was also an aerial supply point for friendly guerilla forces located at La Khang, Laos, near the North Vietnamese border.

The CH-3Cs made their first pickup on the 27th of July. The pilot was Frank Tullo.

Lieutenant Colonel Robert Hanson, USAF, Ret. wrote the story of that rescue for *Air & Space/Smithsonian Magazine*. It was titled "Tullo and the Giant," and is reprinted with his permission.

Tullo and the Giant by Lt. Col. Robert Hanson

That was Frank Tullo's first day as a captain, and he's never forgotten it. He was 25 years old and flying from Korat Royal Thai Air Base, one of two F-105 bases in Thailand. News of his promotion had come through late the evening before, and he had sewn a pair of shiny new captain's bars on his flightsuit. He was wearing those bars when North Vietnamese gunners on the outskirts of Hanoi shot him down.

I heard Tullo's story a few years ago when he was an airline captain and I was negotiating the sale of radios to his airline. I flew 122 missions in F-4E Phantom IIs, also out of Korat, but at a later time in the war. Many of my friends had been shot down over there, and a lot were never heard from again. Most fighter crews were not optimistic about their chances for rescue.

Pilots of the F-105 Thunderchief, or "Thud," in particular, suffered a high loss rate. There was a standing joke among the often chain-smoking Thud crews that the definition of an optimistic Thud driver was one who thought he would die of lung cancer. In fact, the Air Force commissioned a study that showed that during a typical 100-mission tour, an F-105 pilot should expect to get shot down twice and picked up once. At about the time that Tullo got his captain's bars, air rescue planners decided to try to improve the pilots' chances.

On July 27, 1965, Tullo was flying as Dogwood Two in a flight led by his good friend Major Bill Hosmer, a former Thunderbird and the best pilot Tullo had ever flown with. Dogwood was to be the cleanup flight -- the last of 24 F-105s, six flights of four, from Korat to hit surface-to-air missile (SAM) sites in North Vietnam. Their job, as cleanup, would be to take out any sites not destroyed by the earlier flights.

The SAM had introduced a new aspect to the war only days before, when an F-4 Phantom II became the first to fall to these new weapons. The missiles were fired from within a no-fly zone near Hanoi, previously immune from attack as dictated by rules of engagement. Tullo's flight would be part of the first attack within the no-fly zone and the first major strike on the SAM sites since the Phantom had been downed.

To destroy the missile sites and take out their command and

control centers, each Thud was loaded with two pods of 2.75-inch rockets. (They were also equipped with an internal 20-millimeter Gatling cannon.) Along with the rockets, the Thuds carried 450-gallon auxiliary fuel tanks under their wings. Tullo's aircraft, which was scheduled to be flown to Okinawa for maintenance, also carried a 600-gallon tank on its centerline. He'd have to jettison the tank once airborne to stay with the flight.

This was part of a maximum effort involving at least 48 F-105s—24 from Korat and 24 from Takhli—and another 50 or so supporting aircraft. At this early stage of the war—the buildup of U.S. fighters in Thailand and South Vietnam had begun only six months before—tactics and weapons for dealing with SAMs had not been developed. The projected learning curve for the months ahead was nearly vertical.

It was mid-afternoon when Tullo's flight came over the hills from the south to clean up leftover targets. Dogwood flight had been listening to the action on the assigned attack frequency since an in-flight refueling midway en route. From the sound of things, some friendly aircraft were down. As the flight cleared the last ridge at treetop level before arriving at the target area, Hosmer, who was Dogwood lead, exclaimed, "Jesus!"

Working to hold his position on Lead's wing, Tullo managed to steal a look ahead. "I damn near fainted," he told me years later. "To a good Catholic boy, this was the description of hell." The whole valley was a cauldron of flame and smoke from the ordnance dropped by preceding flights, and North Vietnamese Army flak filled the sky. In the five months he had been in the war, Tullo had seen his share of anti-aircraft artillery, but this was the worst yet.

Hosmer had the flight on course for the first SAM site they were to check out. Tracers were flying past the canopies and the smell of cordite was strong—the pilots depressurized their cockpits when they neared the target area so that if hit, smoke from an onboard fire would not be drawn inside. Only days before, Tullo had seen a column of smoke stream from his wingman's still-pressurized cockpit after the canopy was jettisoned prior to ejection.

The flight pressed lower. The Thud would do nearly 700 mph on the deck. Tullo was sure they were less than 200 feet and was working hard to stay in position on Lead. Without warning, Hosmer broke hard left, exclaiming, "Damn, they just salvoed!" Sometimes SAM batteries would fire all their missiles at once in an effort to save the valuable control vans. Tullo could see only the huge wall of smoke and flame coming at the flight from the NVA guns protecting the SAM sites.

Their tremendous speed caused the flight to turn wide enough to be carried directly over the gun site. As they passed over, Tullo looked right into the flaming muzzles of a battery of quad guns. They (the two F-105s) were at 100 feet or lower, and still near 700 mph. He glanced over at Lead to check his position, and then back into his cockpit. That's when he noticed the fire warning light.

"Lead, I have a fire light," he radioed. Three called, "Two, you're on fire. Get out!" Hosmer kept the flight in the turn, saying, "Two, loosen it up. I'm going to look you over."

Tullo assumed the lead and headed for the mountains in the distance. Hosmer said, "Better clean off the wing, Frank."

To give himself more speed and maneuverability, Tullo jettisoned the tanks and rocket pods on his wings and felt the Thud lighten. Three was calling again, his voice tight with urgency. "Two, the flames are trailing a good 150 feet behind you. You better get out!"

In spite of the fire and the calls from Three, Tullo felt a sense of well-being. He was still flying, he had control, and he was with Hosmer. Nothing bad would ever happen with Hoz leading. It would work out. The fire would go out, the aircraft would keep *flying, and he would make it back. They were still over Hanoi. Houses were below them. The mountains to the west, which would come to be known as Thud Ridge, offered refuge. A good bailout area, just in case.*

"*You better get out, Frank, it's really burning,*" *Hosmer said in a calm voice.*

"*Negative,*" *Tullo replied,* "*It's still flying. I've lost the ATM (the noisy auxiliary turbine motor, which provided the Thud's electrical power but left many of the aircraft's pilots with bad hearing), but I've got the standby instruments, and I'm heading for that ridge straight ahead.*"

In the early days, several pilots whose aircraft were on fire ejected over the target and were either killed or taken prisoner. There had been incidents in the Thud's checkered past when a burning aircraft had exploded before the pilot could eject, but many others had flown for a considerable time without blowing up. Many pilots, like Tullo, had decided to take their chances staying with their aircraft as long as they could, rather than eject in the target area.

The ridge was still well ahead of the aircraft. The flight had climbed some but was still very low and being shot at from all quarters. Tullo's aircraft dropped its nose slightly. He pulled back on the stick. No response. He pulled harder. Still nothing. When he heard muffled explosions in the rear of the aircraft, Tullo hit the mike button: "*I've gotta go, Lead. I'm losing controls. It's not responding.*"

At 200 feet, there was no time to wait. If the aircraft nosed down, physics would be against him. Even if he managed to eject, he would likely bounce just behind the aircraft, still in the seat. He pulled up the armrests, which jettisoned the canopy, locked his elbows in the proper position, and revealed the trigger that fired the seat. The results were the most horrific Tullo had ever experienced. At the speed he was moving, the noise, the roar, the buffeting—it was unbelievable. Everything not bolted down in the cockpit went flying past his face. He froze for a matter of seconds before he squeezed the trigger to fire the seat.

The ejection process that followed was so violent that today Tullo's memory is blank of everything that happened immediately after he squeezed the trigger. He doesn't remember leaving the cockpit, the seat separating, or the chute opening. He had the low-level lanyard hooked, which attached the parachute directly to the seat and caused it to deploy almost immediately. After tumbling violently, whump! He was swinging in the chute.

A little battered by the violent ejection, Tullo prepared for the landing. Floating down in the chute was serene and the soft rush of air soothed him. He did not see his aircraft crash. During his descent, he eyed the city of Hanoi about 25 miles away. A small U-shaped farmhouse sat near a clearing, just to the west. He passed below the 100-foot treetops and landed in an area of 10-foot elephant grass.

At that moment, listening to the sound of his flight disappearing to the southwest, the only thing in his mind was that he was on the ground in North Vietnam, armed only with a .38 Special. His first concern was to hide the billowing white parachute. Working hard to control his breathing, he stuffed the parachute under the matted grass and covered it up with dirt. After shedding his harness and survival kit, he removed the emergency radio from his vest, extended the antenna, and prepared to contact Dogwood flight. He could hear them returning, and he had to let them know he was all right.

As the flight drew closer, Tullo turned on the survival radio. Cupping his hand around the mouthpiece, he whispered: "Dogwood Lead, this is Dogwood Two."

Hoz responded immediately: "Roger Two, Lead is reading you. We're going to get a fix on your position."

The flight turned toward Tullo, who had landed on a hillside west of Hanoi. He could hear heavy anti-aircraft fire to the east and see puffs of flak dancing around the flight. Within seconds, hot shrapnel began to fall around him.

"Frank, we gotta go. Fuel is getting low, and we've been ordered out of the area. We're gonna get you a chopper." Hosmer's voice dropped: "And, Frank," he said, "this may be an all-nighter."

Tullo roger'd Hosmer's message and told him he was going to try to work his way higher up the slope to make the pickup easier. He had no doubt that he would be rescued.

As the sound of Dogwood flight faded to the southwest, Tullo prepared to move up the hill to a better vantage point. He decided to open the survival kit and remove useful equipment. In a normal ejection, once stabilized in the chute and prior to landing, a pilot would reach down and pull a handle on the kit's box to deploy it. It was advisable to deploy the kit prior to landing to avoid possible leg injuries, since the case was hard and fairly heavy. Tullo hadn't had this option because he had ejected at such a low level. He rotated the kit's red handle, and with a great whooshing roar, a dinghy began to inflate. The dinghy! He had forgotten all about that! And it was bright yellow! He had to stop the noise. Tullo drew a large survival knife he wore strapped to the leg of his G-suit, threw himself on the dinghy, and began stabbing it. The first two blows merely rebounded. With a final mighty effort, he plunged the knife into the rubber and cut a large hole so the air could escape. With that emergency solved Tullo lay back to catch his breath and get a drink of water. Then he started up the hill.

The elephant grass was so dense that at times he couldn't separate it with his hands and had to climb over the tough, wide blades. After climbing about 50 to 75 feet, he realized he wasn't going to make it to the top. His flightsuit was soaked, and his hands were cut by the sharp edges of the grass. Rather than waste more energy, he flattened out a small space in the grass and faced southeast to have a good view of any threat coming up the slope. Time to set up housekeeping.

Tullo's survival vest and kit included a spare battery for the radio, emergency beeper, day and night flares, pen flares, six rounds of tracer ammo, a "blood chit" printed in several languages that promised rewards for assisting downed American airmen, gold bars for buying freedom, maps, a first aid kit, water purification tablets, two tins of water, two packets of high-energy food, tape, string, 250 feet of rappelling line, a saw, knife, compass, shark repellent, fishing kit, whistle, signaling mirror, sewing kit, and two prophylactics for keeping ammunition or other equipment clean and dry. He extracted the ball ammo from his .38, loaded the tracers, and stuffed everything not immediately useful into the knapsack-type pouch. Then he sat back, tried to relax, and waited for the rescuers he knew would come.

Tullo heard the sound of prop-driven aircraft approaching from the north. He correctly assumed they were Douglas A-1s, or "Spads," as they were called. He stood up and keyed his radio. "This is Dogwood Two, do you read me?"

"Dogwood Two, this is Canasta, and we read you loud and clear. Transmit for bearing." Tullo warned Canasta of the flak to the east, and as advertised, the guns opened up as the aircraft approached Tullo's position. As soon as Tullo could see the aircraft, he began giving vectors. On the second circle, Tullo was looking right up the wing of Canasta, a flight of two Navy A1-Hs. He called, "Canasta, I'm right off your wingtip now."

Canasta Lead said, "Gotcha! Don't worry; we're going for a chopper." As the Spads droned out of the area, Tullo felt sure he would be picked up.

Within a few minutes, he heard the unmistakable sound of Thuds. Thinking it could be Hosmer again; he turned on the survival radio and called, "Any F-105 over Vietnam, this is

Dogwood Two." An answer came from a flight of two Thuds, which approached his position in a wide sweeping turn from the north. The flight Lead, whose voice Tullo recognized, asked Tullo to pop a smoke flare for location.

"Smoke?" Tullo replied. "Are you out of your mind? There's no way I'm going to pop smoke here!"

The pilot told Tullo to calm down. He had just spotted trucks unloading troops to the south of Tullo's position. He also reassured Tullo that they were working on getting a helicopter to him. Tullo heard shots. They built to a crescendo, and then stopped. The shooting had started at some distance but had grown closer. Soon he was able to hear voices as the troops worked their way up the hillside. He burrowed into the dense grass and waited—his heart pounding. He raised his head and saw an older man about 150 to 175 feet away wearing a cone-shaped straw hat. It was all Tullo could do not to make a run for it, but that was exactly what they wanted him to do. He forced himself to sit quietly. The troops made a lot of noise but they kept moving to the east, down the hill. Silence returned and Tullo continued to wait.

George Martin was flying his Sikorsky CH-3C helicopter to Lima 36, a remote staging area in Laos about 120 miles from Hanoi, to prepare for another day of rescue alert duty. Only a few weeks before he had been flying cargo support at Eglin Air Force Base in Florida. Today, he was commanding a small detachment of men and helicopters on a 120-day assignment in Vietnam. He and his crew had been tasked with learning a new mission for which they had little preparation.

In 1965, as the number of U.S. airstrikes and reconnaissance missions in Vietnam multiplied, pilots faced the increasing possibility of being downed deep inside Laos or North Vietnam. Crews flying the small and slow Kaman HH-43 Huskie originally designed as an air-base firefighting and rescue helicopter, were already pushing the aircraft to its limits. There was clearly a need for a faster rescue helicopter with longer legs. The cargo-carrying CH-3C fit the bill, and the Air Force began sending crews from Eglin for specialized training. The crews practiced mountain flying, ground survival, and rescue operations, which involved coordination with controller and escort aircraft. The training was projected to last several months, but the escalating conflict wouldn't wait.

Martin, who was too close to retirement to be selected for the additional training and the accompanying extended tour, was ordered to fill in with 21 men and two CH-3s until the fully trained crews arrived. "I found out Friday afternoon and was gone Sunday evening," Martin says. "It was just like in the movies--I said, 'When do I leave?'"

They said, "How fast can you pack?"

Martin was about to land at an intermediate refueling base when he was asked by radio to divert and try to rescue a downed F-105 pilot. Martin still needed to proceed to Lima 36 to drop off cargo and extra crew. He had to lighten his aircraft to take on as much fuel as possible and still be able to pick up the pilot. "The big consideration in helicopter pickup is gross weight," Martin says. "If you're too heavy to hover, all you can do is fly around and wave at him."

Upon landing at 36, Martin's number two engine warning lights indicated an "overtemp" condition, which meant significant problems, possibly foreign object damage or a compressor stall from air starvation, and under normal circumstances would have grounded the aircraft. The crew looked to Martin for a decision. Everybody was pretty apprehensive. I told them, "We're his only hope. If the engine will start again after cool-down, we'll go." His crew reluctantly agreed.

The engine restarted without incident and Martin's CH-3, call sign "Jolly Green 1," took off for Hanoi. Martin had no idea where to locate the downed pilot. He was unescorted until he was about 50 miles from Hanoi, at which point he was joined by Canasta flight, flown by Ed Greathouse and Holt Livesay from the USS Midway's Attack Squadron 25.

The oppressive heat of the afternoon wore on. Finally, Tullo heard the sound of prop-driven aircraft again. Darkness was about 40 minutes away as he turned on his radio. The aircraft responded immediately. "Dogwood Two, this is Canasta. I have a chopper for you." Seconds later, Canasta flight flew directly over Tullo's position, and there, not far behind, came a helicopter. Tullo was expecting a small chopper, but this one was a big green monster, Martin's Jolly Green, the first in the theater and headed for its first combat recovery—Frank Tullo.

"Dogwood Two, this is Jolly Green. How am I doing?" Martin said to the man on the ground. He was coming right up the valley from the south-southwest.

Tullo said, "You're doing great!" and popped his pen and smoke flares. The chopper's blades made the smoke swirl as Tullo aimed his .38 straight up and fired all six tracer rounds. Crew chief Curtis Pert spotted the pilot through the thick ground cover as soon as the smoke made its way above the trees. As Martin hovered, Pert lowered a "horse collar" sling.

Later, better equipped rescue crews would have a specialized hoist attached to a "jungle penetrator" designed to pierce thick tree canopies. "We just had a jury-rigged cargo winch that you could turn into a 10-cent, Mickey Mouse rescue hoist," Martin says.

On the ground, the down blast was tremendous. Debris flew everywhere, and the trees and grass were whipping and bending wildly. Tullo holstered his pistol, slung the survival kit over his shoulder, and slipped the horse collar over his head. He gave the crew chief in the door a thumbs-up.

The cable became taut and Tullo began to rise off the ground. After being lifted about 10 feet, the hoist jammed and the cable stopped.

The crew chief was giving hand signals Tullo did not

understand. Tullo looked up. Pert and pararescueman George Thayer were in the door lowering a rope. The horse collar was cutting off the circulation in Tullo's arms and he was tiring, but he grabbed the rope and tied it around the top of the horse collar.

Finally the chopper began to move and dragged Tullo through some bushes. Everybody's trying to kill me, he thought. The Jolly climbed and circled as Pert and Thayer struggled with the hoist. The overworked number two engine had begun to overheat and a fire light came on in the Jolly's cockpit. As they circled, Martin hoped that the air flowing through the engine would cool it down and the light might extinguish.

Pert and Thayer were joined by copilot Orville Keese, and the three men strained to pull the dangling man aboard. The pain was becoming so great that Tullo was thinking about dropping from the sling.

Martin spotted a rice paddy next to a house and lowered Tullo to the ground. The exhausted pilot rolled out of the sling as the chopper swung away and landed 50 or 60 feet away from him. Pert and Thayer frantically shouted to Tullo, who sprinted and dove through the door. He could hear an automatic weapon firing and saw both pilots in the helo ducking their heads.

The Jolly had problems: low fuel, a sick engine, darkness, and clouds at altitude. Martin and his crew had been in the war zone slightly more than two weeks and did not even have maps of the area. The crew relied on flares lit inside 55-gallon drums at Lima Site 36 and the landing lights of hovering helos to find a place to land.

"We held only about a quarter of the area around the site," Martin says. "That was the only corridor you could fly through without getting shot at, because the Pathet Lao held the other three-quarters." Martin finally landed with a shaken pilot and just 750 pounds of fuel aboard.

Tullo learned his aircraft was one of six Thuds and one EB-

66 electronic countermeasures aircraft shot down that day. Of three surviving pilots, Tullo was the only one rescued—the others were to spend more than seven years as POWs. Tullo returned to a Thunderchief cockpit and completed his tour. His story was later told in Thunder From Above by John Morocco.

Tullo's rescue was the farthest north that a successful pickup had been made, thanks to the determination of Martin and his crew and the long range of their CH-3C. It was the first of 1,490 recoveries that Jolly Green Giants would make in Southeast Asia. Soon a dedicated air rescue version would be built, the HH-3C, with in-flight refueling capability, armor plating, a powerful hoist, and shatterproof canopies. However, the Jolly Green Giant would find its ultimate form in the HH-53 Super Jolly, an even larger and more powerful helicopter still flown in various versions today (1997). The technology improved, but rescue crews still had to meet the same basic requirements: a willingness to fly into hostile territory, hover in a big green target, and find a man whose only hope arrived on a cable and sling. (Courtesy of Lt. Col. Robert A. Hanson, USAF, Ret. as it appeared in Air and Space/Smithsonian Magazine.*)*

George Martin, as Aircraft Commander, prepared his pilot's report of the mission. The narrative that follows was taken directly from his mission report:

George Martin: *On 27 July, I was proceeding north to Lima Site 36 to assume alert status. There was difficulty proceeding northward due to adverse weather. Eventually we joined up with two HH-43s out of Udorn and were able to land at Lima Site 98. While refueling at 98, I attempted to get further info on the weather between 98 and 36, but before leaving 98 we were informed of a downed pilot and urged to scramble immediately.*

En route to 36 we were advised as many as four F-105s were down and we were being queried as to how many trips we could make between 36 and the target area on one fuel load. I informed Saigon Control that landing at 36 was necessary to offload unnecessary equipment and personnel in view of possibly picking up more than one pilot. As we touched down at 36, number two engine flamed out as a result of a deceleration stall and subsequent over-temp of 900° was encountered and lasted for some four to five seconds. This is 60° above transitory high and an engine change is required.

The decision was made to attempt a restart after cool-down and if the engine would develop power, we would proceed with the mission. During the cooling period additional fuel was taken aboard. And the crew was reduced to four personnel. The engines started and departure was made with 3800 pounds of fuel. The time to target was approximately an hour and twenty minutes. We were escorted by Spad (A-1) aircraft to within 50 miles of the target and flew unescorted until contact was made with Canasta Flight—two A-1s from Attack Squadron 25 aboard the USS Midway.

We made our descent from 10,000 feet over the Black River and accomplished our join-up with Canasta Flight. The three aircraft flew low level at approximately 2000 feet to the target. This took about 12-15 minutes at 130 knots. The A-1s' directions to the target were excellent. About five minutes out from the target Healy Flight, two F-105s, arrived and provided additional cover.

Contact was made with the downed pilot exactly where Canasta Lead directed us. The pilot was on an approximately 40° heavily wooded slope and while he was not visible to me, red smoke marked his position. I established about an 80-foot hover position and lowered the hoist. A relatively quick engagement was made and the pilot had been hoisted some 10 feet when the hoist failed. All of our attempts to operate the hoist proved ineffective, so we dropped a rope to the pilot and attempted to pull him up. This also failed, so I sent the co-pilot back to help and the three still could not raise the pilot, and then the rope began to fray. By this time I had been hovering over 15 minutes and the "fire warning" light on my suspect number two engine came on. I moved the aircraft slightly and had a momentary light out condition. The light illuminated twice more and I decided to move off to gain airflow over the engines. At this time the survivor was hanging on the rope, approximately 60 feet below the helicopter. After ascertaining that he was clear of the trees, I commenced a slow 360 degree climbing turn at 30 knots. This apparently gave me the desired airflow as the red lights remained out. During this time it became apparent that the three men in the rear couldn't pull the pilot up. A landing was then decided upon and a flat spot was looked for. I saw a rice paddy bearing NW of my position and dog-legged first west a half-mile and then north a half-mile. We deposited the pilot in the paddy and landed the helicopter for the pickup. There were many buildings adjacent to the paddy, but there was no sign of life.

Once the pilot was aboard we made an immediate departure—first to the west and then south. About a half mile after departing the landing site we encountered ground fire. It was an automatic weapon and approximately ten shots were heard—rapid fire. At that time, I did not think the helicopter had been hit.

We turned southwest toward the Black River and began a climb back to 10,000 feet. It was full dark at 36 upon our arrival and the site was difficult to find. With the help of two Air America aircraft, call sign "Hotel," and flares on the runway a subsequent safe landing was made with 750 pounds of fuel remaining. We decided to RON at 36 and assess the battle damage to the aircraft in the morning.

The next morning we found three hits that resulted in minor sheet metal damage. One slug passed through the hull equidistance between our two non-self-sealing fuel tanks and two passed through the right sponson.

Frank Tullo (*far right*) shakes hands with CH-3C pilot George Martin. Crew Chief Curtis Pert is shown descending the ladder from the aircraft.

The crew included Capt. George C. Martin (AC), 1/Lt. Orville N. Keese (Co-Pilot), SSgt. Curtis W. Pert (Crew Chief) and A/B Gordon C. Thayer (Paramedic). The rescued pilot was Air Force Captain Frank Tullo, who had flown his F-105 from Korat RTAFB, Thailand.

The next morning, a C-7 Caribou came for Tullo and returned him to Korat. George Martin and his crew cranked up the CH-3C and returned to Nakhon Phanom where the ailing engine was replaced.

THEY CALLED IT NAKED FANNY

The now-declassified Combat Mission Narrative for the Tullo mission reads as follows:

> Four F-105 aircraft were downed while flying against surface to air missile sites in North Vietnam. Of the four downed aircraft only one chute was reported. A CH-3C helicopter which was prepositioned at a forward site in Laos was launched to recover survivors. It entered the same area where the four aircraft had been downed, approximately 40 miles west of Hanoi, and was led to the downed pilot by RESCAP aircraft. The survivor was on a heavily wooded slope and marked his position with red smoke. The helicopter was forced to hover at approximately 80 feet above the pilot due to the high trees. After the pilot had put on the hoist harness and was raised 10 feet a hoist malfunction occurred. The crew was unable to lift the pilot the remaining 70 feet manually. The crew decided a landing would have to be made in order to rescue the survivor, so they flew to a rice paddy ½ mile away with the survivor dangling 70 feet below the helicopter. Immediately after landing and recovering the survivor the helicopter came under automatic weapons fire and received 3 hits, one of which missed the fuel tanks by 6 inches. The remainder of the return journey was uneventful. CH-3C aircraft commander was Capt. George C. Martin, and rescued F-105 pilot was Capt. Frank Tullo.

The following is a postscript to the rescue of Frank Tullo who sent me this message as he reflected back on that day in 1965:

> *It's hard to put into words how I feel about the brave people doing their jobs to their utmost that ended up with a successful rescue under really horrible conditions. All of us pilots knew that many of the rescue efforts started at NKP so we held that location in special esteem. Being on the ground that close to Hanoi; with*

North Vietnamese soldiers clamoring in the elephant grass looking for me; and firing volleys of gun fire to get me to bolt is horrifying beyond description.

I had been involved in rescue attempts both successful and non-successful during my tour and I knew the chances were grim in my situation. It was two Navy A-1s that found me and brought George's helicopter to my position. I can never describe how I felt when I saw that chopper coming in over me in spite of the ground fire. We had our problems that day, with the sling motor, but they hung in there and carried me to a dry rice paddy, set me down and landed next to me so I could get in. All of this was done under fire. What unbelievable courage that took. We were complete strangers but it didn't matter; they did their job! Where do we get such men?

George and I never lost contact with each other and every year on the anniversary I would call him and we would talk. It took me 28 years to contact the two Navy pilots, Ed Greathouse and Holt Livesay, and we ended up having a reunion with all four of us on the 30th anniversary. On the 40th anniversary we met again and I presented them with a crystal paperweight with the inscription Eternally Grateful, 27 July 1965, Dogwood 2.
Hopefully we will all be alive for our 50th in 2015 and we can get together again. —Frank

Unfortunately, due to health conditions, the four were unable to meet in 2015.

Joe Ballinger: *After recommending George and his crew for Silver Stars for the Tullo rescue, and it was downgraded to DFCs, we put them in for DFCs on every mission they made a rescue on.*

Side story—When Col. Allison Brooks, Commander ARS came through for a visit, he was to award the DFCs to George Martin and his crew for the Tullo rescue, they found that they didn't have any DFC medals available for presentation. So believe it or not, they used a Commendation Medal of which they only had one. It was pinned on and taken off after the reading of the citation to be used for the next crewman. The PJ on that pickup was Gordon Thayer, who had been reduced to Airman Basic before he came to us, and was slick-sleeved. I didn't think about it, but George sure did. He asked Colonel Brooks who, as the Commander of ARS, had the authority to give him one stripe back. He said he would after checking the circumstances of the reduction and I believe he did.

George Martin: *It was about this time we began to have personnel problems. One of our two young co-pilots developed appendicitis and was lost to the schedule. This loss, along with our earlier loss of one of our aircraft commanders, reduced our personnel to minimum crew status, as the CH-3 requires a two-man flight crew. This explains why Phil Stambaugh and I were flying together on the 24th of August, the day we rescued Pogreba. So, needless to say, in my daily telephone reports to Saigon, I constantly requested replacement of our two lost air crew.*

Phil Stambaugh: *On one of the days that Lt. Orville Keese was on alert at LS-36, he suddenly had an attack of appendicitis. He was immediately flown to Udorn and then transferred to Bangkok so he could undergo surgery. Everyone figured that Orville was headed back to the states and so we were rather shocked a few days later when he came walking in to Operations. Although he'd had surgery, he'd recovered enough to go water skiing with some of the tech reps at the beach south of Bangkok. Appendicitis— hard way to get a little R & R.*

Scott Harrington

Crystal paperweight given by Frank Tullo to the men who rescued him on the occasion of their 40th anniversary reunion.

THEY CALLED IT NAKED FANNY

27

A PIECE OF CAKE

JOE BALLINGER: *AS WITH MOST OF OUR MISSIONS, this one started sometime shortly after our noon crew change-out. On July 28th we got the call that there was a Navy pilot down over on the Ho Chi Minh Trail north of Mu Gia Pass. That pilot was a Navy lieutenant named Grant Townsend.*

Grant Townsend was the first rescued pilot allowed to be interviewed by the news media. The interview was written by Associated Press reporter Peter Arnett. First Lieutenant Walt Turk was the pilot for this mission, Captain Joe Ballinger was co-pilot, SSgt. Roberto Rodriguez was crew chief and Robert Evans was the PJ. Pilots of the second helicopter were Capt. Dick Laine and Capt. Bruce Hepp.

The following is from Arnett's AP story, and is reprinted here with permission:

Navy LT Grant Townsend had been pulling his A-4 Skyhawk jet out of a bombing run when a sudden explosion jolted the plane.
"I was engulfed in a ball of flame," he said. "It swirled around me. The aircraft was completely out of control."
Townsend jerked the ejection handle and spun into the air.

"Then I was swinging down, my parachute safely above me," he said. "Just 1,500 feet below was North Vietnam."

Townsend drifted toward the edge of a mountain valley. He noticed a river and a cluster of houses to the north. But he couldn't see any people.

"I wasn't surprised," he said. "The way we'd been working that place over with bombs, everyone would have been well hidden."

He prepared for a gentle landing on what appeared to be a grassy slope. He dropped into elephant grass 14 feet deep.

Townsend was 65 miles inside enemy territory.

He instinctively performed his survival routine, tearing off his parachute and tossing away such impeding items as his life raft, helmet and oxygen mask.

"My instinct told me to move up hill," he said. "But I didn't figure I had much of a chance. This was a populated area and the Communists surely could reach me before my own people did."

Townsend began moving through the tough grass, discarding additional equipment on the way. He tossed aside his gravity suit, or G-suit, and his flashlight.

"I wanted to streamline myself," he said.

But he kept his tiny but powerful radio transmitter, which could guide friends to his rescue. He moved 50 yards up from his parachute and made contact with the three other Skyhawks from his carrier, the Midway. The planes circled in, but their fuel supply was running low. The Skyhawks were replaced by two Navy A-1 Skyraider fighter-bombers. They kept flying near him. Before long he was calling for their assistance.

Crouched deep in the grass, Townsend began hearing voices. People he presumed were soldiers were shouting at each other and there was rustling nearby.

He called in the Skyraiders for a strafing run on the area of voices and the noise subsided.

Two Navy A-1s escorting the HH-43s home.

"The aircraft told me that I could expect a rescue helicopter in 40 minutes," he said. "But that was a long time. I tried to keep my mind occupied. I said prayers, I manicured my fingernails."

At 2 p.m., one hour after he had parachuted from his plane, Townsend heard the voices again, this time closer. He called in another strafing run.

The Skyraiders fired rockets, and this set the grass blazing at the valley floor. The flames raced through the undergrowth.

Townsend mistook the rustle of the flames for the Communists.

"I figured well, this is it," he said.

THEY CALLED IT NAKED FANNY

Joe Ballinger: *It was a pretty routine flight for us until we crossed this mountain ridge and heard the downed pilot asking the covering Navy A-1s where the helicopter was and was told that we were about ten minutes out. Still not sounding too excited, he told them the bind he was in—that the grass on one side of him was on fire, and the enemy was searching on the other side so he couldn't move anywhere. Hearing this, Walt put our bird into a dive down the side of the ridge going past redline of 105 knots to 120. When I pointed this out, he just nodded as we all knew the machine had been tested at Edwards to 140 knots and a 4-G pullout and we figured it was okay as long as we didn't push it too far. The Navy A-1s started giving us headings to the downed pilot using port and starboard. Walt told them that we were Air Force and to use left and right if they wanted us to get over him, which they did from then on.*

As we came down the "trail" with the two A-1s doing chandelle loops in front of us and strafing the trail, the pilot, Grant Townsend, fired pen flares up out of the tall elephant grass. The problem with that is the flares don't necessarily indicate exactly where the guy on the ground is located. So, in a hover about five feet above the grass we crossed over him and now he gets excited.

"Hey! Hey! Where you going? I'm behind you!"

At the same time I'm looking out my side window at a line of trucks on the trail looking for something to shoot at. Walt calmly pedal-turned the HH-43 180 degrees and the rotor wash blew down the grass exposing Townsend in a flight suit waving at us.

As Walt pulled up over Grant, I suddenly realized that my side is towards a hill and looking across the cockpit through the bubble I can see a truck with a guy on the other side of the hood. Thinking, "Christ! If he starts shooting, I gotta shoot back through the bubble!"

Thank God, he just watched us as I watched him back. By then, Rod (SSgt. Roberto Rodriguez) had Grant in the cabin and Walt made a max performance climb back across the "trail" and into the mountains towards NKP.

Not knowing at the time we had just made the first rescue of a U.S. Navy pilot from North Vietnam, we quickly found out as the Navy blew our cover with a news release to the fact. Saigon still stuck with the fiction of where we were based and I sent Walt to Saigon for a press interview. That's where, when asked how difficult the rescue was, he made his famous answer, "It was a piece of cake!" He became forever afterwards, "Piece of Cake Turk."

Walt Turk later received a handwritten note from Townsend, which read:

Dear Lt. Turk,
This is just a short note to express my many thanks to you and your crew.

The "Black Knights" of Attack Squadron Twenty Three wish to express their thanks by presenting you and your crew with a few small tokens of our appreciation.

The larger patch is our squadron patch. The smaller patch entitles you to guest membership privileges in the "Tonkin Gulf Yacht Club." It is hoped that you will wear these patches with pride as we do and that they will increase your luck.

Our Tonkin Club Yacht Master tells us that you may also wear the club patch while on Sunday afternoon cruises up and down the Mekong.

Again let me say thank you and I hope that I have an opportunity to see you gentlemen again, preferably in an officers' club.

Best of Luck,

Frank Townsend

Joe Ballinger: *While Walt was down at Saigon giving his interview with the press for Grant Townsend's save, I had recommended him*

THEY CALLED IT NAKED FANNY

Navy LT Grant Townsend shares a grateful moment with his rescuers. *Left to right*: A2C Robert Evans, SSgt. Roberto Rodriguez, LT Townsend, Capt. Joe Ballinger and 1st Lt. Walter Turk.

for a DFC and the rest of the crew the Air Medal. Walt turned down the recommendation for a DFC unless the whole crew got the same. When the "powers that be" told him that they were cutting back on the medals as we were getting too many, he told them that his commander believed that when the entire crew participated in a save they should get the same medal, and he believed the same. So we all got Air Medals and Walt didn't get the DFC that I thought he deserved.

Soon after that, Admiral Sharp, PACAF Commander, flew in for a briefing on our operations. He wanted to know what we needed. That was the day that some USAF captains (us) and a Navy Admiral divided up the war. The U.S. Navy would take over water and coastal combat SAR, and we would take inland SAR with cover of Navy A-1s if they were available. They would also provide us with daily locations of submarines and ships off shore in the event we got hit bad and couldn't make it back to NKP.

28

JOLLY GREENS MAKE IT NUMBER TWO

WHEN THE TWO CH-3Cs ARRIVED AT NKP IN early July, little did anyone know that there was a celebrity in our midst. And while it was 63-09685 that made the first Jolly Green pickup with the rescue of Frank Tullo, it was actually her sister ship, 63-09676, that was bound for stardom. Dubbed the "Black Mariah," 676 would ultimately spend her retirement at the National Museum of the U.S. Air Force at Wright-Patterson AFB in Ohio. We'll share 676's performance trail after she does the job assigned to her at NKP.

It was on August 24th that Phil Stambaugh, George Martin, SSgt. Francis Hall, A1C James Armenia and PJ SSgt. George Thayer were tasked with the pickup of a downed Thud pilot. Major Dean Andrew Pogreba's F-105D was the victim of AAA as he flew to his target some twenty-five miles west of Thanh Hoa, North Vietnam.

Phil Stambaugh recalls that for the CH-3C crews that were on alert, their days started early.

> **Phil Stambaugh**: *We'd leave out of NKP about 15 or 20 minutes before daylight so we could get to Lima Site 36, refuel and be ready to go if we got a call. We normally headed out northwest,*

would then turn north going around the PDJ, and then northeast toward 36. We had just turned on our second leg when we got a call, "Downed pilot!"

Instead of going around the PDJ, we flew parallel to it as we would have to pick up the escort aircraft and this would make it shorter for them than having to go to 36. And from our current position the downed pilot was almost due south. We continued to a smaller refueling site, topped off our tanks and waited. Still no escort birds.

Being only too aware of the fact that the longer a pilot is on the ground, the less the chance that he'll be picked up, they decided to go and let the A-1s catch up with them.

The Combat Mission Narrative reads:

Major Dean Andrew Pogreba was flying an F-105 which was hit immediately prior to bomb release while running on a target in North Vietnam. He bailed out a short distance from the target and hid in a fallen tree as he had heard the voices of people searching for him. A-1E RESCAP aircraft arriving over him came under 37 millimeter AAA fire, one A-1E was hit, but made its home base safely. A CH-3C was scrambled and was directed to Maj. Pogreba's position by the A1-E RESCAP aircraft that had visual contact with him. The CH-3C helicopter made a pickup from a 60 foot hover due to high trees. The CH-3C aircraft commander, Capt. James (Phil) Stambaugh, then made an uneventful flight to Udorn with the survivor.

But the combat mission narratives don't always tell, as Paul Harvey would say, "The rest of the story…"

Phil Stambaugh: *We were at about 5,000 feet and picked up the pilot on the radio well before we got to his location.*

> The area where Major Pogreba had gone down was an agricultural area with some plowed fields and a grass strip. There were some houses to the east of the fields. He was talking to us all the time—giving us his location in relation to where we were. We dropped down to 300—400 feet and flew across the area several times without seeing him.

Co-pilot George Martin says the pickup almost didn't happen because they couldn't see Pogreba when they went to pick him up. Finally, getting close to "bingo fuel," they decided to make one more pass over the area when someone saw a red cloth (that was all he had and he'd been carrying it the whole time). After that, it was virtually a routine pickup. They lowered the hoist into the clump of trees where he was hiding, picked him up and headed toward home.

George gave Pogreba a chewing out when he got on board because they couldn't see him until they saw the red cloth against the green trees. Martin says the cloth was a square yard of bright red silk folded to fit in the switch-blade knife pocket located on the right front thigh position of the standard flight suit. It was to be used as a last ditch attention-grabber, and in Pogreba's case it worked. Fortunately, he was not injured.

Phil says they ran into a bit of a controversy on the flight back to NKP.

> **Phil Stambaugh:** *The Invert controller told us they wanted us to fly the Major to Udorn instead of taking him back to NKP. Since we were running low on fuel and were directly north of NKP, we were intent on going one place—home. Once we finally got whoever it was that wanted us to bring him to Udorn to understand that we were nearly out of fuel with no Lima Sites handy, we headed home."*

Using the Call Sign "Jolly Green 76," the pickup of Pogreba was the second for the Jolly Greens.

Pogreba was a white-haired major. The crew told him it was a good

THEY CALLED IT NAKED FANNY

Major Pogreba is shown here (*silver hair, fourth from left of those standing*) with his rescuers from CH-3C Jolly Green 676. (Photo courtesy Jim Burns, RotorheadsRUs.us and Jim Howerton)

thing the North Vietnamese didn't get him because they would think we were down to using "old" men to fight our war.

Major Dean Pogreba would be shot down again, only the second time he would not be rescued. Reports indicate that his aircraft overflew the North Vietnam/China border and that he actually ejected over and landed in China where he was taken prisoner. At least two attempts to get him released, either by the Chinese or to free him by clandestine means, failed. Hopes for his release were raised when Brig. General Tom Lacy reported that he had seen and spoken to Pogreba. Lacy's credibility was questioned by a "closed door" Senate panel. Pogreba's fate remains a mystery to this day.

Now, on to the story about the celebrity of 676. The green chopper was relieved of her duties at NKP in January of 1966, and transferred to the 20th Helicopter Squadron's "Pony Express" run (supply missions to Lima

The "Black Mariah" at Davis-Monthan with a shark mouth sheet tucked in the nose compartment door. Besides the sheet, the shark mouth was also painted on the nose door using water colors, circa 1987 or 1988. (Photo courtesy Chuck Ruth and rotorheadsrus.us)

Sites) between Da Nang, Tan Son Nhut and Cam Ranh Bay. Later, in the spring of 1966, she was transferred, with all other CH-3s in the Vietnam theatre, to Udorn, Thailand.

Just when or why 676 was painted black has now apparently been documented.

Doug Lawson, MSgt. USAF, Retired, told RotorheadsRUs.us, "I was assigned to NKP where CH-3C 676, the Black Mariah, was painted black." (Doug was assigned to NKP from January 1966, to December 1967, as NCOIC on CH-3Cs/Es.)

"It was not the lack of paint," Lawson said. "I was directed to have all insignia, etc., painted out and all lights to be disconnected to prevent an inadvertent turning on of a light. One of my maintenance crewmen decided to use black paint and just slopped it on. When I saw what he had done I told him to paint the whole aircraft black. It was miserably hot that day and he was very unhappy, as was I.

The "Black Mariah" on display at the National Museum of the U.S. Air Force. (Photo courtesy U.S. Air Force)

"I don't remember the tail number of the other CH-3C, the first aircraft sent to Thai-Am for repair, but I believe it was #689 (it was actually #685). It had gone down in Laos and we did some repairs and flew it out to NKP. We didn't have the capability to repair it so we trucked it to Bangkok for Thai-Am to repair.

"I later went down to check on the repair because it was taking too long. While there I picked up a local English newspaper with a front page picture of 'The Black Mariah' among other CH-3s at NKP with the caption, 'A sister in mourning.'"

The Black Mariah flew many support and counter-insurgency missions while assigned to the "Pony Express." It was rumored that the VC had a $50,000 bounty on the Black Mariah.

In 1969, the 20th SOS CH-3s were reassigned to the 21st Special Operations Squadron at Nakhon Phanom RTAFB.

In 1971, 63-09676 was reassigned to the 6200th ABW, Clark AFB,

Philippines and in 1974, to the 405th FW, Philippines. It is believed that somewhere between Vietnam and Clark she was repainted either camo or silver.

March 31, 1976, found the former Black Mariah assigned to the 302nd SOS, Luke AFB, Arizona.

In December 1986, 676 moved to the 304th ARRS, Portland, Oregon, and in October 1987, to the 71st SOS, Davis-Monthan AFB, Arizona, where she was again redecorated.

In 1990, CH-3E #63-09676 (the CH-3Cs were redesignated CH-3Es after the installation of more powerful engines in 1966) was selected to be refurbished and sent to the National Museum of the U.S. Air Force. The story goes that when the aircraft was being prepared to be repainted the technicians discovered a coat of black under the existing top coat. Knowing that black was not the standard primer color an investigation was begun to uncover some of this helicopter's history and the story of the "Black Mariah" began to unfold.

She is believed to be the only "black" CH-3 to serve in Southeast Asia. What better way to enshrine this aircraft than to return it to the color of its glory days. The "Black Mariah" left Tucson on February 15, 1991 and is now proudly on display at the National Museum of the U.S. Air Force, Wright-Patterson AFB, Dayton, Ohio.

George Warren: *According to Phil's notes, 676 didn't fly between August 25, 1965, and September 26th, which confirms there was no high bird that particular day. On Sept. 26th, it flew a test flight for an engine change. My guess is that we must have used the last spare engine sometime prior and had to wait for a new one to be shipped.*

THEY CALLED IT NAKED FANNY

29

THE INEVITABLE HAPPENS

SEPTEMBER 20, 1965, BEGAN, AS WALTER CRONKITE was wont to say, as "A day like all days." It may have begun that way in Vietnam and the rest of Southeast Asia, but it certainly wouldn't end that way. Chris Hobson, in his book Vietnam Air Losses, would call it "a bad day for U.S. airmen."

An armed recce mission near Sop Cop, close to the Laotian boarder resulted in the shootdown of an F-105D. The pilot, USAF Captain Edgar Hawkins, did not survive the crash.

Air Force Captain Phillip Smith's F-104C lost its navigational system over the Gulf of Tonkin resulting in his being shot down by Chinese Mig-19s and being taken prisoner by the Chinese.

Two of his squadron mates, also in F-104s, collided while trying to locate Smith, but survived and were rescued.

Navy LTJG John Harris had to vacate his A-4E east of Hanoi and became the first pilot to be rescued over land by a ship-based Navy chopper.

The shootdown of USAF Captain Willis Forby in his F-105D would trigger the involvement of the "men of steel" from Naked Fanny.

THEY CALLED IT NAKED FANNY

Joe Ballinger: *It was on Monday, September 20, 1965, that Tom Curtis as aircraft commander, with Duane Martin as co-pilot, Airman 1st Class William Robinson, flight engineer, and PJ Airman 2nd Class Arthur Black were aboard one of the two HH-43s scrambled to pick up Captain Willis Forby, the pilot of Essex 04, an F-105D near Ha Tinh, North Vietnam.*

Scott Harrington: *Duane had only been with the detachment a short period of time before I returned to Clark. I really hadn't gotten to know him yet, but recall sitting next to him during Chapel the Sunday before I left. He was a 1st Lieutenant at the time.*

Joe Ballinger: *That morning as we used High, Low and Off on our daily crew scheduling, Walt and I were on alert with the Low Bird until noon, when we did our crew change-out. There was one CH-3 in commission and it had been sent up north to Lima Site 36. The other CH-3 was down for a power deteriorated engine change. Of the three HH-43s, 4510 was the Low Bird and 0280 was High Bird with 0279 down for an engine and transmission change. Both (the engine and transmission) had metal particles in their oil samples.*

I had no premonitions about a bad day or anything else, but I asked Chet Rainey if we needed 0279 for an emergency, would he fly on it? After telling me, "Sure. It wasn't chips, but just a bad SOAP (Spectrometric Oil Analysis Program) sample," I didn't give it another thought.

It had to be just after noon when the call came in of a pilot down. Tom hadn't time to change out his equipment, so I threw him my survival vest and they scrambled off for the pickup. I went up to Invert to monitor the mission.

Combat Mission Narrative: *The HC-54 on precautionary orbit was informed of the successful bailout of an F-105 pilot over*

North Vietnam. Two HH-43 helicopters were scrambled from Nakhon Phanom, Thailand along with two A-1Es RESCAP aircraft from Udorn AB, Thailand.

Dick Laine was the RCC of the second bird. Bruce Hepp was flying as co-pilot, SSgt. Roberto Rodriguez was the flight engineer and A2C Michael Henebry was aboard as the PJ. Both aircraft were using a Duchy call sign with Tom's aircraft Duchy 41 and Dick's 43 as Duchy 22. The flight from NKP to the downed pilot's location was over 80 miles, putting him approximately 35 kilometers (21¾ miles) southwest of Ha Tinh and 20 kilometers (slightly less than 12½ miles) east of the Laos/Vietnam border in the North Vietnamese province of Nghe Tinh.

Combat Mission Narrative (continued): The HC-54 picked up the downed pilot's beeper as the HH-43s and RESCAP were en route to the incident site. The A-1Es made low passes over the bailout area in an attempt to establish voice or visual contact with the survivor. They experienced no ground fire and felt they had the area the pilot was down in pinpointed. Soon after this, ground activity in the area increased. Troop movement was noted in adjacent areas and ground fire commenced, resulting in minor damage to one of the A-1Es. Shortly after this red smoke was spotted, and one of the HH-43 helicopters proceeded in accompanied by A-1Es.

The weather was inclement, and the visibility was poor. The downed pilot was located in a small bowl-shaped canyon approximately 800 ft. in depth. The canyon was completely enclosed by steep slopes. The width at the top of the canyon varied from approximately 200 to 500 yards. At the southeast end of the canyon was a narrow gap. Using the downed F-105 pilot, Capt. Willis Forby, as bait, the canyon was a perfect place to trap a helicopter rescue crew. Evidently, this is exactly what the North Vietnamese did.

Duchy 22 stripped down for repairs at NKP.

At approximately five miles from the scene of the downed pilot one helicopter, call sign Duchy 22, took the position of "high bird," and initiated a holding pattern. The second helicopter, call sign Duchy 41, took the position as "low bird," the lead aircraft. Duchy 41 proceeded to Captain Forby's location under the direction of the A-1E fighter aircraft, already on station.

> **Combat Mission Narrative (continued)**: Visual contact was made with the downed pilot, when suddenly ground fire broke loose from all around the survivor's position. The HH-43 crashed while attempting to make a pickup. Hostile fire is thought to have been the cause of the crash.

Duchy 41 located the F-105 pilot and came to a hover approximately 100 ft. above his location. The helicopter began receiving ground fire from two sides of the canyon and was observed to settle to the ground by the A-1E pilot who immediately called a "May Day," announcing that Duchy 41 had crashed.

Combat Mission Narrative (continued): The second HH-43 that had been orbiting short of the pickup site immediately proceeded toward the crash scene. The helicopter crew jettisoned the internal auxiliary fuel tank to make room for survivors. They encountered ground fire en route to the area and spotted the helicopter wreckage which seemed fairly well intact, on the first pass. As the helicopter positioned itself for a suitable approach to the pickup area it was under continuous ground fire and as it came to a hover 50 feet above the wreckage a massive and continuous barrage of automatic weapons fire erupted around the helicopter. A white pen flare was also observed at this time although no survivors were spotted. The helicopter was taking a series of hits at this time and initiated an immediate takeoff. Continual heavy fire was received for the next three minutes. The pararescue man was hit on his flak vest by flying debris but did not suffer any injury. Fuel was now running into the aft section of the cabin; however, the helicopter was able to return to Nakhon Phanom without further incident. The CAP aircraft remained on scene until darkness and reported vehicles and personnel moving into the area. The mission was suspended because of the high probability of additional hostile defense buildup which would make the area impenetrable for search and recovery forces the following day. The crew of the downed helicopter was Captain Thomas J. Curtis, 1st Lt. Duane W. Martin, A1C William A. Robinson, A3C Arthur M. Black. The pilot of the second helicopter was Capt. Richard A. Laine.

THEY CALLED IT NAKED FANNY

Duchy 22 quickly began its response to its crashed sister bird under the direction of the A-1E pilot and arrived on the scene in approximately five minutes. Duchy 22 started its descent to attempt to pick up any survivors from the crashed helicopter. The pararescueman (PJ) dropped the auxiliary fuel tank from the rear of Duchy 22. As he watched the trajectory of the tank to the ground, he spotted the wreckage of the helicopter. He observed that the helicopter had dropped into a small clearing on an incline and was held upright by the trees and undergrowth. The only major damage that he noted was that the rotor blades had been sheared from the hubs and the hubs were still turning. The PJ began to direct the pilot into a hover over the wreckage. At an altitude of approximately 50 feet the PJ observed extensive ground fire in the area of the wreckage. The ground fire was very intense. Duchy 22 was struck numerous times on the right side by the ground fire, damaged, and forced to abort the rescue attempt. As the pilot of Duchy 22 initiated his climb from the hover position, a pen flare passed in front of the helicopter.

Due to the dense foliage, no survivors or casualties were observed by the crew of Duchy 22, nor did they see any of the enemy who was firing upon them. Although damaged, Duchy 22 did return to its home base.

Dick Laine, the RCC of Duchy 22, in a personal letter to Joe Ballinger on October 20th of 2010, wrote the following:

> **Dick Laine:** *20 Sep 65. Bruce and I were flying high-bird; Tom and Martin the low. We proceeded over Laos above the clouds and penetrated an opening into NVN. We were near the downed pilot. We were instructed to hold our position. The A-1 led low-bird to the pickup site. Soon thereafter the A-1 reported the chopper was down. We followed it toward the site. We were just above a mountain range, perhaps a hundred feet or so with a cloud just above us. We pulled up into the cloud base part of the way in order to not be visible from the ground. As we broke out the A-1 was directly in front of us and reported that we were over the target. We couldn't see any sign of the chopper. We then descended into a deep bowl-shaped canyon just below us.*

We dropped our fuel barrels and came to a hover above the trees. I noticed something on a bare spot that seemed to move but soon realized it was gunfire striking the dirt. The guys in back then said they could see the fuselage of the downed chopper on its side but still no personnel. We started the hoist down anyway. By this time we started taking hits which could also be felt through the controls. The N-1 power gauge reading dropped off and fuel began leaking down through the overhead radio and electrical panel into the cockpit. Still no visual on the crew. Rodriguez called over the intercom that he was hit.

That's when I pulled the collective, rising up the left side of the canyon wall. A pen flare shot up out of the trees on the way out. By this time ground fire was quite audible and as we rolled left over the canyon crest, maybe 50 to 75 feet, a troop was pointing his gun straight at us. I flinchingly jerked the cyclic. Not sure if we could make it, we headed down the slope toward rice paddies. My thinking was that if we had to, we could possibly go down in a paddy near the mountain and have access to tree cover if needed. However, flying parallel to the border between the fields and trees the aircraft seemed to be functioning so we began gaining altitude allowing the option of an autorotation if needed. Ground fire was no longer audible as it had been continuously from leaving the canyon until the climb.

We avoided transmitting due to the cockpit fuel leak. An electrical arc by keying the mic had the potential of starting a fire. We climbed quite high (12,000 ft.) on the way back over the mountains of Laos giving us more autorotative options if required. By this time we were told an Air America chopper (H-34) was trailing us. A message was relayed stating he refused to continue following us as we were headed toward an anti-aircraft site. We deviated direction about 20 or 30 degrees to the right. A message was received stating the new direction was acceptable. Later our third and only remaining HH-43 escorted us to NKP.

I learned that the event occurred very near a NVN military base, which explained why so many troops appeared into the area so rapidly. It was reported in a Bangkok newspaper out of NVN. The chopper took hits in the fuselage, rotor blades, engine and transmission and all of which had to be replaced. A starting fuel line had been ruptured accounting for the fuel leak into the cockpit. When filling out the damage report, I expressed my disdain that up until that time all of our crew members had not been provided a personal two-way radio as were the fighter pilots.

Joe Ballinger (Inside Invert Control): *I was there as they (4510/Duchy 41) were in the hover on the pickup. I heard that they had gone down and crashed on site, and that 0280 (Duchy 22) was going in to recover them. That's when I notified our maintenance to fuel and prep 0279 for a mission and asked for a volunteer to fly with me.*

After hearing that 0280 was shot up and leaving the site, I came down, signed off both red Xs, and took off with Walt, Devers and Wallace. After crossing the Mekong, we found out that 0280 was still airborne and coming back to NKP! That's when the "Fog of War" set in with me and I was determined to go in and get them back. An Air America H-34, flown by Herb Baker, joined up with us for backup.

Near the border of Laos and North Vietnam, we were told not to go in as the crew had been captured! Still determined that I could do it, I ignored the orders and continued on until the second call! It was only then that I made the decision to turn back and follow 0280 home to NKP, or to any site or safe area they could make.

I questioned myself for that decision for years after. Did I make it as a Commander who needed to be ready tomorrow to do the same thing over again with the aircraft and crews that remained? Or did I take the easy way out not having the balls to attempt it and leaving my men behind?

North Vietnamese propaganda photo of Airman William Robinson taken prisoner. David Cutillo provided a newspaper clipping with the same photo. The cut-line read: "Purported Capture." This photo, released in Budapest by MTI, the Hungarian news agency, had accompanying caption that read: "Militiawoman capturing U.S. air pirate. Over 1,600 U.S. aircraft have been brought down over North Vietnam, hundreds of air pirates paid for their crimes." No date was given on the photo, which originated in Hanoi.

THEY CALLED IT NAKED FANNY

After finding 0280 and joining up, we followed them the rest of the way back to NKP where we landed without further incident.

Rodriguez wasn't seriously injured as his flak vest took most of the hit. 0280 was another matter, really shot up. Many of the hits—if the pocked hole in the main transmission was a fraction deeper; a hit an inch off the blade control flap or the nicked fuel line—could have been fatal.

We were all in shock and depression as the day came to an end. And that night wasn't any better as we packed and inventoried all the missing crew's personal gear.

An electronic search was made for the remainder of the day and again at first light the next morning with negative results. The pilot in command of Duchy 22 felt that there was a strong possibility that at least some of the men survived the crash. However, because of the terrain in the area of the crash site, and the A-1E pilot's observation of enemy trucks and ground troops in the area, he did not have high hopes for the crew's success at evading capture. This concern was later proved valid when Radio Hanoi announced that "September saw the first U.S. helicopter down in North Vietnam and the capture of its entire crew."

Joe Ballinger: *The next day I was given orders from Saigon to ground the HH-43s and crews until further notice. Not much to ground as 0280 needed a lot of repair, along with an engine, transmission and blade replacement. And 0279 still needed an engine and transmission change. That left us with only one CH-3C for rescue alert. And they did call, that same day, 21 Sep 65, with the CH-3C picking up Greenwood from the panhandle of North Vietnam for the last rescue of the TDY group at Naked Fanny!*

The same day I got a message from PARRC (Pacific Aerospace Rescue and Recovery Center) in Hawaii questioning flying 0279 and misreporting of NORS-G (Non Operational Report Status-Grounded) with metal particles in the engine and transmission. The bean counters at PARRC had caught the time we reported flying and sent us a TWX. At that point, I could have cared less if signing off on the aircraft for a one-time flight was legal or not, or about anything they could do to me! I called 38th ARS and asked Colonel Krafka to take care of that as he knew what I had to do. I never heard of it again.

By the time that both HH-43Bs were test flown and back in commission (around the 28th or 29th of September), I realized that we (HH-43B aircrews) were falling apart from depression. And that if we didn't get back in the saddle, we would never be able to face ourselves with the CH-3C guys carrying the load and with the HH-43B Udorn Det standing the alert for us while we just sat around. So I called a meeting and told everyone the bad news: that I was calling Saigon and putting us back on alert. I didn't get a single negative comment from them and since we were now short one crew, two of the Udorn pilots volunteered to fill in. One of them was Lt. Bill Wirstrom.

Captain Curtis, Airman Black, Airman Robinson, and Captain Willis Forby, the F-105 pilot, were captured by the North Vietnamese and returned to the United States in 1973. Lieutenant Martin evaded immediate capture in North Vietnam and made his way into Laos where he was subsequently captured by the Pathet Lao and imprisoned.

At the end of June 1966, Martin, along with a Navy pilot, LTJG Dieter Dengler; Air America civilian Eugene DeBruin; a Chinese national; and three Thais escaped from the Houay Het Prison camp in Central Laos. Martin and Dengler evaded the enemy together for seventeen days before Martin was killed by a machete wielding villager. Ironically, Dengler was rescued five days later in the Demilitarized Zone between North and South Vietnam.

THEY CALLED IT NAKED FANNY

Joe Ballinger: *After receiving a copy of the now-declassified History of the 38th Air Rescue Squadron from 1 July—30 September 1965, from which the Combat Mission Narratives were taken, I noticed a huge discrepancy. For some reason, while the tallies of the missions, sorties, objectives were all properly accounted for, the totals under the headings listing number of ARS aircraft lost and ARS men wounded in action/killed in action/missing in action show zeroes. I guess 20 September 1965 didn't count!*

All four crew members of Duchy 41 received the Air Force Cross (AFC). (The Air Force Cross is awarded to U.S. and Foreign military personnel and civilians who have displayed extraordinary heroism in one of the following situations: while engaged in action against a U.S. enemy, while engaged in military operations involving conflict with a foreign force, or while serving with a Friendly nation engaged in armed conflict against a force in which the United States is not a belligerent party. The AFC is awarded when the heroic actions fall just short of warranting the Congressional Medal of Honor.)

BLACK, ARTHUR NEIL (POW) Airman Third Class, U.S. Air Force, Detachment 3, 38th Aerospace Rescue and Recovery Squadron, Tan Son Nhut Air Base, Vietnam, Date of Action: September 20, 1965.

CURTIS, THOMAS JERRY (POW) Captain, U.S. Air Force, Detachment 3, 38th Aerospace Rescue and Recovery Squadron, Tan Son Nhut Air Base, Vietnam, Date of Action: September 20, 1965.

MARTIN, DUANE WHITNEY (POW/Died while attempting to escape) 1st Lieutenant, U.S. Air Force, Detachment 3, 38th Aerospace Rescue and Recovery Squadron, Tan Son Nhut Air Base, Vietnam, Date of Action: September 20, 1965.

ROBINSON, WILLIAM ANDREW (POW) Airman First Class, U.S. Air Force, Detachment 3, 38th Aerospace Rescue and Recovery Squadron, Tan Son Nhut Air Base, Vietnam, Date of Action: September 20, 1965.

Although Joe had recommended that Dick Laine's crew (Duchy 22) receive Silver Stars for the mission, nothing ever came of it, apparently because Col. Krafka had gone and there was no one to push it through after they left NKP.

> **Don Williams, 5th TAC**: *I served with Black and Robinson at NKP in 1965. They, and the whole bunch who flew north with those HH-43Bs, known as Pedros, were real heroes. They pulled a lot of guys out of the jungle with puddle jumpers that had absolutely no armor or weapons. One of the three HH-43Bs had a bullet hole right through the floor between the pilot's legs and out through the windscreen. None of that stopped them. They went when called.*
>
> *I was at Travis when they came back and tried to see them, but the intelligence bunch wouldn't let me.*

THEY CALLED IT NAKED FANNY

Scott Harrington: *I spoke with Tom Curtis a year or so after his release while he was attending War College at Maxwell Air Force Base in Montgomery, Alabama. Later on, after having lost touch, we reconnected by e-mail. I learned that he was scheduled to come to Naval Air Station Pensacola for both physical and psychological evaluations as part of a military program to monitor POWs. On at least two occasions we were foiled in our plans to meet due to unforeseen schedule changes. But finally, in February of 2009, nearly 44 years after we had last seen each other, we were able to meet. He and his wife met me at McGuire's restaurant in Pensacola for a grand reunion. There was no mistaking that it was the same Tom Curtis when he walked through the door. Before we started eating our meal I asked Tom if he would mind if I offered a prayer. Of course, he had no objection. During the course of my prayer I attempted to thank God for allowing us to have this wonderful reunion, and I totally lost it. I finally regained control of my emotions and finished the prayer, at which point Tom said, "You know, I'm usually the one who does that."*

Our conversation at dinner was as if we had just seen each other the day before. Tom would later e-mail me saying, "How great that comrades in arms are able to reconnect so easily."

To add more detail to the story of their being shot down, Tom said they had actually recovered the downed pilot, Willis Forby, and had him in the chopper when the ground fire brought them down.

Tom also told me of a rather amazing thing that happened while he and the others were POWs. The full story follows in the next chapter.

During the course of writing this book, because I had no idea how Tom would feel about retelling the story of the shootdown, I was very hesitant about asking him if he would do so. I wanted to have his perspective, but didn't want to cause him any discomfort. When I finally bit the bullet and asked if he would mind talking about what happened that day I was thrilled when his reply was, "Sure, I don't mind talking about the shootdown."

Tom said his memory was that the same crew stood alert for a calendar day and that he, Duane Martin, Bill Robinson and Art Black had the duty. (You may remember that Joe Ballinger's recollection was that it was at the time of a crew change that the call came in.)

So almost 49 years after the fact and having survived seven and a half years as a prisoner of war, here is the story of the shootdown of Duchy 41 as told by the pilot, Tom Curtis:

Tom Curtis: *We got the call and it was an F-105 that was down and that the pilot had ejected in North Vietnam. This was the first mission that I flew with the Air Force A-1s, call sign Sandy. Previously, the A-1s (Navy) had launched off a ship and we joined up with them wherever. (Air Force A-1Es were based at Udorn.) And this was the first mission I flew in North Vietnam. So, there were a lot of "news" here—new things.*

Duane Martin was the co-pilot. He had not been with us long. He came to us from a local base rescue detachment in Taiwan. We had one of our guys that elected to go home. I thought he went to resign his commission, but later I discovered that when he got home, "Rescue" offered him a job in California, which he took. I still have trouble with—well, I don't have trouble with it anymore because he recently passed away. But I thought about that a lot, with Martin just having gotten there and he got there because somebody else vacated his post, if you will.

Anyhow, a normal flight of two H-43s and we headed toward the scene where the pilot was down and as I recall there was an SA-16 or a C-54, I can't remember which, that was on-scene commander.

So we're homing in and getting into the area—it was across

THEY CALLED IT NAKED FANNY

Tom Curtis "relaxing."

Laos—probably 20-25 miles into North Vietnam and in the general vicinity of Vinh. We finally got the beacon and the guy was, of course, on the ground. We didn't see any evidence of 105 (F-105) wreckage, we just homed in on his locator.

The crewmen, as you know, were Bill Robinson and Arthur Neil Black. They called him Art then and he since has decided he wants to be known as Neil. He was the PJ and Bill Robinson was the flight mechanic.

I left the wingman (Duchy 22) about five miles away when I went in to try to execute the recovery. We got into the area; got over the survivor; had the two Air Force A-1s that were flying their "daisy chain;" and went into the hover. Robbie was on the hot mic (microphone) and he's telling me what to do with the helicopter. We got right over the survivor and he kept telling me "down, down, down," because he could see the horse collar, but the survivor couldn't reach it yet. By the time I finally got the horse collar down—all the cable was out—I could look out at the tips of the blades and I didn't have but less than a foot of clearance between the rotor blades and the trees, so I just shoved the rotor blades down into the trees in order to get that rescue device down to the survivor. Robbie's on hot mic and he's still talking "steady, left, right" or whatever. He said, "Survivor's in the sling, survivor coming up," and I felt when the survivor left the ground and I had to add just a touch of power. Somewhere in this critical juncture one of the A-1s that was running with his 20mm got hit in the rocket pod and caught on fire. He called, "I'm hit!" And he pulled up.

The author (*left*) in a more recent photo with Tom Curtis.

In my mind, this is what the other guy (A-1 pilot) is thinking; they were still in South Vietnam, he wasn't on a SAR mission and wasn't doing what he was supposed to be doing so he pulled up to check out lead. That left me sitting high and dry. That may have happened anyway, I don't know. But about that time I lost power from 100 percent and fell into the trees and because the blades were made out of laminated wood, they disappeared in a hurry. I created enough tooth picks to last that section of Southeast Asia for the duration.

We didn't tumble—we went straight down and my thought was, "I'm gonna kill that guy in the sling." There was no way I could miss him—he was still in the sling and I'm coming right on top of him. But as luck would have it, as God would have it, that didn't happen. When we hit, I had an M-16 parked right next to my seat and it broke it in two. That was the power of the impact. We were following normal procedures of a crash—get out and collect over here to make sure everyone is out and so we did that. And this co-pilot, he was very, very excited. He was trying to get out of his harness and had his weapon and he fired a round and almost shot himself in the foot. So I tried to calm him down and I undid his snaps and about that time the 105 pilot came up. I asked him if he was injured and he said "no." Robbie is there and he rode that thing on his knees—he hit on his knees. I was surprised that he was as agile as he was. I told the 105 guy that we were gonna get away from the crash because they were gonna come here next. There was a very steep slope so I led the way down to a stream. We crossed the stream—just a little creek—and we went about two-thirds of the way up the other side, still a steep slope. I don't know what happened to Duane Martin, the co-pilot. I guess as I went around the tree or as we three (Tom, Robbie and Neil) went around the tree we maybe went to the left and he went to the right. Anyway, our paths diverged and he was not with us. And we got to a big old, old fallen tree; this was about two-thirds of the way up. So I told the guys we're going to get behind this tree and we'll either wait until somebody comes in and tries to snake us out or until it gets dark and we can make our way west and get back into Laos in one of the same areas where we'd have a better chance of evasion. So we are there and the guy that I had left about five miles away (Duchy 22), he came in and I fired a pencil flare and they came almost to a hover over us, but I could hear the rounds impacting that 43. Then I did what I thought was a very courageous thing, I started waving them off. Later, when I talked to those guys they said, "You didn't have to wave us off, we could feel those rounds. They said they never did actually see us on the ground. I guess they got pretty busy. So the second 43 made their way back over Laos and across the Mekong and just barely got across because of losing so much fuel.

So, we're sitting there, the three of us, waiting for dark. The F-105 pilot, Will Forby, had some bad knees so he went back to where he was before we got there. So we've got Martin somewhere and Forby in his little enclave and the three of us off the helicopter.

I don't remember the time, but in my mind's eye now almost 49 years later, it was probably a couple of hours, and the Vietnamese were down here in this creek and they're yelling and shouting and finally one of these guys decided he was going to climb up the ridge. And as fate would have it, his path to the ridge took him right on to the log that we were behind. And I told the guys, "I'm not going to fight a war with a .38 aircrew pistol." And so we were captured. They secured our hands behind our backs and marched us down into the creek and then we started going to villages. And it seemed in every village there was a political officer and he would get the villagers all stirred up. They isolated us—they didn't want Americans seeing other Americans so they separated us and we didn't have any opportunities to converse for the next seven days.

Their journey would eventually take them to Hanoi and the infamous Hanoi Hilton prison camp. Curtis, Robinson, Black and Forby all would spend the next seven and a half years as POWs. Curtis was moved 13 different times during his imprisonment and endured torture and punishment, as did many of the 591 men who were finally released beginning on February 12, 1973. The four were among the first 142 prisoners who boarded the C-141 Starlifters that took them to Clark Air Base in the Philippines.

Duane Martin evaded capture in North Vietnam, making his way into Laos where he was captured and held prisoner by the Pathet Lao. On June 19, 1966, while prison guards were eating, some of the prisoners slipped out of their hand and foot restraints and grabbed the guard's unattended weapons. The Pathet Lao guards spotted some of the other prisoners trying to escape. A shootout ensued with fellow prisoner Navy LTJG Dieter Dengler, killing at least three of the guards. Dengler and Martin headed for the Mekong River to escape into Thailand. Several days after the escape the two were hiding out near an Akha village in Laos. Martin had been severely weakened due to a bout with malaria. He was further demoralized when an attempt to signal a C-130 flare ship that came over them produced no results.

He told Dengler that he was going to die. Later that day he said he was going to try to steal some food from the village. Dengler told him it would be suicide but accompanied him on the venture. As they neared the village, a boy alerted the village of their presence and a villager came running toward them with a machete. Martin knelt down on the trail with his hands clasped before him in supplication, but the man swung at Martin, first hitting him in the leg. His second swing struck Martin in the back of the neck, killing him.

Ironically, Dengler managed to escape back into the jungle and was later rescued in the demilitarized zone (DMZ) after forming an SOS with some rocks and being spotted by an Air Force A-1E pilot who spotted the signal and directed a helicopter to pick him up.

Postscript

Joe Ballinger: *As I would imagine, most USAF and USN guys were watching the guys get off the Freedom Bird at Clark. I was, too. And there were Tom, Robbie, and Blackie looking far better than I could have imagined. I didn't pay any attention to the guy who got off the plane behind them. Somewhere around seven to 10 days after that I was flying out on a night air-refueling training mission at Hill AFB, where I was now Squadron Chief of Standardization on the CH-3s. About halfway into the training flight I got a call from Hill to return to the base ASAP. When I questioned why, I was told there was nothing wrong with my family, but I was ordered to return home and await a priority phone call. When I got home, my wife told me that I would be getting a call from Tom. It seems they were given unlimited phone privileges. When the call came in, it was a conference call* *with Tom, Robbie and Blackie on the other end. [It felt] like it was only the day before. They called me "Captain," and I didn't correct them. (Joe had been promoted to major during the seven and a half years they had been POWs.) We joked and talked for 20—30 minutes. I even asked Black if he was ready to swim the Mekong again. When I asked what happened to the pilot they went in to get, they laughed and told me he stepped off the plane (Freedom Bird) right behind them. And that they had just made the longest rescue in Air Rescue history: it only took them seven and a half years. I was choked up and couldn't really believe how normal they sounded.*

A short time later, Jay Strayer took over the squadron and became my boss. I don't know how he did it but he set up a Dining In (a formal military function designed to promote camaraderie among a unit) on 4 August 1973, shortly before my retirement. Tom Curtis was brought in as the guest speaker. Walt and I met him as he was getting off the plane at Hill and had two hours alone with him. After his talk he called me up to the stand and gave me a signed hand receipt for my M-16, .38 and survival vest and apologized for the time it took to do so.

Recall that earlier in the chapter that the crew changeover was in progress at the time the call came in for the mission. The survival vest was mentioned, but the weapons in the aircraft were also Joe's.

About a year and a half later, after Joe's retirement, he flew in to Salt Lake City and drove out to Hill AFB and checked in with his former commander, Jay Strayer. Jay informed him that Colonel Tom Curtis had just been stationed there. They drove out to Tom's new house and Joe, being out of the military and now with long hair and a "Ho Chi Minh mustache," went up to the house and knocked on the door. When no one answered the door, Jay encouraged Joe to keep knocking and Tom finally came to the door giving Joe a suspicious once-over.

Joe Ballinger: *When I finally told him who I was, he pulled the door open and hugged me like a long lost brother. Then he looked at me and told me, "I thought you were an itinerant salesman begging for something."*

30

JOLLYS MAKE THIRD RESCUE

JOE BALLINGER: *It was the day after Tom, Duane, Robbie and Black were shot down. Saigon had ordered the HH-43s and personnel to stand down until further notice. Since 676 was also down for repairs, it left our combined unit with one bird to stand alert.*

Sure enough, we got a call on an F-105 down in the mountains northwest of Mu Gia Pass. Anti-aircraft batteries around the target, somewhere east of Mu Gia Pass, had forced Capt. Frederick R. Greenwood to eject from his Thud.

Senior Master Sergeant Robert L. LaPointe, USAF, Ret., has generously given his permission to use the description of this mission from his book *PJs in Vietnam: The Story of Air Rescue in Vietnam as Seen Through the Eyes of Pararescuemen*:

Bob LaPointe: *On the 21st of September, the day after Duchy 41 was lost, Capt. Frederick Greenwood ejected from his F-105. Once again an F-105 was down in North Vietnam. Two CH-3s scrambled from NKP. The downed pilot's wingmen remained on the scene to CAP their teammate until the SARTF arrived. With A-1s in protective formation, the low bird went in for the pick-*

up. Piloted by Capt. George Martin, it began to take ground fire, which continued throughout the pick-up. The downed pilot was perched on a ledge on the side of a cliff forcing the CH-3 to hover next to a vertical wall of solid rock. Despite the difficulties of terrain and hostile fire, a successful hoist recovery was made. The rescued pilot was treated for a broken ankle by the PJ and returned to NKP. The CH-3 suffered minor battle damage but no crew members were wounded. If any pilot in Southeast Asia still wondered if Air Rescue crews would persist, even after losing one of their own planes and crews, they now had the answer.

Sergeant LaPointe's description would have sufficed as a description of the mission. But who can resist "the rest of the story" when a blow-by-blow account is available from the pilot of that CH-3C, Captain George Martin.

George Martin: *On 21 September we had a call for help near the Mu Gia Pass. This was approximately 100 miles due east of NKP. Our second helicopter was just coming on line after routine minor maintenance. The HH-43s were not available, so I said George (Warren) and I would go. The target was an F-105 bail-out. We proceeded uneventfully until we were right up next to the Mu Gia Pass area. All of a sudden a voice came in over the rescue channel saying, "He's right there," and as we were frantically trying to look everywhere at once, this F-105 came up behind us on the left side heading downward into the canyon at a rather steep angle. We concentrated looking at where the jet's flight angle indicated and finally spotted a parachute way down below us caught in some trees at the bottom of the canyon. I immediately started to wonder how I was going to position myself over or near the parachute, assuming the man would be close by. The terrain was extremely rugged and, as I was maneuvering the helicopter closer to the tree, suddenly a voice came in on the radio stating, "You're way below me."*

Now, there was a very steep cliff, just about vertical, and I scanned upwards not seeing anybody. I called the voice asking him for his exact position. He again said, "You're way below me." Since the first time he said it, I figured he must be on the cliff face. I was at a high hover and inadvertently applying a little up-collective. I called again and asked if he had the helicopter in sight, which of course he did, and he kept repeating I was way below him. This cliff face appeared to be 400 or 500 feet above me. So I just continued my up-collective, and the helicopter was doing a slow climb up the cliff. All of a sudden the crew chief, Lee R. Diggs, called out, "There he is."

At about the same time, it seemed, I saw him. He was sitting on a small ledge with his radio up to his right ear and, when I looked out and being even with him, we were close enough to see each other's eyes, and he abruptly put the radio down on the ground beside him. I right away began to wonder how I was going to get the helicopter above the ledge in order to lower the hoist down to him. The vertical distance was not a problem. It was all about the lateral clearance, or lack thereof. I raised the helicopter about 25 or 30 feet above him but was looking straight out to a solid rock wall.

There was, I remember, a little bush with yellow flowers on it swaying violently from the rotor wash that I was using as a hover reference. At this point I had brought the helicopter to a standstill and thinking I was as close to the wall as I wanted to get.

Suddenly Diggs said, "You'll have to move it in a little more," and I replied to him that the rotor tips were getting mighty close to the wall.

His reply to me, "Go ahead and move it in closer, I can see better than you can."

So, using my little yellow bush as a reference, I realized Diggs could see better than me and that I was allowing more room than was absolutely necessary, so my little yellow bush was 50-100 feet ahead of me on the right side. I intended to move the helicopter in maybe 3-5 feet closer. I moved it that far and stopped, getting ready to tell Diggs if we still couldn't reach the man with the hook I was going to have to pull off.

About that time Diggs said, "He's coming up."

So I moved the helicopter laterally to my left and paused to allow Diggs to get him in the cabin. Diggs did a good job of keeping me minutely informed. It seems the pilot had certain injuries. I subsequently learned he had two broken ankles and other injuries suffered during the bail-out.

About this time abruptly and unexpectedly came the sound of rifle fire. It seems Sheldon Tart, who was our engine man and had been an AR-15 instructor, managed to talk his way on board our flight. As Diggs and the paramedic were attending to the rescuee, Tart was looking all about and spotted four enemy soldiers coming up on the left side of the aircraft making ready to fire at us. Tart fired first and took care of that threat.

George and I were just beginning to exhale a bit and thinking about getting out of there. I had just initiated a climbing left turn when suddenly the aircraft went into a violent left and right bank out-of-control situation. I immediately looked at George to see what he had done with the controls and found him looking at me. I gathered up the controls and, stabilizing the aircraft, resumed my left-climb position. No sooner was the aircraft stabilized when the same thing happened all over again. About that time an A-1E pilot identified himself as having fired a set of rockets at enemy troops on the ground, and then his wing man came up and repeated it. I remember giving them a few choice words as we headed back west to NKP.

We arrived back at NKP to find everyone standing by, ready to offer help to our rescued F-105 pilot. I recall a C-54 was on the ground ready to pick him up. I climbed aboard while they were

Scott Harrington

securing him and got his name—Captain Frederick Greenwood. I never saw him or heard from him again.

Captain George Martin, 1st Lt. George Warren, SSgt. Lee Diggs, A1C Sheldon Tart and A2C R. E. Scherzer, PJ, made the run and the successful rescue.

THEY CALLED IT NAKED FANNY

31

DEPARTURE AND CHILLY HOMECOMING

JOE BALLINGER: *I STARTED SENDING OUR GUYS home in groups, beginning the 8th of October. Since we had no priority going back, I put one officer in charge with orders that enlisted men went before them. Dick Laine went first, then Walt with his group.*

On the 10th of October, only Bruce, Airman Hart and I were left. The C-130 that we were to go out on only had seats for two, so I got Hart and Bruce on, as per my orders to the rest. As I was standing on the ramp with my bags watching the C-130 taxi out, I saw it stop; a crewman got out and waved to me. Bruce hollered, "Bring your bags! You're going out with us!"

Bruce had remembered that I was a rated Navigator, too, and convinced the Aircraft Commander to put me on as a crewman. You can gross out a bird with crewmen and they don't count for seating. So I logged Navigator time on my last flight out!

When we returned home, I got a call from the supply guys at Kirtland complaining about the hand receipts we had from turning our weapons over to the new guys at NKP. I went down to see if I could straighten it out with the MSgt. in charge When

THEY CALLED IT NAKED FANNY

I explained to him that they needed them more than anybody did here, he got all the personal supply records of our aircrew, and threw them in the trash can. He told the records guy to write it off as Combat Loss for all of us.

Bruce Hepp: *I have tried to forget how scared I was for the six months I spent at NKP. With a lovely wife waiting for me at home and three very young children in her care, I only wanted to live long enough to be reunited with her and my children. I arrived at NKP weighing 168 pounds and not knowing what to expect. I received the required mission briefing and found myself on alert for the next pilot pickup mission.*

Six months later I boarded an aircraft with Joe Ballinger to head back to the U.S. My weight was 143 pounds. I ate well, as we all did, but the mental pressure of 24-7 just waiting to be killed, took its toll. At the time I figured that as we crossed the Mekong River heading North on a pickup mission, my chances of getting back to NKP were about 50%.

I was overhead when four great men and their aircraft were shot out from under me and we were unable to pick them up. Three somehow managed to survive the Hell of prison camp for nearly eight years, but my bunk mate, Duane Martin, met with the horrible death of being beheaded while attempting to escape through the jungle.

Arriving in San Francisco, Joe and I were being driven through the city in a staff car and were dressed in our Class A uniforms. Numerous times during this trip we were flipped the "bird," spit at and shouted down by the long haired hippies protesting the war. What a rotten reception for our return from war.

I am still very proud of what we all did to save the numerous lives behind enemy lines.

My first pilot pickup as the Rescue Crew Commander was

256 miles north of the DMZ. As I am sure you already know it produced 8 Silver Stars for the crews of the two aircraft. I was also awarded 3 additional DFCs for pick-ups that followed.

In today's world there are only a few people who have knowledge of why we were in Vietnam or what we did there, let alone why there were over 60,000 men and women killed getting the job done.

With October came the end of the four-month TDY for George Martin and the rest of their number as the group that had gone to the various survival schools arrived at NKP. George and his people briefed them, and some of those on TDY elected to stay with the new arrivals. George said this was his third war (WWII, Korea, Vietnam), and he was going home.

THEY CALLED IT NAKED FANNY

32

CATS AND DOGS MISSIONS

WITH ONE CREW AND ONE CHOPPER OFF DUTY WHILE the other two crews stood standby, there were many opportunities to impact the area around Nakhon Phanom with such things as medical checkups. And there were also necessary trips with ordnance disposal teams to dispose of undetonated ammunition.

> **Joe Ballinger**: *We had our share of these missions, flown by the OFF crew and the spare helicopter. These were NOT in our job descriptions, but we did them anyway.*

> **Neil McCutchan**: *We were on an EOD (Explosive Ordnance Disposal) mission. A fighter had jettisoned a load of ordnance and it included CBUs (Cluster Bomb Units). We took an EOD disposal crew out to the site. They searched the area and picked up the bomblets putting them in a cardboard box. They asked us to fly them to a central location near the "dump" site to dispose of them. We did. None of us on the flight crew knew what was in the boxes, though.*

> **Bruce Hepp**: [Different incident than above.] *We had the EOD team with us and found the bombs but some were without the*

detonator. After a long wait at the bomb pickle site, the team attached charges to the bombs which had the detonators removed, and rolled out the entire roll of wire which was used to detonate the bombs. Notice I said bombs. I think it was a complete "pickle" (release or dropping) of all ordnance from an F-4. Could it have been 7 bombs?

All of us were told to take cover as far away from the site as we could, as they were about to shoot the charges. I could not have imagined the enormous blast which took place. The earth shook and rocks, soil, foliage and branches, everything the jungle had to offer, fell around us. Fortunately none of us was injured. After everything settled down we were invited to inspect the blast area. It was an enormous hole. Oh, and the detonator? It was found under the Village Chief's bed.

Joe Ballinger: *I got a call from ASOC about taking a Radar Survey Team to a high plateau north of NKP to check out the area for a new radar site. This plateau was where some Buddhist Monks lived in cliff dwellings. We had been up there before on an area training mission. I didn't think there was much chance of a radar site being approved for that area, but agreed to take them.*

As it happened, it was Walt's and my day off, so I took the flight with Walt as my copilot. The plateau was pretty well jungle covered but I found a flat rock space big enough for us to land. The Team then took off to do what they came for. I lounged around the chopper and was suddenly surprised by two native Thais coming up a trail out of the jungle growth. When I did my "sawasdee kap" greeting, I was more surprised by being greeted in very good English. It turned out that the one with me in front of the HH-43 was an English teacher in a village about thirty miles away. They were Buddhists who had come on foot all this way to pay their respect to the monks. I told him about the survey team and, having a camera on me, requested a shot of us shaking hands.

Joe Ballinger and Thai English teacher posing in front of the HH-43.

He wrote down his address and I sent him copies of the picture after I got back to the States. And as far as I have ever known, no radar site was ever placed there. I heard later that this area was the birthplace of Buddha, but in Southeast Asia that is a little like Washington Slept Here!

This picture [see page 266] was taken after giving some Laotian VIPs a helicopter ride and tour of NKP in 1965. I'm standing in the center between Lt. General Vang Pao (commander of the Hmong forces of the Laotian Army) to my right and Brig. General Thao Ma (commander of the Royal Laotian Air Force). The three of us were in our early 30s at the time! I don't remember

THEY CALLED IT NAKED FANNY

Joe Ballinger (*center*) with a group of Laotian VIPs, 1965. Also shown: Lt. General Vang Pao (*left of Joe, with beret*), commander of the Hmong forces of the Laotian Army, and Brig. General Thao Ma (*right of Joe*), commander of the Royal Laotian Air Force. Dick Laine, (*far right*), was the co-pilot.

the general at Vang Pao's right, but I believe he was Vang Pao's boss—the commander of the Royal Laotian Army. Dick Laine, at my far left, was my co-pilot that day. General Ma was later shot down at Vientiane during a coup attempt. I heard he was shot while in the cockpit after crash landing. The HH-43B 62-4510 in the picture was later shot down in NVN and the crew was taken POW.

I recall the time when General Ma's chopper was out of commission and Tom and Bruce went down and evacuated Colonel Lee's wounded troops off the panhandle plains.

Bruce Hepp: *I recall crossing the Mekong and heading inland a few miles to a designated landing spot. We were told that we would be met by another person that spoke English. His name was "Cadillac," and he would supply all the information we needed to locate the injured men. We located the landing site and after landing, we shut down. A couple of minutes later a man in a sage green flight suit came out of a small building and walked toward the front of our aircraft. He had no other markings on his clothing. I got out and walked toward him. We met and shook hands. I asked him if he was Cadillac and he replied, "Yes, I am." I asked if he was American military. He looked me in the eye, tapped two fingers on my captain's bars and replied, "Just like you."*

At that time I believe the rest of the crew headed toward him and he said he would tell us exactly where to locate the casualties. He had a map and gave us particulars on the location.

We had all the extra seats stripped out of the AC, no rear doors and we took off with a lightened fuel load knowing we would be evacuating battle casualties. After locating them, we landed. The mechanic and the PJ spread a large tarp out in the back of the chopper. I believe there were either seven or nine men, one of which was holding his entire innards in his T-shirt. The other men were all seriously injured—some worse than others. We had the net up in the rear of the AC; they all were bleeding and there was a lot of jellied blood running down the floor toward the rear of the AC. That was the reason for the tarp. I will never forget the smell. As we loaded them in the rear cabin they either crawled, if they were able, or were helped in any way we could, to find a place to lay or sit. Several were leaning against the AC cabin walls and a couple of them were leaning on each other. I doubt that any one of them weighed 135 pounds. No seats or seat belts were available for the casualties. I will never forget this vivid picture, which is still in my mind, of the man with his innards in his blood soaked T- shirt, holding them with his left arm and holding himself seated against the stringers in the fuselage with the fingers of his right hand. I cannot imagine his pain. It gave me an insight into the courage and guts these little men had! I will surely die with this image in my head. We flew them back across the river to NKP. They were picked up shortly thereafter and flown to the hospital at Korat. We received word a few days later that they all survived.

Joe Ballinger: *The next day, Walt and I took them all the malaria pills and medicine we could spare. We got a briefing from Col. Lee and were buzzed by General Ma in a T-28. When we got back to Savannakhet, Gen. Ma told us to get out of Laos ASAP as the ICC (International Control Commission) was trying to catch us there. On the way out to Mukdahan across the Mekong, there was a loud bang that shook the helicopter, and I thought we had taken a hit. I did a near autorotation to a rice paddy where the crew chief told me that an empty fuel drum sitting on end had expanded, hitting the floor. We took off and got across the river without being caught. I heard later that it was only because the Thai Air Force had buzzed the ICC H-34 and forced it down for not filing a proper flight clearance that we got away without being detected.*

The Jolly Greens were no exception to these types of missions, getting involved when Major Ercy Carver of the 6235th Air Base Squadron was informed by a local Thai policeman that three of his policemen had been wounded in a gun battle with bandits in the southern part of the province. The police official requested use of a helicopter to evacuate the wounded officers to the city hospital in Nakhon Phanom. Capt. Fred Liebert and 1st Lt. Orville Keese went to the village, some 23 miles south of the base.

One of the victims had died when the helicopter arrived, but the other two were picked up and brought to Nakhon Phanom to be rushed to a hospital.

One of the two wounded men, a provincial police Colonel of Nakhon Phanom, was so badly injured that he required surgery. At the request of a Thai government official, Major Carver arranged to fly the wounded Colonel, his wife and a doctor to Bangkok for surgery.

We flew the Flight Surgeon out to villages for med visits. Just landed in a ville and set up shop like the guys had been doing before we got there. We passed out little American flags and candy to the kids that always crowded around. Learned you could never have enough candy, so we took cigarettes and passed out one each. Later, the same Flight Surgeon, suffering from a bad state of depression was sent back to the States. Good guy, but not suited for the business we were in. In all honesty, I don't know that any of us were either, but we did it anyway.

THEY CALLED IT NAKED FANNY

33

OFFICERS' LOUNGE— NKP AIR BASE

SCOTT HARRINGTON: *BECAUSE THERE WERE JUST A FEW officers on the base we had an opportunity to get to know each other fairly well. There were probably ten or so from the Invert group— a communications officer, a Flight Surgeon and a half dozen helicopter pilots. We had a small building overlooking the ramp area for our Officers' Lounge. A young Thai woman named Pen Pit, pronounced* Pen Pete, *served as our barmaid. We were often treated to a fresh Thai pineapple that she would peel and slice for us.*

Dick Laine recalls "Saturday Night Spider Fights." He says Pen Pit would introduce a foreign spider into one of the webs that had been woven in the club rafters during the week. Naturally, the spider that had spun the web would defend its territory and the two would fight to the death.

We were all members of our Afterburner Club. In order to join, you had to drink a shot glass of burning cognac which, in the dark, looked just like the flames shooting out of an aircraft when the afterburner was ignited. The key was to roll the shot glass over your thumb and drain it as quickly as possible. If you

THEY CALLED IT NAKED FANNY

Pen Pit, our barmaid.

took a breath during your attempt, you likely would singe the inside of your nose and without a doubt set your moustache (if you had one) ablaze.

One special member of our Afterburner Club was the wonderful comedienne Martha Raye. She didn't like cognac, but did like vodka, so we lit a vodka afterburner for her and she drank it like a pro. She was among the many entertainers who were part of the USO troupes that came to visit and entertain. I had the opportunity, since I was off duty, to spend a couple of hours with her in the afternoon prior to her USO performance. She was a grand lady.

Few of us knew that she was a colonel in the U.S. Army Reserve and a nurse with a surgical specialty. In 1967, during a visit to a Special Forces outpost that came under attack while she was there, "Colonel Maggie" assisted wounded troops aboard the

Comedienne Martha Raye downing a burning cognac and officially becoming a member of the "Afterburner Club."

Chinook helicopter ferrying dead and wounded. She also filled in at the Pleiku Army Field Hospital giving other nurses a well-deserved break. She is the only woman buried in the Special Forces Cemetery at Ft. Bragg, NC.

When I arrived at NKP, Izzy Freedman was the manager of the Officers' Club. His signature appears on the front of my membership card. Raymond Burr's signature is on the back.

Joe Ballinger: *In the Officers' Club, we didn't have a great selection of beer, mostly Thai, so we drank whatever we had from the cooler. Somewhere, somehow we got into the habit of telling Pen Pit, "Gimme a Coors, please!" and she would give us whatever was cold. At the time, Coors beer was not pasteurized and didn't travel*

THEY CALLED IT NAKED FANNY

Scott Harrington's NKP Officers' Lounge card.

well, so we knew we wouldn't get it there. Imagine our surprise when one night with a big grin she placed some cans of Coors on the bar for us. It seems that the fighter pilots had heard about our little joke and had two cases of Coors flown in for us. One went to the NCO Club.

34

THIS AND THAT MEMORIES

JOE BALLINGER: *A SHORT TIME AFTER THE RAINY day adventure, a Ubon HH-43 flamed out on the way back from an NKP visit. They crash landed in a clearing full of stumps about halfway between NKP and Ubon. We picked up the crew and brought them back to NKP. Then we gave them assistance at the crash site while they recovered their bird when their own Det CO never went out to the site.*

Somewhere in here, we got a VIP visit from General Joe Cunningham, former Commander Air Rescue Service. It was damned good for morale knowing he took the time to come up and see us. He remembered Walt from a time when he was a helicopter mechanic on a tool box inspection; and me from when he cleared me from a Flight Evaluation Board. It was quite different from the later visit by General "Whip" Wilson, 13th AF Commander. He called the place a "God damn jungle camp," and fired Major Carver, who was down in Bangkok trying to get supplies for us.

Martha Raye was a hit with the guys who gave her a lasting memory of NKP by painting the Naked Fanny logo (without her knowing it) on the bottom of her luggage. During her visit, Davey

THEY CALLED IT NAKED FANNY

TSgt. Wade Ketron with the great Martha Raye.

Allen (Udorn Det) threw a blade tip weight and we went out to get him. Davy was pissed when I wouldn't send any guys back until the show was over.

Bruce Hepp: *I remember the visit by the USO when Martha Raye was the honored guest. We gathered in the NCO Club to see her show. She asked if someone would autograph her suitcase which was leather. No one had a marker to do the job so she asked if anyone had a knife? I said that I did. She asked me to please do the job with my knife. The photo is of me on the floor with her suitcase. Moments later we received orders to scramble on a downed pilot. She fought with us saying she was an RN and she was going to go with us. We left and missed the show as she couldn't go with us.*

Bruce Hepp autographing Martha Raye's suitcase.

Joe Ballinger: *There was the time the fuel truck pump broke down and the young A2C in charge couldn't get it fixed, so he put 55-gallon barrels on a flatbed and hand pumped fuel for our birds. Then, he couldn't get any action out of Bangkok for more fuel, so I picked up the phone and called Saigon. I used a "Flash" priority and busted the Radar Major (that would have been Major Douthit) who was trying to get radar parts, off the line. He was a little torqued, but not nearly as torqued as the general I got connected with. Since I couldn't get through on a "Flash" priority, I went to a little known priority just below "Presidential" called "Rescue Emergency." It seems the general stayed on the line as I explained our problem to the 38th ARS Commander, Lt. Col. Ed Krafka. As I was telling the colonel that all the fuel we had left was in our helicopter tanks, the general, whoever he was, broke in and told me, "Don't worry! I'll take care of that* problem!" About two hours later a C-130 flew by and low level air-dropped rolagons of fuel on our runway. Some bounced all over and into the trees, but we got our fuel.

Another day we found a Conex box (intermodal shipping container) in a ditch out by the runway. Once we cut the padlock, we opened it and found it was full of M-16 and .38 caliber ammo. Don't know how it got there, but it was timely as we were running out of what we brought over with us. (Jim Burns wonders if it wasn't from the first TDY group since they had a CONEX and that is where they stored their guns.)

Our use of interconnected barrels internally for range extension wasn't kosher, but they worked fine until we got the internal F-model (a later model of the HH-43) bladders.

Our guys at NKP got F-model hoist drums and cable and installed them so we had 250 feet of cable. That wasn't put in the books!

Also, Ruben Hardy, the Sikorsky Tech Rep., got Jeep fan belts from Bangkok for the CH-3 transmission oil cooler. It just shortened the inspection time.

And when we were very, very short of 43 rotor blades and finding the only set left in a container full of water, Tom Curtis spent several hours on the ramp running a shaking bird until it smoothed out getting all the water out of them.

Bruce Hepp: *Izzy Freedman was in charge of the Officers' Lounge, but apparently touched 'nary a drop of the witches brew. That is until he was made to drink an "afterburner" the night before his departure from NKP. Everyone assumed that he had gone to bed, but after a couple of hours and a heavy rain storm, somebody stepped on him on their way back to their hooch. He was face down on the board walk and quite wet. This may have been his first alcoholic drink as I can't remember him drinking with the rest of us.*

Photo of a "rolagon"—a 500-gallon rubber blivet resembling a very fat tire that can be airdropped out of planes and rolled around to where they are needed. Rolagons have an axle in the center that allows them to have both ends hooked up to a vehicle.

Wade Ketron: *Coffee was first made in large tubs until we got urns. After a few weeks of using the urns, the coffee began to have a funny taste and complaints were made about it. The cooks said they had removed a scrub brush that had been left in the urn at the first cleaning. They decided to put it back in the urn and the coffee returned to its previous good taste again.*

There was a situation that I became aware of and brought to the attention of the right people. Baht was the Thai currency and the rate of exchange was enough to make a few cents, or more, if you exchanged $20 bills. I noticed when I, and others, would use American money at the NCO Club; we would be given our change in Baht. I didn't think much about it until I was in town one day and saw the Manager of the NCO Club and his friend go into the local bank. Then the light came on—they were exchanging money for a profit and the U.S. money was then going to the Viet Cong for their use.

As I neared my time to return to Clark, permanent party troops were arriving from the States, including a new commander. He was a colonel and had been there no time until he went down on the flight line and sat in a helicopter unnoticed. He then demanded better security. After that incident, while my crew was working a swing shift, I shared that information with them and said that I expected he would try to pull the same thing around Operations. I told them I didn't believe in playing games in a combat area. It wasn't too long after that I got a call from the switchboard that the guard, A1C Yancey, had someone he didn't recognize on the ground outside stating that he was the new commander. I went outside and sure enough, that is who it was. I identified him, gave him a salute and he left.

The only time that I really got scared was shortly before I left and it was after dark. I was in my bunk when an alert was called. Someone had seen a flare and movement across the flight line. My duty position and weapon were in Operations. I had a five cell flashlight that I carried at night to watch for snakes. As I walked up the road toward Operations I could hear these young voices saying, "How do you get the safety off." All I could think of was one shot and everyone would be shooting at each other. I turned my flashlight on and held it toward my chin. Someone yelled, "Turn that light off!" I replied, "No, I don't want to get shot." When I got to Operations I got my maps and extra clips of ammunition and was ready to survive, even if I had to go by myself.

Joe Ballinger: *We got a request from ASOC to support the U.S. Embassy, Thailand, in taking some of their U.S. Aid personnel*

Pilot Jay Strayer (*left*) and Invert Weapons Controller Bud Myers modeling the latest in sarong wear. In Thailand, men as well as women wear sarongs. Made of a lightweight cloth, they are sewn as a complete circle that must be doubled back and tucked. Worn without skivvies, they are cool and airy.

on a tour of a village, south of NKP. So I took them down to the village where a Thai Colonel would give them a briefing on how the U.S. Aid money was spent in the local area. The Thai Army ran most of the U.S. Aid projects. Dick Laine was my CP. One of the more interesting subjects at the briefing was the use of the new roads in an area where there were very few vehicles. The Thai colonel told us that as soon as a new road was built, there would be a jitney bus on it taking passengers and excess produce to the local city markets.

We again got a request from ASOC to support the Thai Police on a night raid at a village south of NKP. After talking it over with the CH-3 guys, they agreed to take it, so I accepted the mission. George Martin assigned Freddie and Orville to fly it. I sat in on the briefing that a Thai Police colonel gave telling us about the suspected communist insurgency activities in that area that they wanted to intercept and capture. And that our people were to be involved only in transporting them to the edge of the village, then back. I noticed that the Thai colonel had a High Standard .22 pistol holstered on his hip and offered him the loan of my .38 pistol. He told me thanks but that he was a good shot with his own pistol. A couple of hours later we got a call that they needed an ambulance as they had wounded on board. According to the story I heard later the Thai colonel got stitched up with three hits but killed his opponent with the .22. As they were being taken on a stretcher from the CH-3 to an ambulance, the Thai colonel waved me over. As I took his hand he told me, "Captain! Next time I take your .38!

After I got to Thailand, I had heard that they had no problem with Communists or Communism. When I asked why, I was told, "We eliminate them by killing them wherever we find them!" I was now a true believer!

Then there was Jim Burns's empty trunk episode. Jim was told by his CO at Clark that he would need a locking trunk to keep valuables in once he arrived at his TDY destination. Not having any success in finding one he "borrowed" a "fly-a-way" parts kit trunk from the squadron parts room. Only one problem—the lid had to be bolted on. And not having an immediate need to use it, Jim just kept it empty.

At every juncture; from boarding the aircraft at Clark to flying to Saigon; to attempting to get it aboard a plane to Bangkok; to getting it into a cab en route to the hotel, the empty trunk became like an albatross. So Jim decided to solve the problem by asking the bartender at the hotel in Bangkok if he had a place he could keep it for four months. The bartender was only too glad to help out and stored the empty trunk in the wine cellar.

After about half of his TDY was over, the detachment commander sent Jim and a couple of others to Bangkok to "get some parts."

"All of us got to go 'chase parts' while we were there, which meant that since the shuttle only ran once a week…we *had* to stay in Bangkok for six days," said Jim. "Damn! And wait to catch a ride back to NKP."

While on his "parts chasing" trip, he again stayed at the same hotel as on his way up-country.

"The Wednesday before I headed back to NKP, I asked the bartender how the empty trunk was doing. He led me down to the wine cellar to show me," said Burns.

"See, trunk where you leave it," said the bartender. Burns said he looked at the trunk for a few seconds, then turned to the bartender and said, "Since you were so kind to store the empty trunk for me, I'm giving it to you. Keep the trunk, I don't want it back."

The bartender was thrilled to death, and so was Burns. He had finally shed himself of the cursed "empty trunk." He figured he'd find some way to explain what had happened to it when he got back to Clark. As it turned out, he was never asked by anyone where the trunk was. It just went MIA from the fly-a-way kit room and no one ever said a thing.

Joe Ballinger: *The transportation equipment we had then was mostly WWII (and Korea) leftovers: 6x6s and one lonely Jeep. The Jeep was the Base Commander's and was named "Nellie Bell!" Major Carver would let some of us use it for going to town at night. One night, I went in with a bunch of base troops and hit the bars with them. As the night wore on, the others found reasons to stay in town overnight and I was the only one left. Not that I was against such extracurricular activities, just wasn't the night* for such for me. So, sometime around 2 a.m., I got into Nellie Bell to head back to the base. There was only one problem, Nellie Bell was a WWII Jeep and there was no key. I could start it with the switches but didn't know the combination to turn on the lights. Now being that I wasn't exactly sober and there being a full moon out, I convinced myself that if I drove carefully I could make the 10 miles back without any problem.

So, driving along at about 20-25 miles per hour and no traffic, I was enjoying the night air with the top down, when I heard a very loud, "Aieee Ayyeeeee Aiiieee." I slammed on the brakes figuring I had run over some poor Thai and was in deep doo-doo. As I looked through the windshield I found, in the center of the road, a large water buffalo loaded down on both sides with what looked like bamboo and a Thai riding in the middle. At this point I moved to the side of the road and parked as he went around and on his way probably wondering what the crazy round eye was doing there with no lights. Myself, using the better part of valor, I just leaned back and went to sleep until the sun came up. When I got back to the base, I got razzed for finding a "tii lak" (actually "tii rak," but often mispronounced as tii lak. It means sweetheart) and staying the night. When I told the truth, it was so far out, most of them believed me. Phil Stambaugh took to calling me "Water Buffalo Ballinger" after that, even at Sheppard (Sheppard AFB, near Wichita Falls, Texas) where he taught me to fly the H-3.

Joe Ballinger: *While we were at Nakhon Phanom, we received notice that Walt Turk had been approved for an upgrade in status from Reserve officer to Regular. Walt had received his commission as a 2nd Lieutenant through OCS. Being a "Regular" officer has several advantages such as having a better chance at promotion and protection against RIF (reduction in force).*

Tom Curtis held the only American flag we could find on

1st Lt. Walt Turk is sworn in as a Regular officer. Joe Ballinger is at left with hand raised; Tom Curtis holds the American flag; and Lt. Turk, also with hand raised, is facing Ballinger.

the base while I administered the oath that swore-in Walt as a Regular officer.

Freddie Liebert brought over a fancy crocheted hammock that he hung in the back of the CH-3C so he could stand by for the next mission in comfort. But that wasn't enough for Freddie, so he hauled lumber and plywood (probably from packing and crates) up to LS-36 and built a lean-to shelter for everyone to sit in, in the shade or out of the rain. It became known as "Fearless Freddie's Flophouse," with a big sign on it to that effect. I wish we had a picture of it!

Southwest of NKP was a town by the name of Sakon Nakhon. It had a lake, Sakon Nakhon Lake and beside the lake was a PSP runway, supposedly built as part of the SEATO agreement. Not a building around it, except for a guard shack. Later we found out that it had a U.S. Army unit located there.

How we found out was one day we came into our O Club hooch and found a very attractive round-eye lady, probably about 24, in a short skirt sitting at our bar. Her husband was an Army captain who was stationed at Sakon Nakhon Lake (actually the commander of the unit). And being a college educated, independent lady with no children, she made the decision to get a visa and come to Thailand to see him. NKP was as close as she could get by air and wanted to know how to get there by ground transportation. There may have been a way, but in the interest of helping out a fellow officer's wife, I got a six-by truck and two of my guys volunteered to drive her down. They did, but there were one or two little problems we didn't know about. First, she hadn't told her husband she was coming and wanted to surprise him. She did that! The second problem was this was one of those secret Listening/Watch Intelligence sites and she couldn't get on it. And we heard later, that the U.S. Army wasn't amused at her living there in Sakon Nakhon with her husband. So they confined him to the site and they couldn't get together. Don't know what happened after that??

Then, there was the time that one of the Air America jocks, Herb Baker, brought a U.S. Aid dolly over from Thakhek, Laos. He had to bunk her in the Parachute Shop for the night since we had no VIP or visitor's area.

A few days later, Blackie and Henebry swam the Mekong to visit the same dolly. They called the next morning from Mukdahan as the boat they borrowed to come back in didn't have any oars. So I flew down and picked them up so they could pull alert that day.

I also recall the day that Walt and I landed at Long Nak Tha, a base between NKP and Ubon with a PSP runway that had *yellow Xs painted on it for no landings! We found a British Engineering Unit housekeeping a base with more facilities—swimming pool, tennis courts, clubs, etc., than we had at NKP. After having tea, using the Queen's finest china, we went on our way again, never really knowing what the base was for, but suspecting (as with the building at the end of our ramp—that wasn't there) more of the same Special Operations stuff.*

Bruce Hepp: *One additional memory was a flight to the Governor's home, in one of the Thai provinces, to have lunch with the Governor. It was to be a thank-you for all the assistance we had provided to the Thai people. (Transportation for their leaders as well as the medical missions to the remote villages.)*

The day of the lunch could only be established when we had three birds in commission and the Thai people concerned were available. As I remember several of the chopper group, who could be spared, went along and not just the crew. We had a member of the local police with us who would assist in getting us to the proper landing spot, adjacent to the Governor's home and act as our interpreter.

After landing we were met by the Governor and his people who escorted us to his home, which was a hundred yards or so up the hill. After entering his home we were given instructions by the Thai interpreter to help us meet the protocol necessary to eat with the Governor. After everyone was seated we were asked individually if we would like ice water to drink. Considering our location in the middle of nowhere, I think some of us wondered where they got the ice. This was evidently an unusual and very proper drink to be served only on special occasions. We found out later that they had a refrigerator. I don't know where they got the electricity to run it.

Having heard stories about the diets of those living out in the jungle, we had previously discussed what we might be served.

THEY CALLED IT NAKED FANNY

Rat and snake were two of the possible choices in the back of our minds. Dog came in third. I am not sure who asked, "What are we were having for lunch," but a huge sigh of relief was heard from more than one of us when the answer was chicken.

Now here comes the fun part! Everything was served family style in large porcelain bowls. As the boiled chicken pieces came to me I was deciding whether it would be white or dark meat when my choice suddenly became beak, foot or comb. The chicken had been prepared with a meat cleaver and, I believe, just about everything a chicken possesses was in the bowl. I was able to locate a recognizable piece of thigh which I quickly placed on my plate. After we began eating I discovered that several very sharp pieces of thigh bone were imbedded in my selection. I'm not sure why but I seem to think we were also served small pieces of corn on the cob?

After the meal was over and the small talk had ceased, we were excused to return to NKP. On the way down the outside stairs we noticed several teen-aged girls at the side of the house with round pans, squatting in the grass, washing the dishes from our meal. We looked at them and in our best Thai, thanked them for their part in the meal. Needless to say this brought blushing and many giggles. I now wonder whether they had ever seen a round eye in their life, especially young men. They stopped their dish washing and watched us very carefully as we headed for the chopper and departed for home.

35

BATTLEFIELD COMMISSIONS

MAJOR WILLIAM D. HOBBS: *THE TIME: JULY 24, 1965. Place: 23,000 feet over North Vietnam. Mission: Fly cover for aircraft bombing troop concentrations. Restriction: Stay between Hanoi and the troop concentrations.*

Air Force Capt. (O-3) Richard P. (Pop) Keirn, flying close formation in a flight of four F-4s, takes the first surface-to-air missile (SAM) hit of the Vietnam War. Keirn, his plane on fire and out of control, ejects and parachutes into the unknown below.

Landing in the trees, but uninjured, Keirn manages to evade the enemy for more than 18 hours before he is captured and taken to the infamous Hanoi Hilton for interrogation. Later, he is moved to a "hell hole" that later would become known to its inmates as the "Zoo."

(One such experience should be enough for any one person in a lifetime, but for Keirn it was POW experience number two. As a young flight officer in World War II, Keirn was shot down over Germany and spent the rest of the war as a prisoner in Stalag Luft 1 near Barth, Germany.)

Four years passed.

THEY CALLED IT NAKED FANNY

The fall of 1969 found 24 POWs in Keirn's cell block. There were five other POW compounds in the camp; altogether there were more than 100 prisoners. But there were only three enlisted men in the whole camp—all in Keirn's compound: Airman Third Class (E-2) Arthur Black, Airman First Class (E-4) Bill Robinson and Staff Sergeant (E-5) Arthur Cormier.

From time to time, little arguments would crop up between some of the officers and one or more of the enlisted men—over baseball or football, nothing of consequence. One day this was going on and one of the officers said, "I can't argue with you. You're an enlisted man and I'm an officer." Another officer quipped: "Well, let's make 'em officers and then we can argue!"

A couple of simple, off-the-cuff statements like that set the idea for an officer candidate school in motion.

Someone asked Keirn, since he had served in World War II, if he had ever seen anyone battlefield-commissioned. He had. Someone else suggested: "Let's battlefield commission them." The idea took hold.

Colonel (later Lt. Gen.) John P. Flynn—"Sky," as he was known then—was the senior POW in the Zoo. Since he was housed in the next compound, Keirn had to communicate with him by tapping out messages on the wall, in code. Flynn endorsed the idea and battlefield-commissioned them.

Robinson says, "We assumed the role of second lieutenants and were treated as such by all the POWs. Needless to say, our morale shot up to new heights."

One might wonder why it was unanimously decided that the three men were officer material. Black and Cormier were both pararescuemen. Black was a high school graduate with less than a year of college. Cormier was a high school graduate and had 45 semester hours of college. Robinson, a helicopter crew chief, had graduated from high school. All had been aboard helicopters that were shot down.

"It's hard to put into words what they did to make us believe they would make good officers," Keirn says. "Their conduct in prison was as good as any officer there and better than some. They supported the officers over them to the best of their ability. They took orders without question. They did more than their share of the work. They helped anyone who was injured or sick and tried to do their best to make things work for everybody."

Keirn suggested that they start a school for the new officers so that when they got back to the States, Air Force authorities would not question the validity of the commissioning. The three enlisted men didn't think the whole thing would work, but they went along with it just to have something to do. No one thought it would be a waste of time to have the school; instructing Black, Robinson and Cormier would give the others something to do, too.

All the officers offered to help in any way they could. The ones who did the actual training were 1st Lt. (now Lt. Col.) Thomas Browning, 1st Lt. (now Lt. Col.) John Borling, and Navy LTJG (now CMDR) David Carey. Browning and Borling were graduates of the Air Force Academy and Carey was a graduate of the Naval Academy. They gave the three men the benefit of everything they had learned.

The teachers and the students went to work: customs and courtesies of the service; the structure of military command; supply and intelligence; and how these things should work together to make a viable military outfit. They conducted courses in math, psychology, writing and grammar. They used any kind of material that was available, such as toilet paper and pencil stubs.

Sometimes the three students were given one day to prepare for a 15-minute speech on a certain subject. Another time, they were given a subject and only two minutes to prepare for a five-minute speech. The instructors gave them math problems, navigation—just about anything that could be studied and questioned. This continued for four hours a day, six days a week, for about four months.

And not one of the men "slacked" in his homework.

The treatment of the Americans seemed to change with the political climate. Early in their captivity, most of the torture came in the form of beatings, solitary confinement, starvation and humiliation.

But by 1970, when this officer training was going on, the North Vietnamese had slacked off on this kind of treatment; the starvation diet had been improved. The food they were getting was adequate for exercising, running in place, playing volleyball or some basketball. And both instructors and students were better able to concentrate.

The policy in most wars has been to separate the officers from the enlisted men. But in this case, there were only three enlisted men. Keirn believes the North Vietnamese thought it wasn't worth the trouble to separate them.

Flynn suggests another idea: "The NV treated us as the blackest of criminals, never recognizing us as prisoners of war. Since they considered us criminals, there was no separation of the enlisted men from the officers. For them to do so would have indicated that they did consider us POWs and were following accepted procedure."

Either way, the NV inadvertently paved the way for this OCS behind bars.

Ironically, the NV did recognize that the American "criminals" had military rank. They posted signs stating that junior officers would be imprisoned for at least seven years; majors and lieutenant colonels would have to stay for 12 to 14 years and colonels and above would never see their families again. Theoretically, commissioning the three airmen could have meant the NV would increase their sentence— had they known what was going on.

In February 1973, freedom came.

For years, Air Force policymakers have been hung up on the notion that all officers should have degrees. Would they honor the battlefield commissions?

John Flynn was uncertain of his authority to bestow a battlefield commission. He had been promoted to brigadier general while he was in prison, but the information had been withheld from the public for two reasons. If the North Vietnamese had found out about the promotion, it could have meant harsher treatment. Second, officials wanted to see whether Flynn was mentally capable before they pinned on a star.

Wasting no time, Flynn went directly to then Secretary of the Air Force John L. McLucas. He told McLucas the story behind the battlefield commissioning. To some people's surprise, McLucas enthusiastically supported it. The only thing he wouldn't go along with was make the commission retroactive to the date of the commissioning in prison.

Considering the time-in-grade factor, that would have made them first lieutenants well on their way to being considered for promotion to captain.

"I think it's important to note," says General Flynn, "that bestowing a battlefield commission on a deserving enlisted man improves the spirit and morale of the enlisted force. I never made the mistake of believing all officers are smarter than all enlisted men."

Where are they now? (This would have been in 1981.)

All three men are captains. Because of his enlisted experience in the field, Bill Robinson went into aircraft maintenance and today is an aircraft maintenance officer with the 33rd Component Repair Squadron at Eglin AFB, Fla.

Arthur Neil Black went through pilot training and flew HC-130s for a year and a half. Today he is a T-37 instructor pilot at Mather AFB, Calif.

THEY CALLED IT NAKED FANNY

Arthur Cormier, the "old man" of the trio, has had a most unusual career. Cormier actually had gone to Air Force OCS back in 1960, but had not completed the course. When he was released from prison on Feb. 12, 1973, he had close to 20 years' service. On official Air Force records, he had been promoted to senior master sergeant (E-8) and had a line number for chief master sergeant (E-9).

With the approval of the Secretary of the Air Force, Cormier waited until he was promoted to chief master sergeant before accepting his commission. That way, if he retired before 10 years' commissioned service; he would be able to retire at his highest enlisted grade. When Cormier did accept a commission, he was given the same time-in-grade as Black and Robinson, who were commissioned earlier.

The article above was written by Major William D. Hobbs, USAF, Ret., and was published in *The Times Magazine*, October 5, 1981. The story is reprinted with permission from Major Hobbs. His permission was granted prior to his passing on November 19, 2014.

Arthur Neil Black retired from the United States Air Force as a Major; Arthur Cormier and William Robinson retired from the United States Air Force as captains.

A second, more recent version of the "Battlefield Commissions" was written by Colonel Leo K. Thorsness, USAF, Ret., Congressional Medal of Honor recipient and also a POW. His book, *Surviving Hell: A POW's Journey*, was published in 2008. His article, "Commissioned in Hanoi," appeared in *Air Force Magazine*. It is reprinted here with permission from Colonel Thorsness and from *Air Force Magazine*, published by the Air Force Association."

Commissioned in Hanoi by Col. Leo K. Thorsness

Art Cormier, Neil Black, and Bill Robinson showed excellence in the POW camps around Hanoi.

In 1967, there was a "unit" of approximately 300 Americans fighting the Vietnam War from within a Hanoi prison. The unit—later named the 4th Allied POW Wing—was located in the drab North Vietnamese capital. Within this unit, every man had the same job: prisoner of war.

All—except three enlisted airmen—were officers, including me. Our job description was to continue fighting for the United States while imprisoned.

The three enlisted airmen were SSgt. Arthur Cormier, Amn. Arthur Neil Black (A3C) and (A1C) William A. Robinson. All were crewmen on helicopters that rescued aircrews from downed aircraft. The three were shot down in 1965.

They were captured, taken prisoner, and ended up in the Hoa Lo prison in Hanoi (the "Hanoi Hilton," in POW parlance).

POWs were dressed in pajamas, and were usually disheveled as a result of infrequent chances to bathe or shave. Given only two daily meals, and those of poor nutritional value, the POWs were thin. Under these conditions, enlisted men, officers, Air Force, Navy, and Marine Corps all looked about the same.

A general rule, though with multiple exceptions, was that the higher ranking a prisoner was, the more torture he suffered. Art Cormier, Neil Black, and Bill Robinson were among the exceptions. They were tortured like the officer POWs.

A Daring Escape

An idea to do the "right thing"—in the absence of knowledge of specific regulations or rules—was hatched in early 1968.

At that time, the POW officers decided to commission the three enlisted POWs, Cormier, Black, and Robinson. Why? The commissioned men saw these three enlisted men show exceptional heroic qualities.

Until late 1969, most prisoners lived in solitary confinement or in small cells with one or two other POWs. The rules were simple: no noise from any cell. If a prisoner was caught trying to communicate with a POW in the next cell, through the concrete walls, he received a beating—or more.

Most of our torture was for propaganda. The North Vietnamese wanted us to write or make a statement of confession condemning the war. They thrived on the growing anti-war sentiment in the United States, and felt statements from POWs would support that movement.

The North Vietnamese put us in solitary because they believed in the divide-and-conquer theory. They believed that if they could isolate us, they could prevent us from communicating. Both they and we knew that if prisoners could communicate, we could organize. If we could organize, we could resist—or at least resist better.

The POWs lived in these conditions until early 1969. Then, some of us were moved into an area that we named the "Annex." It was part of the POW camp called the "Zoo," located a couple of miles southwest of the Hanoi Hilton. The Annex had larger cells holding up to about 10 POWs.

The cells had a high-walled tiny outside area where we could spend a few minutes on most days.

It was from the Annex that Capt. John A. Dramesi and Capt. Edwin L. Atterberry escaped on May 10, 1969. John and Ed escaped through the roof of the cell in which they lived with several others. They made it over the prison wall.

At daybreak the next day, they could find no cover and were spotted and recaptured. Atterberry was subsequently tortured to death, while Dramesi survived months of torture.

Following that escape, the POWs were taken back into the small Zoo cells. The systematic and horrendous torture that followed was long-lasting and as severe as any we experienced the entire time we all served as POWs.

This was the environment that the officers and enlisted men

endured. We served our country and endured torture to our best ability. Over time, we strengthened our solidarity and, in our way, showed leadership in battle.

Our collective memory fades, but it is agreed that the idea to commission the enlisted airmen germinated in Annex cell #3, which held 12 men—eight Air Force and four Navy.

The five Air Force officers were Darrel E. Pyle, Harry D. Monlux, Michael L. Brazelton, Ralph "Tom" Browning, and John L. Borling. The Naval officers were Richard M. Brunhaver, David J. Carey, Read B. Mecleary, and James B. Bailey. All were O-2s (LTJGs) when they were captured. The Air Force enlisted men were there as well.

By date of rank, Skip Brunhaver was the SRO, or senior ranking officer.

Once the commissioning idea was hatched, it consumed a lot of time—but having a new subject to discuss was refreshing. When the same men are together in the same cell 24 hours a day with no pencils, papers, or books, new subjects are welcome.

All men enthusiastically joined in. The three enlisted airmen found all of this interesting, but appropriately held back from offering opinions.

Conversation often centered on "could it be done?"

A frequent question was, "Skip, what do you think—you are the SRO?" Of the nine officers in the cell, Borling and Browning were Air Force Academy graduates, and Carey and Mecleary were Naval Academy graduates.

Brunhaver generally responded with something like, "How in the world do I know? You, John, and Tom are the Air Force graduates. Did you flunk the battlefield commission course?"

Brunhaver was never shy when expressing his opinion.

Battlefield Commissions

Borling and Browning did not think the Air Force had had

experience or regulations covering battlefield commissions. The Air Force had become a separate service in 1947 and there were no opportunities in Korea for enlisted airmen to receive a battlefield commission. Until Vietnam, the subject simply never came up in the Air Force.

As the conversation heated up, Borling and Browning would turn to Carey and Mecleary, their Annapolis counterparts, saying, "The Marines fall under the Navy. Marines have had a lot of battlefield commissions. What do your regulations say?"

Carey once tried to hoodwink the Air Force members. He said, "I recall in our plebe year, we had a course titled 'History of Battlefield Commissions in Blood and Guts Eyeball Warfare,'" adding that "it was covered under Naval Regulation 291-41-3A." Carey said it confidently, with a straight face. He turned aside to avoid looking at anyone and then, as if talking to himself, added, "Yes, the more I think about it, I'm sure that was the regulation." At best he was believed for maybe 25 seconds before he turned back to the troops with a big grin.

One topic we discussed was whether, if the prisoners went through with their plan, the North Vietnamese would find out that Cormier, Black, and Robinson had become officers. If they found out, would the former enlisted men be tortured more?

This was one time all three enlisted spoke up, saying, "We have been tortured already, we have nothing to lose."

After a week of conversation, Brunhaver declared that it was time to decide: "I would like your vote up or down to promote Art, Neil, and Bill to second lieutenants."

Without hesitation, the other eight officers raised their hands high. Brunhaver looked at Cormier, Black, and Robinson, who felt it was not their position to vote about a battlefield commission for themselves. Brunhaver didn't accept their deference, and sharply said, "Men, do I get the impression you don't want to be officers?"

When the three of them realized that Brunhaver truly wanted

to know how they felt about being promoted to second lieutenant, the hands of all three shot up.

Brunhaver, as cell SRO, decided it was time to run the commissioning idea by the Annex's ranking officer, Capt. Konrad W. Trautman. There was a problem, however: how to contact him. In buildings with a common wall—and with time and a rusty nail—a small hole could be drilled from one cell into the next. Drilling a pencil-sized hole took time, but time was something the POWs had plenty of, and the hole could be covered or disguised when not used.

Cells without adjoining walls posed another problem. Fortunately, in the first few days we were in the Annex, we discovered that we could toss a stone from one courtyard to the next. Tossing a stone with a note attached significantly increased the risk of being caught, however.

Bits of red tile roof, ground into powder and mixed with water, can make a faint ink. Blood makes a bold ink, and under the circumstances the POWs were willing to do whatever it took.

Generally, something could be found to write on. Our toilet paper, for example, was large (squares were about 15 inches across), very coarse, and tan-colored. Parts of the sheets were thick and parts had holes; sometimes small wood fibers were embedded in the papers.

It Won't Hurt To Try

We carefully tore the sheets into squares of about three-and-a-half by three-and-a-half inches. We did not get much toilet paper, and even if paper was used for a secret note, the receiver recycled it back into toilet paper.

A cryptic note was written, asking for permission to commission Cormier, Black, and Robinson. It was rolled tightly and pushed through a hole from cell #3 to cell #4. This was big news to the POWs in cell #4.

Once cell #4 had it, they glued the note with rice paste to a stone, and airmailed (threw) the note from Yard 4 to Yard 5, where Trautman was imprisoned. He consulted his "staff of eight officers" in cell #5, and with little discussion, the decision was unanimous.

Trautman returned his answer—"Yes, commission Art, Neil, and Bill"—by airmail to cell #4 and back through the wall hole to cell #3.

The bottom line in all conversations about promoting Cormier, Black, and Robinson from enlisted to officers boiled down to: "It won't hurt to try. The Air Force can sort it out when we get home."

Basic to all conversations, however, was the quality of the three enlisted men. All had "kept the faith" in America during four long and brutal years, from 1965 to 1969. All had withstood individual torture, kept their integrity, and served honorably in terrible living conditions with inadequate food. Despite all of this, they had kept their dignity intact.

We saw firsthand that these men exhibited heroic qualities in our daily POW battlefield.

With Annex SRO Trautman granting his approval, the day arrived. Although it had been several years since any officers had been sworn in, they collectively reconstructed the oath. All remembered that you repeat your name and swear to defend the Constitution of the United States against all enemies, and take on the obligations without reservation. So help me God.

The oath that was administered was not perfect, but it was close enough under all circumstances. Never had the oath been taken more seriously—nor, likely, taken in prison pajamas. Cormier, Black, and Robinson each repeated the oath standing at attention and proud. It was a solemn, memorable occasion.

After commissioning, the officers created an "in-cell Officer Candidate School." Cormier, Black, and Robinson gladly attended, took instructions serious, and were on their way to becoming fine officers. The courses were taught by the Air Force and Naval Academy graduates, with the other officers helping out.

Then came the failed Son Tay raid of Nov. 20, 1970. Son Tay was about 23 miles west of Hanoi. The raid was perfectly executed, but when the American rescue troops landed in the POW camp there, the prisoners had already been moved.

Indirectly, however, the mission was a success. The North Vietnamese realized we could be rescued and they moved the prisoners into large cells in the Hanoi Hilton. Treatment started to improve, and living with up to 45 POWs in one cell was a much better arrangement.

Once in the Hilton, we settled into a routine. We now were allowed to talk out loud, and some of the barred windows were not bricked up, meaning we could see the sky.

With between 15 to 45 POWs in a cell, there was a lot of knowledge available, and we began to inventory who knew the most about subjects.

Eventually the POW with the most knowledge about a subject, if willing, began to teach, although it was hard to teach certain subjects like math without pencils or paper.

The last year we were held prisoner, we began to receive some medicine. We really didn't know what ailments the bottle of blue medicine treated, but it was great ink. If we got ahead and had extra toilet paper, with bamboo pen and blue medicine, we could make class notes.

When the guards found these notes they typically destroyed them, but sometimes they did not mind us having a few math notes or Spanish vocabulary word lists.

At the Hilton—also called Camp Unity by the POWs—the O-5 and O-6 rank prisoners were kept separate from the more junior officers. Col. John P. Flynn was the ranking POW in Unity, and occasionally we were able to get a note to or from him at a "note drop" (small crack) at a common toilet. The toilet itself was, of course, a squat-over-the-hole model.

We were able to tell Flynn about the commissioning ceremony for Cormier, Black, and Robinson, and in his return note he enthusiastically approved.

Flynn made it a personal priority to make the commissions official when he got back to the United States. He also directed the academy graduates to teach a three month "officer" program to Cormier, Black, and Robinson. The word spread throughout Unity, so that whatever cells they were moved to, their training would follow.

The courses centered on leadership, management, motivation techniques, character development, command decision-making, and one combined course on supply and logistics. It was surprising how many POWs, officers all, listened in while the courses were being taught to the new second lieutenants.

President Nixon sent the B-52s—finally—over Hanoi in December 1972. The bombers came, wave after wave and night after night. The bombing started Dec. 18, and the B-52s, supported by F-105 Wild Weasels and F-4 Phantoms, came every night, except Christmas night, until Dec. 29. The B-52s were allowed to drop their bombs within 2,000 feet of the Hanoi Hilton. When a string of 72 bombs goes off within 2,000 feet of you, it makes a thunderous noise. The plaster falling off the cell ceiling was another good signal, as was seeing SAMs streak into the sky, and hearing the flak from every direction and the sound of many B-52 engines—first in the distance, then slowly getting louder. Combining the visual, audio, and "feel" senses together was the most wonderful experience for the POWs—we had waited years for it to happen.

Forced to the Table

This massive show of strength forced the North Vietnamese to go back to the bargaining table in Paris. Twenty-nine days after the final bomb, on Jan. 27, 1973, Henry Kissinger and Le Duc Tho signed the Paris Peace Accords, officially ending the Vietnam War.

POWS were released in four groups, one group about every 15 days starting in February 1973. The longest-held prisoners were released first. That group included the three new second lieutenants.

After our release, Flynn, by then a brigadier general, and Admiral James B. Stockdale, a former POW, joined forces to push for official recognition of the battlefield commissions that Art Cormier, Neil Black, and Bill Robinson had received (Cormier asked that his commission be delayed until he was promoted to chief master sergeant.)

Flynn and Stockdale wrote a document explaining the rationale, process, and training for the battlefield commissions. They gave their strongest recommendation that the Hanoi commissioning of Cormier, Black, and Robinson be accepted.

Initially, Flynn and Stockdale took their request to the Air Force, since the three enlisted men were all airmen. On first contact, there was resistance by the Air Force because there were no regulations or precedents for USAF battlefield commissions.

Stockdale then unofficially talked to the Navy which, of course, had regulations and ample precedents involving both the Navy and Marine Corps. Soon the Air Force figured a way to be on board, and the battlefield commissions moved up the line. They were accepted and approved through the Secretary of Defense. The Defense Secretary decided, however, to take the request to the White House for final approval.

Nixon was briefed on the 1969 battlefield commissions in the Annex prison in North Vietnam for the three outstanding enlisted men. It was reliably reported Nixon's response to the commissioning request was, "Hell, yes!"

THEY CALLED IT NAKED FANNY

The promotion date was slipped from 1969 to the date of final approval, which was April 9, 1973. Flynn and Col. Fred V. Cherry, outstanding POWs both, administered the oaths of office at Andrews AFB, Md.

After the war, Black, Cormier, and Robinson demonstrated exemplary service as officers. Cormier and Robinson focused on support and maintenance duties. Black went to pilot training and spent many years as a rated officer. All three served honorably with distinction after prison, as they had while they were POWs. Cormier and Robinson retired as captains, while Black retired as a major.

Commissioning the three enlisted POWs in prison was one of the few positive events during those long years. It was the right thing to do for them, and it was the right thing for all of us, even though no one official was looking. We were cut off from our country, our military branches, and our homes. We didn't know how our lives would turn out, but we were—and are -- proud to have lived this experience while serving our country during those extraordinarily difficult times.

AFTERWORD

JOE BALLINGER: WE LIVED BY THE MOTTO, *"These things we do that others might live!"* But there was another difference of Air Rescue Service pilots. ARS qualified their pilots as Rescue Crew Commanders (RCCs), something like SAC Bomber pilots. To be a RCC, you not only checked out as an Aircraft Commander, you were fully trained in all Rescue operations; qualified to be a Mission Commander; and were certified by a Squadron Flight Board (to be able to carry out any rescue operation without any support). In order to do this fully, without jeopardy to your career, you were protected by what we called the "Calculated Risk Clause" in the Air Rescue Operations Regulations! That when prosecuting a life or death rescue mission as a Rescue Crew Commander, you could take a "Calculated Risk" with your aircraft and crew in prosecuting a lifesaving mission.

I didn't use this terminology, so as not to confuse the issues as to pilots and co-pilots used throughout the flying world. But as far as I know, until Duane Martin and the TDY TAC CH-3C pilots arrived, all of our helicopter pilots for CSAR were RCC qualified. Thus, while we were not combat experienced, we were highly qualified helicopter pilots and (the number of RCC pilots) were used up very early in the Vietnam War.

Like all services, co-pilots were just trained to be RCCs as their hours and experience developed.

We never really paid much attention to the "Calculated Risk Clause" after we got into Combat SAR, but I'm sure it was always in the back of our minds. All the time that I was there as *the Commander, as I told the C-54 Mission Commander when Tom didn't go in for the pickup, our Low Bird Pilot (RCC) was the On-Scene Commander and his decisions I backed up fully until they replaced me.*

Actually we were tasked not by ARS but by ASOC out of Udorn after the first mission I agreed to go on. Which, by today's rules, made us Special Operations, whether we liked it or not. And they backed any decisions any of us made! What can I say, it was a messed up war, but we made it work, because as I said as captains and lieutenants we held the hammer.

Like dealing straight with Admiral Sharp, we made the decision to share the war with the USN without any interim bosses. All my boss, Lt. Col. Krafka, out of Saigon, would tell me is you guys are doing great, keep it up and good luck. A lot of the fighter targets were supposedly selected by the White House, but we were so far out of the loop; we got ignored except by the fighter jocks.

When Lt. Colonel Krafka accepted the Presidential Citation for the 38th ARS, and his promotion to colonel at the White House, I was the first he called and told me to call all of my guys and tell them to put it (the Presidential Citation ribbon) on, and to tell them that he owed his promotion to us!

For its "extraordinary gallantry" during rescue missions in Southeast Asia, the 38th Aerospace Rescue and Recovery Squadron was awarded the Presidential Unit Citation on 19 January 1966. In his remarks President Johnson said, "The 38th has inscribed its name on the honor scroll of American heroes. Time and time again, these men have risked their lives so their comrades could live." The unit earned the citation for its outstanding record in combat operations from 1 August 1964 to 31 July 1965. The President credited the unit with saving 74 downed pilots during the period covered by the citation. (That would include all detachments, not just the NKP detachment.)

Joe Ballinger: *Later when I got passed over for major, I got a call from Col. Krafka and he asked if I had punched out a General. And when I told him I was putting in my resignation and going to fly for Air America, he flew in and talked me out of it by promising me a plush job in Saigon. I told him no, I wanted a Combat Command again. He told me that majors and lieutenant colonels were now taking over the Dets. But if he could get me a command, would I pull my resignation. I did on his word, and somehow he got me DET CO for the CSAR unit at Nha Trang when I went back in Jan 67, the only captain having that job.*

Also, I would mention that General Heinie Aderholt gave me a Regular Life Membership in the Air Commando Association, instead of an Associate Membership, telling the ACA that my guys had been further behind the lines than his. And that any of them were eligible to be Air Commandos!

I would be committing a great disservice if I failed to talk about the great support we received at NKP. For example, the Mess Hall (the Ponderosa), that was run by a Tech Sergeant along with local Thai helpers who served us great meals. Breakfast, lunch, dinner and Midnight Mess! They would hold meals for us when we came in late at night from Laos. I remember one time when all he got for meat in our supplies for about five days was spareribs. He had them cooked in every different way he could to keep the guys from complaining too much. One day when I was off (not on alert status), I went to town to look around and found him at the local market. Assuming that he was checking on local produce, I chatted with him and found out he was buying local spices. When I saw him pay for them out of his billfold, I asked who was funding it. He said he was. He had to make our food better somehow. I gave him what money I had and went back to the base and talked to Major Carver telling him what the Tech Sergeant was doing. After suggesting that we could tap the officers more for meals subsistence, he agreed with me that it wasn't right for this to come out of the sergeant's pocket and that he would find funding!

As the senior fly guy on base, I became Base Operations Officer by fiat! Basically, what that meant was that I was in charge of the runway, taxiway and ramp, as we didn't have a tower. It also meant sitting in on the Base meetings and giving advice on such. When available I would meet transient aircraft. There weren't very many but A/1C Stewart, our HH-43 engine man, volunteered to be a Follow-Me driver and meet the aircraft to park them. This was surprising to me as Airman Stewart was not the sharpest man I had brought over. There was even some worry among the maintenance crew about him taking proper care of our engines. I had already heard there was no problem on that account as he was constantly working, tweaking them up in top condition. He even went downtown and had a "Follow-Me" vest made up and shined up his boots. One night, while over at the NCO Club buying some drinks for my troops, I saw Stewart and complimented him on his work. Telling him that he would have been a Staff Sargent by now if he had performed that way before and I asked him why now? He told me that this was the first time in his life he knew what his job was all about! That his engines took us up north and helped us to bring another guy back. He was proud of that!

He wasn't the only one who felt that way! Scott says, "Katy Bar the Door!" when we came back with a rescued pilot. I can tell you this; nearly the whole base shut down and was on the ramp as a welcoming home committee. They all knew by supporting us, they had a piece of the action too!

The reality of what we did out of NKP was unreal in many circumstances; but I am glad we didn't know what the Air Rescue Service prediction of our losses would be!

In the book United States Air Force, Search and Rescue in Southeast Asia by Earl H. Tilford, Jr., written while assigned to *the Office of Air Force History as a captain, and published by the Office of Air Force History, United States Air Force, Washington, D.C., 1980, on page 62 it states: "...Brig. Gen. Adriel N. Williams, Commander of the Air Rescue Service, in a letter to the Chief of Staff of the Air Force Gen. Curtis E. LeMay, cited ARS Programming Plan 563, which estimated that the HH-43B/F force would suffer a forty percent attrition rate in the first year of combat operations."*

We had a 33.3% loss of aircraft at NKP; but thanks be to God, while our loss of personnel was bad enough, it was a lot less than predicted.

THEY CALLED IT NAKED FANNY

APPENDICES

(A) HELICOPTER PERSONNEL ASSIGNED TO NKP
(B) INVERT PERSONNEL ASSIGNED TO NKP
(C) NEW HONOR COURT STATUE
(D) WHERE ARE THEY NOW?
(E) AIRCRAFT TIMELINE
(F) MISSION TIMELINE

THEY CALLED IT NAKED FANNY

HELICOPTER PERSONNEL ASSIGNED TO NKP

DET. PROVISIONAL 3, PARC
Nakhon Phanom RTAFB, Jun-Nov 1964

Capt. Robert W. Davis (P)	33 ARS Det. CO
Capt. Lucian A Gunter III (P)	33 ARS
Capt. Leonard Fialko (P)	Augment from 36 ARS, Det. 1, Misawa AB, Japan
1st Lt. Michael C. Tennery (P)	33 ARS
1st Lt. Kenneth Franzel (P)	Augment from 36 ARS, Det. 4, Osan AB, ROK
1Lt. James W. Crabb (P)	
TSgt. Alvin C. Reed (FE)	
SSgt. Albert B. Parker (FE)	33 ARS NCOIC
SSgt. Charles D. Severns (FE)	33 ARS
SSgt. John Willcox, Jr. (EM)	33 ARS
SSgt. David H. Blouin (MT)	51st USAF Dispensary
SSgt. Donald L. Watson (MT)	51st USAF Dispensary
SSgt. William J. McDougal	Augment from 36 ARS
A1C Daniel E Galde	Augment from 36 ARS, Tachikawa
A1C James W. Burns (FE)	Augment from 31 ARS, Clark AB, PI
A1C Fred D. Scott (FE)	33 ARS
A1C David C. Black (MT)	51st USAF Dispensary
A1C Morris Johnson, Jr. (MT)	51st USAF Dispensary

THEY CALLED IT NAKED FANNY

DET. PROVISIONAL 2, PARC
From Da Nang AB, RVN and Nakhon Phanom RTAFB, Nov 1964-Jan 1965

Capt. Alva G. Graham Det CO	Minot AFB, ND
Capt. Tom Kelly RCC	Minot AFB, ND
Capt. Joe Leech RCC	Minot AFB, ND
1st Lt. John Christianson RCC	Minot AFB, ND
1st Lt. Jim Sovell RCC	Grand Fords AFB, ND
1st Lt. Robert Osik RCC	Selfridge AFB, MI
A1C George Fink ADM	Minot AFB, ND
MSgt. Robert Bradfield Maint Sup	Minot AFB, ND
MSgt. Eldrid Lusk Maint NCOIC	Minot AFB, ND
SSgt. Charles Husby FE	Minot AFB, ND
SSgt. Robert Julian FE	Kincheloe AFB, MI
SSgt. James Tabor FE	Glasgow AFB, MT
A1C Roman Jennissen HM	Minot AFB, ND
A2C Larry Smith HM	Minot AFB, ND
A2C John Zielinsky HM	K. I. Sawyer AFB, MI
SSgt. Robert Bennett PJ	
A2C Andre Raymond PJ	
A2C Albert Dobson PJ	
A2C Richard L. Graham PJ	
SSgt. Arthur Saintheart ABR	Minot AFB, ND
SSgt. William Dickerson ABR	Minot AFB, ND
A1C Jerry Wolford ABR	Minot AFB, ND
A1C Edward Bevens ABR	Minot AFB, ND

DET. PROVISIONAL 2, PARC
Nakhon Phanom RTAFB, Jan-Apr 1965

Capt. Warren K. Davis (RCC) Det. CO
Capt. Israel Freedman (RCC)

Capt. James C. Rodenberg (RCC)
Capt. Jay M. Strayer (RCC)
1st Lt. Neil McCutchan (RCC)
1st Lt. Fred Glover (RCC)
TSgt. John J. Kelly (HM)
SSgt. Enson J. "E-J" Farmer (PJ)
SSgt. Harold G. Stroud (HM)
A1C Herbert H. Romish (PJ)
A1C Cecil A. Boothby (HM)
A2C Eric A. Anderson, Jr. (PJ)
A2C Michael T. Henebry (PJ)
A3C Frank P. Hanutke (HM)

DET. PROVISIONAL 2, PARC—DET. 1, 38th ARS
Nakhon Phanom AB, Apr-Oct 1965

Capt. Joe E. Ballinger (RCC) Det. CO	Kirtland AFB, NM
Capt. Bruce C. Hepp (RCC)	Kirtland AFB, NM
Capt. Stanley O. Schaetzle (RCC)	Kirtland AFB, NM
Capt. Thomas J. Curtis (RCC)	England AFB, LA
Capt. Richard Laine (RCC)	Grand Forks AFB, ND
1st Lt. Walter F. Turk (RCC)	Kirtland AFB, NM
1st Lt. Duane Martin* Det. 9, WARC	Portland IAP
C/MSgt Tom Luty (HMFE)	
T/Sgt Chester E. Rainey (HMFE)	Kirtland AFB, NM
S/Sgt Roberto Rodriguez (HMFE)	
A1C Harry L. Hart, Jr., (Admin. Clerk)	Kirtland AFB, NM
A1C John H. Stewart (HMFE) .	Kirtland AFB, NM
A1C Francisco Alverado (HMFE)	
A1C William A. Robinson, (HMFE)	
A1C Richard A. Wallace (PJ)	
A2C David M. Cutillo (HMFE)	Kirtland AFB, NM
A2C Arthur N. Black (PJ)	

THEY CALLED IT NAKED FANNY

A2C Marvin Brenamen (PJ)
A2C Michael T. Henebry (PJ)
A3C Darwin L. Devers (HMFE) Kirtland AFB, NM

*(On 20 July 1965, 1st Lt. Duane Martin was added as a pilot to replace Capt. Stan Schaetzle, who was reassigned during the TDY period.)

DET. 1, 38th ARRC—CH-3C GROUP
Nakhon Phanom AB, Thailand, Jun-Oct 1965

Capt. George C. Martin	4488 Test Sq. (Heli) Det. CO
Capt. James P. Stambaugh	4488 Test Sq. (Heli)
Capt. Fred Liebert	4488 Test Sq. (Heli)
1st Lt. George Warren	4488 Test Sq. (Heli)
1st Lt. Orville N. Keese	4488 Test Sq. (Heli)
TSgt. Michael Hoffman	4485 OM Sq.
SSgt. Eddie Walker	4485 A&E Maint. Sq.
SSgt. Jim P. Byrd	4485 OM Sq.
SSgt. Francis L. Hill	4485 OM Sq.
SSgt. Curtis W. Pert	4485 OM Sq.
SSgt. Lee R. Diggs	4485 OM Sq.
SSgt. George A. Johnson	4485 OM Sq.
SSgt. George Thayer	
A1C Bing Gibson	4485 A&E Maint. Sq.
A1C George R. Alston	4485 OM Sq.
A1C Jerry H. Price	4485 A&E Maint. Sq.
A1C Sheldon C. Tart	4485 OM Sq.
A1C James E. Armenia	4485 OM Sq.
A2C Harry W. Hylander, Jr.	4485 OM Sq.
A2C Garold L Isenhour	4485 OM Sq.
A2C Bibbye J. Gonzales	4485 OM Sq.
A2C R. E. Scherzer	

In reviewing the listings of the various units it is important to note that, beginning with the second TDY detachment, the pilots who flew the HH-43Bs had a special designation.

Appendix B

INVERT PERSONNEL ASSIGNED TO NKP

INVERT PERSONNEL (including Communications)
From Official USAF orders, mission reports and personal recall

Maj. Howard Douthit
Capt. Wayne Griggs
Capt. Gerry Swenson
Capt. Frank Troth
1st Lt. Harvey A. Childress
1st Lt. Michael G. Coover
1st Lt. James E. Foote
1st Lt. Richard Grannis
1st Lt. Phillip Hamilton
1st Lt. Scott Harrington
1st Lt. Earle Myers
2nd Lt. Michael R. Sweet
CWO Albert C. Clough
CWO George Wolfram
SMSgt Thomas E. McMenamin
SMSgt Robert B. Weekley, Jr.
SMSgt Thomas W. A. Haney
MSgt Herbert Mathews, Jr.
TSgt. Wade Ketron
TSgt. Barney Parker
TSgt. Richard Pitzer
TSgt. William R. Tipton
SSgt. Antonio V. Lewis

THEY CALLED IT NAKED FANNY

SSgt. Harold Lewis
SSgt. Charles M. Lierman
SSgt. Elmer Z. McWilliams
SSgt. Eugene Ogle
SSgt. Dennis Stace
SSgt. Frank Seal
SSgt. Noel Tennant
SSgt. Francis A. Wiley
A1C Joel Alexander
A1C Ronald A. Craft
A1C John Curtis
A1C Jay Easy
A1C Austin Kallman
A1C Clifton J. Keys, Jr.
A1C Rodney Jones
A1C Harlan Tuxtow
A1C Albert Yancey
A1C Conrad Demartine
A2C James L. Salvaterra
A2C Lloyd E. Wimbish
A3C William F. McGinty

It is my duty, as a member of the Air Rescue Service, to save life and to aid the injured. I will be prepared at all times to perform my assigned duties quickly and efficiently, placing these duties before personal desires and comforts. These things I do that others may live.

—Code of the Air Rescueman

Appendix C

NEW HONOR COURT STATUE

John Christianson, Pedro Rescue Helicopter Association president (who also served at Nakhon Phanom and contributed to this book), and Chris Taylor, Pedro Rescue Helicopter Association treasurer are shown unveiling the new Honor Court statue at the U.S. Air Force Academy. An identical monument was earlier placed at the Air Force Enlisted Heritage Research Institute at Maxwell-Gunter AF Base, Montgomery, AL. Plans call for a third monument to be located at Lackland AFB, San Antonio, TX in 2018. Taylor's father, James Taylor, now deceased, designed the memorials. (Photo courtesy John Christianson)

On September 19, 2014, the Pedro Rescue Helicopter Association presented the U.S. Air Force Academy with a Southeast Asia, Vietnam Pedro Rescue Helicopter Monument, dedicated to the pilots, firefighter/rescue, medics and crew members of the HH-43 Helicopters of the Air Rescue Service.

THEY CALLED IT NAKED FANNY

The four sides of the monument are engraved as follows:

SIDE ONE: DETACHMENTS WERE DEPLOYED WORLDWIDE AT U.S. AIR BASES WITH CALL SIGNS SUCH AS "FIREBIRD," "RESCUE 1," "PEDRO." THE HH-43 HELICOPTER AND ITS AIR AND GROUND CREWS MAINTAINED AN ALERT STATUS TO AID AIRCREWS WHO WERE DOWNED AND SOME IN BURNING AIRCRAFT. AT THE SOUND OF AN ALARM THE AIRCREW WOULD BE AIRBORNE WITHIN 2 MINUTES, HOOK UP A SPECIAL FIRE SUPPRESSION KIT (FSK), WHICH COULD PRODUCE 690 GALLONS OF FOAM. THIS WOULD ALLOW FIREFIGHTERS TO REMOVE THE AIRCREWS FROM A BURNING AIRCRAFT. FOR A DOWNED AIR CREW, THE HH-43 ALERT CREW WOULD COORDINATE WITH HEADQUARTERS OR KING BIRD, THEN WOULD DEPART ON A SET HEADING TO MAKE A PICKUP OR RECOVERY. THE MOTTO OF THE AEROSPACE RESCUE AND RECOVERY SERVICE IS "THAT OTHERS MAY LIVE."

SIDE TWO: HH-43 LIVES SAVED AS REPORTED BY AIR FORCE TIMES 1964-1972 IN SOUTH EAST ASIA MORE THAN 1880 PERSONS WERE SAVED FROM CERTAIN DEATH OR CAPTURE. PARARESCUEMAN WILLIAM H. "PITTS" PITSENBARGER WAS POSTHUMOUSLY AWARDED THE MEDAL OF HONOR FOR HEROIC ACTIONS ON 11 APRIL 1966. HE WAS LOWERED 100 FEET BY HOIST FROM THE HH-43B RESCUE HELICOPTER TO RESCUE U. S. ARMY SOLDIERS. HE VOLUNTARILY REMAINED ON THE GROUND TO TREAT AND ASSIST THE TROOPS AND WAS SUBSEQUENTLY KILLED WHEN THEIR POSITION WAS OVERRUN.

SIDE THREE: DEDICATED TO AIR AND MAINTENANCE CREWS WHO FLEW AND MAINTAINED THE H-43 AND THE ONES WHO MADE THE SUPREME SACRIFICE. "THAT OTHERS MAY LIVE" AND LET US NEVER TAKE LIGHTLY THE FREEDOM FOR WHICH THEY DIED. MEMORIAL DEDICATED BY THE PEDRO HELICOPTER RESCUE ASSOCIATION PedroAFRescue.org

SIDE FOUR: MEMORABLE HH-43 RECORDS AND EVENTS 18 OCTOBER 1961 AN HH-43B ATTAINED AN ALTITUDE OF 32,840 FT. SETTING THE WORLD RECORD FOR CLASS E-1 HELICOPTERS. IN 1964 IT WAS THE FIRST USAF RESCUE HELICOPTER DEPLOYED TO SOUTHEAST ASIA. IN 1963-1964 THE AIRCRAFT AND CREWS SUPPORTED THE U.S. MAPPING MISSION IN NEW GUINEA AND 1964-1966 IN ETHIOPIA AS IT WAS THE ONLY HELICOPTER AT THAT TIME ABLE TO WORK IN THE HIGH ALTITUDES. THE HH-43 HELICOPTER WAS MANUFACTURED BY THE KAMAN AIRCRAFT CORPORATION OF BLOOMFIELD, CT.

Appendix D

WHERE ARE THEY NOW?

James E. Armenia: Died in a military helicopter crash.
Joe Ballinger: Retired as a major, lives in Kansas.
Neil Black: Retired as a major, lives in Pennsylvania.
Jim Burns: Retired as a SMSgt, lives in Florida.
Al (Allen) Childress: Retired as a major, died in 2009.
Tom Curtis: Retired as a colonel, lives in Texas.
David Cutillo: Retired, lives in Arizona.
Warren K. Davis: Died July 19, 1969 while trying to rescue the crew of a B-52 that crashed on take-off at Utapao RTAFB, Thailand.
Leroy Diggs: Died December 10, 2009.
Howard Douthit: Retired from the Air Force, deceased.
Leonard (Len) Fialko: Lives in Alabama.
Izzy Freedman: Wonders if he's retired, lives in Thailand.
Dan Galde: Retired as a SMSgt, lives in Arizona.
Scott Harrington: Retired from Gulf Power Co., lives in Florida.
Bruce Hepp: Retired from United Airlines, lives in Colorado.
Orville Keese: Died in a civilian helicopter accident.
Wade Ketron: Retired as a SMSgt., lives in Ohio.
Dick Laine: Works as a physician's assistant in California.
Fred Liebert: Retired from Petroleum Helicopters, deceased.
Duane Martin: Killed during a POW escape.
George Martin: Retired as a major, lives in Alabama.
Earle "Bud" Myers: Retired, lives in North Dakota.
Neil McCutchan: Retired as a major, lives in Florida.
William Robinson: Retired as a captain, lives in Tennessee.

THEY CALLED IT NAKED FANNY

Stan Schaetzle: Retired a Lt. Col., died Feb. 2013.
Phil Stambaugh: Retired as a major, lives in Florida.
Jay Strayer: Retired as a colonel, lives in Ohio.
Walt Turk: Retired as a colonel, lives in Texas.
George Warren: Retired as chief pilot from Columbia Helicopters, lives in Oregon.

Appendix E

AIRCRAFT TIMELINE

17 June 1964—Kaman HH-43Bs 62-4565 and 62-5978 were flown from Naha AB to Udorn AB, Thailand, in two C-130s. Both were reassembled at Udorn and flown to NKP. A third HH-43B, 62-4564, arrived later (possibly in August).

10 Nov 1964—HH-43Bs 60-0279, 60-0280 and 62-4510 arrived at NKP from Da Nang.

20 Nov 1964—(Approximate Date) 62-4564, 62-4565 and 62-5978 were shipped back to Naha AB, Okinawa.

May, 1965—Det. 5, 38th ARS, arrives at Udorn RTAFB, Thailand, with their HH-43Bs for local base rescue and SAR.

6 July 1965—Sikorsky CH-3Cs 63-09676 and 63-09685 arrived from Eglin AFB, Florida.

20 Sep 1965—HH-43B 62-4510 was shot down on a rescue mission near Ha Tinh, NVN.

4 Oct 1965—The first Sikorsky HH-3s arrived and became part of Det. 5, 38th ARS at Udorn RTAFB, Thailand bringing the detachment strength to 3 HH-43Bs, 1 CH-3C and 6 HH-3Cs.

THEY CALLED IT NAKED FANNY

10 Nov 1964: HH-43Bs 60-0279, 60-0280 and 62-4510 arrived at NKP from Da Nang. Helicopter 62-4510 is shown on fire suppression alert prior to being shipped to NKP. The round ball on the trailer is the FSK, or Fire Suppression Kit, a large fire extinguisher carried by the HH-43 to a crash site to help rescue the crew. This aircraft, 62-4510, after moving from Da Nang to NKP, was flown on missions during 1965. On Sept 20, while on a rescue mission into North Vietnam, it was shot down. The entire crew—Capt. Tom Curtis (RCC),1st Lt. Duane W. Martin (CP), A1C William A. Robinson (FE) and A3C Arthur N. Black (PJ)—was captured and taken prisoner. The other two aircraft, 279 and 280, were moved to Phu Cat, Vietnam, and were still being flown in 1968—thus the two oldest HH-43s in Vietnam. Good machines. (Photo courtesy John Christianson)

Appendix F

MISSION TIMELINE

18-19 Nov 1964—The first large scale CSAR operation of the Vietnam War involved two HH-43Bs (possibly 62-4564 and 62-4565) call signs Pansy 88 and Pansy 89 from Nakhon Phanom RTAFB, Thailand in an attempted rescue of Capt. William Reynolds Martin who had ejected from his F-100D (call sign Ball 03) near Ban Senphan, Laos. This was the first USAF rescue attempt in Laos. Capt. Martin's body was found on Nov. 19 having died during his ejection. Rescue crew members were Jim Crabb (P), 1st Lt. John Christianson (CP); TSgt. Alvin C. Reed (FE) and SSgt. Robert Bennett the PJ. 1st Lt. Jim Sovell was co-pilot on the second aircraft.

2 Mar 1965—The first night Combat Rescue occurred in Laos when an HH-43B (62-4510) call sign Brandy 41 from Nakhon Phanom RTAFB, Thailand, crewed by Capt. Israel Freedman (P), Capt. James Rodenberg (CP), A3C Frank P. Hanutke (FM) and A1C Herbert H. Romisch (PJ), rescued F-105D pilot Major George W. Panas, near Tchepone, Laos. The "high bird" on the mission was HH-43B (60-0279) call sign Brandy 21, Capt. Warren Davis (P), TSgt. John J. Kelly (FM), and SSgt. Enson J. Farmer (PJ). (The co-pilot on the mission was the NKP Flight Surgeon, a rated captain.)

31 Mar 1965—An HH-43B (60-0279) call sign Alban 21 from Nakhon Phanom RTAFB, Thailand, crewed by Capt. Jay Strayer (P), Capt. James Rodenberg (CP), A1C Cecil Boothby (FE) and SSgt. Enson J. Farmer (PJ) rescued F-100D pilot, Capt. Ron Bigoness, after he had flown his

stricken aircraft from near Ha Tinh, NVN to about twenty miles into Laos. The "high bird" (60-4510) was piloted by Capt. Israel Freedman with Capt. Warren Davis (CP), A3C Frank Hanutke (HM), SSgt. Harold Stroud (HM) and A2C Eric Anderson, Jr. (PJ).

27 April 1965—An HH-43B crewed by Capt. James Rodenberg (P), Capt. Jay Strayer (CP), A1C Cecil A. Boothby (FM) and A2C Michael Henebry (PJ), rescued a U.S. Navy A1-H pilot, LTJG Scott B. Wilkes, who had bailed out of his ground fire damaged aircraft that he had flown to with two miles of NKP.

12 May 1965—An HH-43B from NKP RTAFB, Thailand, with Capt. Joe Ballinger (P), 1st Lt. Walter Turk (CP), A2C David Cutillo (HMFE) and TSgt. Chester Rainey (HMFE), made the pickup of Capt. Ralph E. Schneider who had ejected in Thailand when the engine failed on his F-105D.

17 May 1965—Two HH-43Bs from NKP RTAFB, Thailand, with Capt. Bruce Hepp (P), Capt. Stan Schaetzle (CP), SSgt. Roberto Rodriguez (HMFE) and A1C Richard Wallace (PJ) in the "low bird" rescued F-105D pilot Capt. James L. Taliaferro, Jr., from near Ban Kia Na in North Vietnam. The "high bird" on the mission was piloted by 1st Lt. Walter Turk with Capt. Joe Ballinger (CP), A1C William A. Robinson (HMFE) and A2C Marvin Brenamen (PJ).

8 June 1965—Crewed by Capt. Thomas J. Curtis (P), Capt. Bruce Hepp (CP), A2C David Cutillo (HMFE) and A1C Richard Wallace in the "low bird," rescued Capt. Harold "Buff" Rademacher from nearly 80 miles north of the DMZ in North Vietnam. The "high bird" crew on the mission included Capt. Stan Schaetzle (P) and 1st Lt. Walter Turk (CP), with A1C Francisco Alverado (HMFE) and A2C Michael Henebry (PJ).

9 June 1965—An HH-43B from NKP, crewed by Capt. Richard A. Laine (P), Capt. Joe Ballinger (CP), A3C Darwin L. Devers (FE) and A2C Michael

Henebry (PJ, landed to pick up Capt. Carroll D. Keeter and Capt. Gerry L. Getman who ejected from their F-4C in Thailand after it ran out of fuel.

23 June 1965—Two HH-43Bs from NKP RTAFB, Thailand, rescued the only pilot shot down over North Vietnam and rescued from North Vietnam without ever setting foot in North Vietnam. The "low bird," piloted by Capt. Bruce Hepp with Capt. Thomas J. Curtis (CP), A1C Francisco Alverado (HMFE) and Airman James E. Poole (PJ), rescued Maj. Robert W. Wilson from 20 miles NW of a bridge near Cha Noi, North Vietnam. Capt. Stan Schaetzle and 1st Lt. Walter Turk piloted the "high bird," while their PJ was A2C Arthur Neil Black.

1 July 1965—The 38th ARS was activated at Tan Son Nhut AB, RVN. Lt. Col. Edward Krafka became its first commander. The 38th ARS acted as a headquarters for all ARS helicopter detachments that became PCS units.

3 July 1965—An HH-43 piloted by Capt. David Allen, rescued the pilot of an F-105D, Maj. Kenneth R. Johnston in Laos some 75 miles north of Udorn, Thailand, after he ran out of fuel.

6 July 1965—Arrival date of two Sikorsky CH-3Cs at Nakhon Phanom RTAFB, Thailand, on loan from TAC.

24 July 1965—F-105D pilot Maj. W. J. McClelland was rescued by HH-43B helicopters from Nakhon Phanom RTAFB, Thailand. Captain Curtis piloted the "low bird" while Captain Bruce Hepp and 1st Lt. Walter Turk flew the "high bird" deep into hostile territory to recover Major McClelland. This rescue mission involved flight in excess of 260 miles over unfamiliar territory, under marginal weather conditions, and without navigational aids.

27 July 1965—A USAF CH-3C (call sign Shed 85), crewed by Capt. George Martin (P), Lt. Orville Keese (CP), SSgt. Curtis Pert (FE) and SSgt. George Thayer (PJ), that had staged out of Lima Site 36 in northern

THEY CALLED IT NAKED FANNY

Laos, rescued F-105D pilot, Capt. Frank J. Tullo (call sign Dogwood 02), after his aircraft had been hit by AAA fire and he ejected. He landed in tall elephant grass near Hoang Trung, about five miles west of the Black River. Capt. Tullo was the first pilot rescued in the Vietnam War by a CH-3C helicopter.

28 July 1965—An HH-43, piloted by 1st Lt. Walter Turk, from Nakhon Phanom RTAFB, Thailand, rescued the pilot of a U.S. Navy A-4E, LT Grant R. Townsend, after he ejected from his aircraft in Laos. The aircraft had been damaged on a bomb run attacking an AAA site fifty miles south of Vinh, North Vietnam.

24 Aug 1965—A CH-3C, piloted by Capt. James Stambaugh, rescued the pilot of an F-105D, Maj. Dean Andrew Pogreba, after he had ejected as his aircraft was shot down while attacking a target on August 22 about twenty-five miles west of Thanh Hoa, North Vietnam. Capt. George Martin was the co-pilot on the mission. Staff Sergeant Francis Hill (HM), A1C James Armenia (HM) and PJ SSgt. George Thayer (PJ) were also crew members.

31 Aug 1965—An HH-43B from Udorn RTAFB, Thailand, crewed by Capt. David E. Allen (P), Lt. John K. Forsythe (CP), George Lepsey (FE) and Bedford Lockard (MT), rescued the pilot of an F-105D, Maj. W. H. Bollinger, after he ejected, about fifty miles southwest of PhuTho, North Vietnam. His aircraft had been hit by AAA fire during an attack on a bridge near PhuTho.

6 Sep 1965—Capt. Gary D. Barnhill was picked up by an HH-43B from Udorn RTAFB, Thailand. His F-105D developed a fuel leak while air-refueling and he quickly disconnected as his aircraft caught fire. He ejected shortly before his aircraft exploded.

20 Sep 1965—HH-43B Huskie #622-4510, call sign Duchy 41, of Det. 1, 38th ARS, Nakhon Phanom RTAFB, Thailand, and crewed by Capt.

Thomas J. Curtis (P), 1st Lt. Duane W. Martin (CP), A1C William A. Robinson (FE) and A3C Arthur N. Black (PJ) was shot down on a SAR in North Vietnam attempting to rescue F-105D pilot, Capt. Willis E. Forby, call sign Essex 04. All became POWs and Martin was later KIA during an escape attempt in Laos. The high bird on this mission was HH-43B #60-0280, call sign Duchy 22, crewed by Capt. Richard Laine (P), Capt. Bruce Hepp (CP), SSgt. Roberto Rodriguez (FE) and A2C Michael Henebry (PJ). Duchy 22 was hit by ground fire and forced to return to NKP.

21 Sep 1965—A CH-3C piloted by Capt. George Martin, rescued the pilot of an F-105D, Capt. Frederick R. Greenwood, after he ejected from his aircraft that had been hit by 57 mm AAA fire which attacking a target near the Mu Gia Pass.

The PSP from the original runway. As with all who installed it, landed on it, and walked on it—it did its job and did it WELL!

GLOSSARY

A-1E, A-1H	Single seat, propeller-driven fighter/bomber aircraft made by Douglas
AAA	Anti-aircraft Artillery
ADF	Automatic Direction Finder
ARRS	Air Rescue and Recovery Service
ARS	Air Rescue Service
BAR	Browning automatic rifle
C-54	Made by Douglas, the C-54 is four-engine transport aircraft
C-123	The Fairchild C-123 Provider is an American military transport aircraft
C-130	The Lockheed C-130 Hercules is a four-engine turboprop military transport aircraft also used as refueling tanker aircraft for helicopters
CEC	The U.S. Navy's Civil Engineering Corps (Seabees)
CH-3C	This was the original Jolly Green Giant helicopter used to rescue downed pilots
CINCPAC	Commander-in-Chief Pacific
CO	Commanding Officer
COMCBPAC	Commander Mobile Construction Battalion Pacific
C-rations	C for "combat," meals used during WWII, Korea and Vietnam
CRP	Combat Reporting Post: Radar operations facility USAF
Crypto	Refers to cryptographic or encoded messages
CSAR	Combat Search and Rescue

THEY CALLED IT NAKED FANNY

F-100	The North American F-100 Super Sabre is a supersonic jet fighter/bomber aircraft
F-101	The Voodoo, by McDonnell, was a fighter/interceptor and photo reconnaissance aircraft
F-105	The Republic F-105 Thunderchief is a supersonic jet fighter/bomber aircraft.
F-4	The McDonnell Douglas F-4 Phantom II is a supersonic jet fighter/bomber aircraft
Feet Dry	Flying over land
Feet Wet	Flying over water
Guard	International Emergency frequency
H-34	The Sikorsky H-34 Choctaw is a piston-engine military transport helicopter
HH-43B	Made by Kaman Corp., the HH-43 was a twin-rotor helicopter used for CSAR missions
HU-16	The Grumman HU-16 Albatross is a large twin-radial engine amphibious flying boat that was used as a search and rescue and combat search and rescue aircraft.
J-57	Pratt and Whitney turbojet engine used in the F-100
JP-4	Jet Propellant. A jet fuel that was a 50-50 blend of kerosene and gasoline
Karst	Porous topography ranging from mountain highs to sunken caves common in Laos
KC-135	The Boeing KC-135 Stratotanker was used to refuel fighter/bomber and bomber aircraft
LIMA SITES	Landing sites in Laos with the Lima the military phonetic designation or the letter "L"
LTJG	Lieutenant Junior Grade: Naval officer rank equivalent to 1st Lt.

M-16	Also referred to as an AR-15, it was the primary assault rifle during the Vietnam War
MAC	Military Airlift Command
MAGTHAI	Military Advisory Group Thailand
MCB	Mobile Construction Battalion
MIGCAP	MIGs were North Vietnamese aircraft–Combat Air Patrol
MOB	Mobile Communications Squadron
NCO	Non-commissioned officer; enlisted with the rank of staff sergeant or above
NKP	The location and airfield designation for Nakhon Phanom
NKPRTAFB	Nakhon Phanom Royal Thai Air Force Base
OIC	Officer in Charge
PARC	Pacific Air Rescue Command
PDJ	Plain of Jars: Laotian landmark, often called the Southeast Asian version of Stonehenge
PE	Personal Equipment
Penetrator	Forest or Jungle: Bullet-shaped device for extracting downed pilots in triple-canopy rain-forest
Pitot Tube	The pitot (pronounced pee-toe) static tube system is an ingenious device used by airplanes and boats for measuring forward speed.
PJ	Pararescueman or pararescue jumper
POW	Prisoner of War
PPI	Plan Position Indicator: Basically the radar scope or screen that displayed reflected radar returns
PSP	Pierced Steel Planking
RON	Remain Over Night
Round-eye	Another name for a Caucasian or white person; as opposed to an Oriental or Asian person

SAC	Strategic Air Command
SAR	Search and Rescue
SOG	Studies and Operations Group, commonly referred to as Special Operations Group
T-28	North American Aviation T-28 Trojan is a piston-engine military trainer aircraft
TAC	Tactical Air Command
TDY	Temporary Duty
TCG	Tactical Control Group
TCS	Tactical Control Squadron
Tech Rep	Technical Representative of the aircraft manufacturer
USNS	United States Naval Ship
VOCO	Verbal Orders of the Commander
VOR	Visual Omni Range: A VHF navigational aid used to determine radial and distance from a specific point

ABOUT THE AUTHOR

SCOTT HARRINGTON IS A GRADUATE of Southern Illinois University, Class of 1962. He received his commission as a 2nd Lieutenant in the United States Air Force on December 21, 1962, and attended Weapons Controller School at Keesler Air Force Base, Mississippi. His first duty assignment was to Sioux City Air Base, Iowa, as a Weapons Controller in the Semi-Automatic Ground Environment or SAGE Center (call sign: Drumbeat).

In November of 1964, Harrington was assigned to the 605th Tactical Control Squadron (TCS), part of the 5th Tactical Control Group, at Clark Air Base, Philippines. He was sent to the Combat Reporting Post (CRP) at Tan Son Nhut Air Base in South Vietnam in December, for 35 days training on the manual radar scopes. (The SAGE system utilized digital computers to display radar images while the manual environment used the raw radar images.) His next assignment, since 5th TAC was designed to set up and temporarily man radar sites in Southeast Asia, was to Nakhon Phanom where he served as Senior Director/Weapons Controller of a radar operations crew for 120 days at the CRP, call sign: Invert.

Based on his performance at Nakhon Phanom, he was tapped for a third TDY by Major Howard Douthit, the site commander at Nakhon Phanom, to assist with the setup and initial operation of a radar site at Dong Ha, Vietnam. Serving initially as Ramp Officer, he expeditiously and safely oversaw the offloading of radar and communication equipment, vehicles, personnel and other cargo with only one aircraft being hit by a single enemy bullet. Once the radar site was operational, he returned to Clark, departing just eleven hours prior to the first mortar attack against the base at Dong Ha.

For his work in support of the Air Rescue Service at Nakhon Phanom, Harrington received the Air Force Commendation Medal. For his skilled handling of various additional responsibilities that led to the successful completion of the Combat Reporting Post at Dong Ha (Waterboy) well ahead of schedule, he received an Oak Leaf Cluster to the Air Force Commendation Medal.

Upon his return to the United States he was assigned to Indian Springs Air Force Station, Nevada (now Creech Air Force Base), in support of the Atomic Energy Commission's underground nuclear test facility at Mercury, Nevada. He served as the controller for air sampling aircraft for sixteen underground nuclear tests and the testing of a nuclear powered rocket engine in the company of rocket technology genius Dr. Werner Von Braun.

Harrington then spent eleven years in broadcasting with stints in Dubuque, Iowa; Indianapolis, Indiana; and at 50,000 watt clear channel WSB in Atlanta, where he won several awards for broadcast excellence as a radio news anchor.

He left the broadcast field in the late '70s, and spent the next twenty-six years with Gulf Power Company in Pensacola, Florida in public relations. He was accredited by the International Accreditation Board, receiving the designation of APR (Accredited in Public Relations) and sat for and passed the Florida Public Relations Association's Certified Public Relations Counselor (CPRC) exam. Harrington won numerous public relations awards and was honored by the Florida Public Relations Association with the Lt. Col. John W. Dillin Award for his service and contributions to the Association and the public relations profession.

Now retired, Harrington and his wife, Jaci, live on ten acres in Northwest Florida.

Printed in Great Britain
by Amazon